D1472939

EXPRESS Yourself

English as a Second Language

Second Year of Secondary Cycle Two

Philippa Parks
Tanja Vaillancourt
Cara Webb

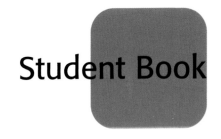

Student Book

ERPI
ÉDITIONS DU RENOUVEAU PÉDAGOGIQUE INC.

5757, RUE CYPIHOT
SAINT-LAURENT (QUÉBEC)
H4S 1R3

TÉLÉPHONE : 514 334-2690
TÉLÉCOPIEUR : 514 334-4720
erpidlm@erpi.com

Managing editor
Sharnee Chait

Project editor
Esmé Vlahos

Copy editors
Jeremy Lanaway
Laura Thomson

Proofreaders
Giselle Nyiri
Katie Shafley

Photo research and permissions
Pierre-Richard Bernier
Élisabeth Côté

Art director
Hélène Cousineau

Graphic design coordinator
Sylvie Piotte

Graphic design and layout
Accent tonique

Illustrations
Josée Bisaillon, Volta Création
Alexandre Couture
François Couture
Simon Dupuis
Vincent Gagnon
Hélène Meunier

Consultants
Rachelle Carr, École secondaire Joseph-Hermas-Leclerc
Commission scolaire du Val-des-Cerfs

Addie Malkus, École secondaire Mgr-Euclide-Théberge
Commission scolaire des Hautes-Rivières

Dear students,

Welcome to another school year! The goal of this book is to encourage you to practise your English every day and to have fun doing it. The three of us are not only second language teachers but language learners as well. Here are some tricks that helped us when we learned a second or third language.

Philippa I grew up in Ontario where most people speak English, but I practised my French by watching French television shows. In high school, signing up for an exchange to France helped me enormously. Going to a place where everyone spoke French was really motivating. When I moved to Montréal, I tried to read the labels on cereal boxes, signs, and posters—anything I could in French. Finally, I made francophone friends and ended up marrying a Québecois! That's a great way to learn another language!

Tanja It took me about three years to learn Spanish and to feel comfortable speaking it. What helped the most is that I was not afraid to make mistakes when I was speaking. During my classes, I improved my vocabulary by listening to Spanish songs and watching Spanish movies. I also had the chance to practise speaking Spanish in different countries, by travelling and working. Learning Spanish changed my life because I met many new friends.

Cara I moved from British Columbia to Montréal to go to university. I lived in a French-speaking area and made friends with a neighbour. We had language exchanges. I enjoy swimming so I joined the local community swim team. The instructions were in French and none of the other members on the team spoke English. I had to speak French if I wanted to communicate. I made the most of every opportunity to use my second language.

We hope that this book inspires you to learn English and that English becomes a language you love to use. Good luck!

Philippa Parks
Tanja Vaillancourt
Cara Webb

Table of Contents

Unit 7

Unit 8

Unit 9

Unit 10

Welcome to **EXPRESS** Yourself

Let's explore the features of your Student Book.

The First Page of the Unit

Each unit starts with a cover page that tells you:

The title of the unit ⋯⋯⋯⋯⋯

What you will do ⋯⋯⋯⋯⋯

The question you will learn to answer ⋯⋯⋯⋯⋯

The Final Task with two options ⋯⋯⋯⋯⋯

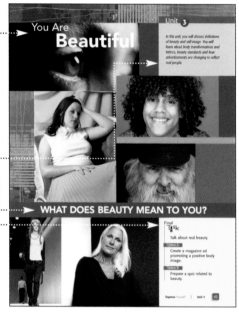

Smart Start ⋯⋯⋯⋯⋯

You begin with activities to find out what you already know about the topic.

Tasks

The units are divided into tasks.

There are activities to complete in each task. ⋯⋯⋯⋯⋯

ESL Competencies

While doing activities, you will express yourself in many ways:

 Speaking and communicating with others ⋯⋯⋯⋯⋯

 Reading and responding to texts

 Listening and responding to audio texts

 Watching and responding to video texts

Writing and producing texts

Resources to Help You

Be Smart shows strategies and tricks for learning English.

Smart Talk suggests conversation starters for speaking.

Self-Evaluate asks you questions about your learning.

Smart Words defines new words in the text.

Special Features

ICT Options makes information and communication technology suggestions.

Go Further provides extra activities for more practice or if you want a challenge.

Smart Facts gives you interesting information about the English culture and the world.

Smart Structure

In each unit, you will review grammar you need in order to complete a task.

> There is a handout to practise the Structure. ············

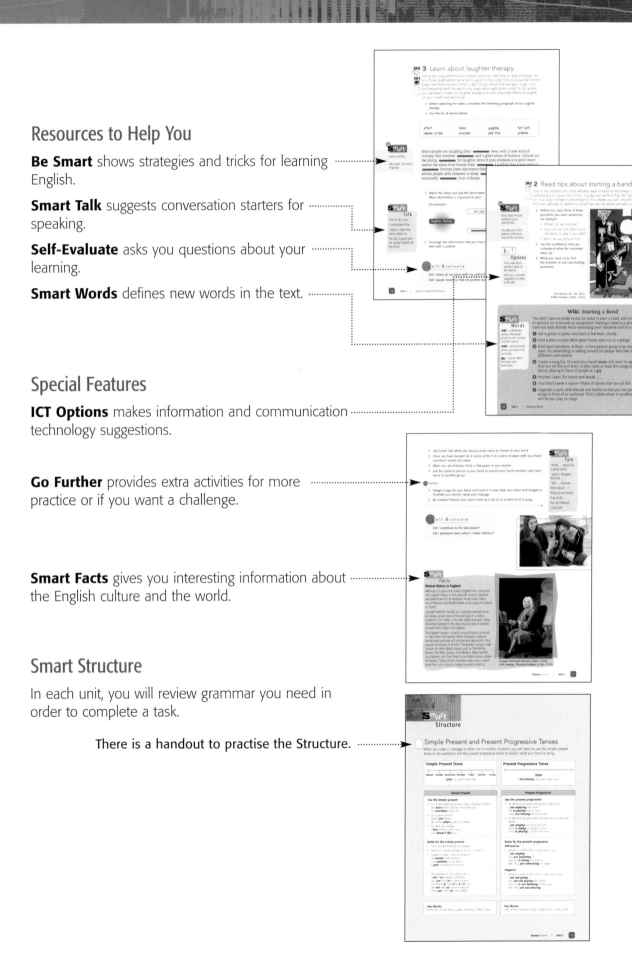

Smart Stop

In each unit, you will learn about text types and their features.

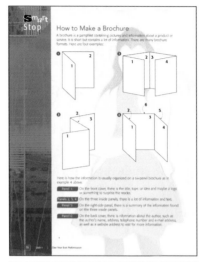

Writing and Production Steps

When it is time to write or produce a text, use these important steps to help you do it right!

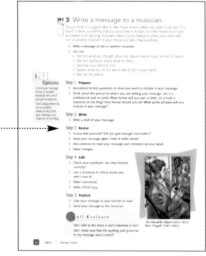

Final Task

The unit ends with a fun project.

This sentence tells you what the project is. ········►

You can choose one of the options. ········

Smart Words Review lists the most important new ········ words in the unit.

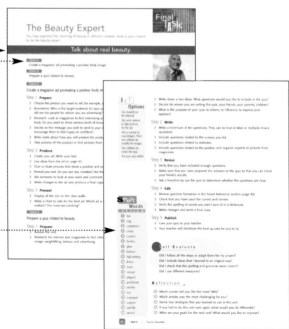

Short Stories

You will read four short stories in the Student Book. Each story relates to a unit.

Smart Facts tells you about the author and background.

You will prepare for reading by doing vocabulary and strategy activities.

You can read the stories aloud with your class or listen to them on the CD.

After you read, there are activities and mini-projects for you to do.

Extra Texts

Each unit includes two extra texts to read. The second text is more challenging than the first.

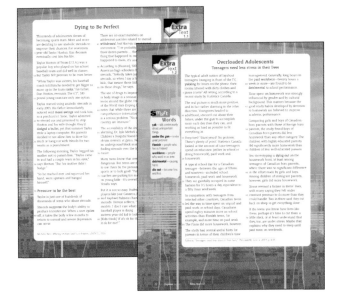

Review

There are two sections to review Smart Words and Smart Structures.

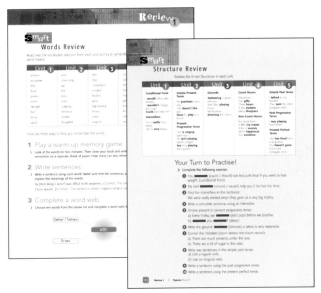

Smart Reference

You can find resources easily at the end of the Student Book.

Smart Talk reviews functional language that you need to communicate.

Smart Words Review is a glossary of all words in the Smart Words Reviews.

Smart Structures includes a chart of irregular verbs.

Smart Texts helps you review text features.

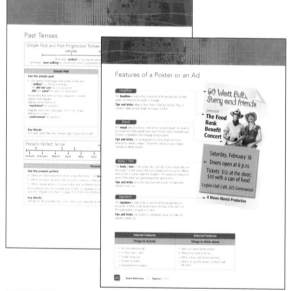

Be Smart Strategies includes Communication and Learning Strategies.

Processes are for responding, writing or producing texts.

Ideas to Improve Your English helps you practise your English outside of school.

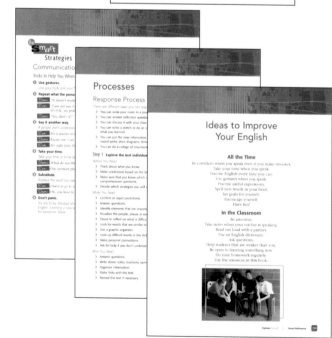

Give Your Best
Performance

HOW CAN YOU ACHIEVE YOUR BEST?

Final
Task

Explain how you achieve success.

Option A

Write a brochure about ways to achieve your best performance.

Option B

Write a story, journal entry, newspaper article or poem about an event that you are proud of.

Smart Start

Achieving goals in life gives you a sense of accomplishment. Doing what you like makes life more interesting and helps you to be happy. Sometimes, you can even receive awards for doing what you like to do!

C1 1 What are you good at?

Make a list of things that you are good at.

> Spend a few minutes thinking about what you are good at. Think of awards that you received for sports or in other fields, such as music, dance, art, science or math.

> Write down at least five examples. They could even be simple actions like helping a friend.

If you don't know a word, try a synonym.

Ask a classmate for ideas.

Ask your teacher for help in translating difficult words.

1	I am proud of my blog.
2	I am a very good skateboarder.
3	I won a gymnastics competition in elementary school.
4	
5	

> Discuss your accomplishments with two different partners.
> Put a check mark in front of those that you have in common.

Talk

I am proud of …
I won …
Really?
What are you good at …?

Self-**E**valuate

Did I share all my answers?
Did I listen to my partner?

2 Interview a partner about competition and performance.

Doing the best you can gives a great sense of accomplishment. Competition often puts you in a state of mind that allows you to push your limits to give your best performance. However, when competition takes up too much of your life, it can make you feel stressed and unhappy. In this next activity, you will discuss your opinion about competition and performance.

> Write your answers to the questions below individually.

> Make complete sentences.

> Then take turns discussing your answers with a partner.

1. On the list of accomplishments that you wrote in the first activity, what are you most proud of? Why?

2. Is it easy or difficult for you to be good at school? Why?

3. Do you always try your best? In which area do you feel most able to succeed—school, sports, science, art, social events, music?

4. Do you prefer to compete by yourself or with others? Do you prefer individual or team activities?

5. Are you busy every night with homework? What do you usually do when you return from school?

6. Who encourages you to be the best you can? Your parents? Your friends? Your teachers?

7. What trophy or award would you most like to win?

8. What do you do when you feel stressed? How do you relax? What do you do to have fun?

Be Smart

Use gestures when you are speaking. Remember— your hands and face speak too!

Take your time. Find examples from your personal life.

Smart Talk

I spend a lot of time …

I won …

I would like to win …

I agree / disagree with you …

What do you think?

Go Further

> Give yourself an award. Celebrate the great things that you do!

> Make a list of all the people you know who deserve an award. Explain why they deserve this award.

This award goes to: _____ for a great performance in: _____

Self-Evaluate

Did I answer all the questions that my partner asked me?

Did I ask the teacher for help when I was unsure how to say something?

Finding the Right Balance

Positive stress is the fuel that allows us to be who we are. It can give us energy and make us forget about the obstacles on our road. However, when positive stress is experienced for a long period of time, it can turn into negative stress and lead to consequences that affect our health and well-being.

1 Read about opposites.

Some teenagers say they feel that they are under constant pressure to achieve. They feel that they have to be the best in every field. At times, they even cut out sleep in order to do everything that they want to do.

Teenagers in this group are called "overachievers." They are almost never satisfied with what they have accomplished because they are always looking to do more.

Then there is the group of "underachievers"—teenagers who have the potential to do great things, but who decide not to use their **strengths**.

The ideal situation is to find the right balance—to have time for work, friends and relaxation. **At the end of the day**, it is important to be satisfied and content with what you do, without always feeling pressured.

Compare the two texts.

Words

strength = quality or ability

at the end of the day = finally

Facts

Perfectionism

Perfectionists are overachievers who set the highest standards of performance in everything they do. They differ from healthy achievers as follows:

Perfectionists	Healthy Achievers
Set standards beyond their reach.	Set high standards.
Are never satisfied by anything less than perfection.	Enjoy doing their best.
Lose energy when they experience failure.	Use failure to create new energy to succeed.
Have a great fear of failure.	Have a normal fear of failure.
Believe that mistakes must never be made.	See mistakes as opportunities for learning.
Can't take criticism.	React well to helpful criticism.

> Read about an overachiever and an underachiever on page 5. Whom do you identify with?

Overachiever

I do so much in a day. I always want to be the smartest, the most athletic, the best dressed and the most popular person in any group. I want to get the best marks in school.

5 I'm always rushing from one activity to the next. In the morning, I have early sports practice before school. After school, I take private piano lessons. Then I babysit my neighbour's children. Finally, after babysitting, I come home and finish my homework. This is a typical day for me.

Last year, my hair began to **thin**. My mother was concerned and took me 10 to the doctor. After the blood tests showed normal results, he informed me that stress might be the cause of my hair loss.

I admit that I overdo it most of the time—I sometimes study six hours in a row and drink five coffees at night to stay awake and do my homework to perfection.

15 I don't really know why I feel that I have to do so much. I feel pressure to perform all the time, and yet I'm not satisfied with what I achieve. I'm a perfectionist.

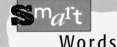
Underachiever

When the teacher asks me to do something in class, I usually don't want to do it. In fact, almost everything the teacher asks me to do, I don't do. I'm 20 more interested in looking outside and watching the birds fly. I look at my pencil and think about what I could do with it. Tap, tap, tap on my desktop. The teacher usually takes the pen away from me. My parents, the teacher and even my friends try to explain to me why it's so important for me to do my schoolwork, but I don't understand them.

25 There are days when I get into trouble for not doing anything. There are also days when the rest of the class is nervous because it's test time, but those days are my best days. I didn't study, so why should I be nervous?

When my parents ask me if I did my homework, I tell them I did. If I tell them the truth, they'll be **upset** with me. When my report 30 card comes, I assure them that my marks will get better next semester. At the end of the school year, I usually **flunk** most of my classes. I don't see it as a problem—if I fail, I'll just make up the classes in summer school.

My parents sent me to see a specialist in school to find out 35 why I never participate in class. She said that my attitude may be caused by many factors. Maybe it's a physical reason—but I don't have a hearing problem. Maybe it's an environmental problem—but my school is okay and so is my family. I just don't want to do what everyone asks me 40 to do.

The Juggler, 1943, Marc Chagall (1887–1985)

> Write your answers to the following questions individually.

1. Which group do you identify with most—overachievers or underachievers? Why?

2. What do you think is better—to be an overachiever or an underachiever?

3. Name three things that the overachiever in the text on page 5 does after school.

4. Guess three things that an underachiever might do after school.

5. What are five characteristics of people who are able to maintain a balance between overachieving and underachieving?

6. Think of someone you know who is an overachiever or an underachiever. Explain how that person resembles the overachiever or underachiever you read about on page 5. Give examples.

Self-Evaluate

Did I answer all the questions?

Did I give my personal opinion?

2 Listen to a dialogue.

Where does teenagers' pressure to perform come from? Sometimes it is the teenager who wants to perform, but in other families, the pressure comes from the teenager's parents. These parents are very competitive and impose their way of living—as well as their stress—onto their children, without realizing the harm it is causing.

Here is the story of Andrew, a fifteen-year-old student who spends most of his time playing hockey. He loves hockey, but he would like to spend less time playing the sport to have time for other activities. However, Andrew's dad is his hockey coach and wants Andrew to play better.

> Before listening to the dialogue, read the statements about Andrew's dad below.

> Decide with your class if Andrew's dad's behaviour is normal or exaggerated.

	Andrew's dad ...	Normal	Exaggerated
1	makes him practise every day.	▬▬▬▬▬	▬▬▬▬▬
2	built a special case for all the trophies Andrew won and will hopefully win in the future.	▬▬▬▬▬	▬▬▬▬▬
3	insults the referees when he thinks that they have been unfair to Andrew.	▬▬▬▬▬	▬▬▬▬▬
4	gives Andrew tricks on how to improve his game.	▬▬▬▬▬	▬▬▬▬▬
5	loves to share his passion for hockey with Andrew.	▬▬▬▬▬	▬▬▬▬▬

Listen attentively.

Take a risk when you are not sure what to answer.

> Now you will listen to a dialogue between Andrew and his friend, Jules.

> When you have finished listening, complete the statements below individually.

> Then discuss your opinion of the story with a partner using these sentence starters:

❶ I think Andrew should …

❷ I think Andrew's dad must …

❸ If my dad was like that …

❹ Andrew is very lucky because …

❺ Andrew feels stressed because …

❻ I think the best solution is …

> Go beyond the story to see where you feel pressure in your life, for example:

❼ In my family, things are very different / similar because …

❽ Sometimes, I feel pressure from my friends when …

 Further

> Read the script out loud with a partner twice. The first time, one partner plays Andrew and the other partner plays his friend, Jules. The second time, partners exchange roles.

> With a partner, write one more page to add to the script. Invent the rest of the story. Perform the new scene for your class.

Self-Evaluate

Did I give my opinion for all the statements?

Did I respect my partner and wait for my turn to reply?

Structure

The Conditional Form

When you give advice or make suggestions, you need to use the conditional form. You just used it in the previous exercise: *Andrew should* … Three modal auxiliaries express the conditional form. They are used in different contexts.

Would
Use would
• For general situations *I* **would** *help you, but I don't have the time.*
• For polite requests **Would** *you help me, please?*
• For a repeated action in the past *When I lived in Québec, I* **would** *go to soccer practice every week.*
• For preference when combined with the word *rather* *I* **would** *rather go to the cinema than stay at home.*
Contracted form
• I **would**–I'**d** I **would not**–I **wouldn't**

Could
Use could
• For capability *I* **could** *help you tomorrow.*
• For polite requests **Could** *you do this for me, please?*
• For expressing certainty in the negative form *Charles-Alexandre* **could not** *have failed the exam.*
• For suggestions *We* **could** *go to the next tournament.*
Contracted form
• She **could not**–she **couldn't**

Should
Use should
• For advice *You* **should** *come early so that we have enough time to do our homework.*
• For suggestions *You* **should** *talk to the art teacher about your project.*
• For high probability *Maika* **should** *do well in her driving exam.*
Contracted form
• She **should not**–she **shouldn't**

Intensifiers

When you are talking about performance, competition, exams or school, you often use intensifiers to express how you are feeling.

Intensifiers are adverbs that enhance other adverbs and adjectives. In English, they come before the words that they modify.

Mr. Bessette, our English teacher, is **really** *busy right now.*   (*really* modifies the adjective *busy*)
I'm a **little** *tired today.*   (*little* modifies the adjective *tired*)

Pay attention when you use the intensifier **very**.

• **Very** cannot modify a verb.

incorrect *I* **very** *like competition.*   correct *I am* **very** *competitive.*

• You can use **very much** to modify a verb.

incorrect *I* **very much** *like competition.*   correct *I like competition* **very much**.

Here are more examples of intensifiers:

too, very, really, fairly, rather, little, enough, totally, extremely, definitely

C3 3 Invent a positive ending.

There are many ways to put balance back into your life. For example, you can change your schedule, do less, spend time with friends, do an activity that you like, explore the great outdoors, eat and sleep well, and avoid stimulants such as caffeine.

In this activity, you will read the beginning of two stories about a mother and daughter who both have stressful lives. You will conclude these stories by proposing ways to solve their problems.

> Continue the stories by finding solutions to the problems.

> Write a minimum of four sentences for each situation.

> Use the pronoun "I" with the conditional form and intensifiers.

> Make sure that you finish with a happy ending.

> Give a title to each story once completed.

Ask yourself what you already know about stress before you start.

Try to write as many sentences as possible.

 forty-two-year-old mom

I'm always rushing. I never have any free time. After work, I have to go grocery shopping, and then I have to pick up my daughter, Elizabeth, from soccer practice. When we get home, I make supper, do the dishes and prepare the lunch boxes for the next day. Twice a week, in the evening, I have Italian lessons. I know that my behaviour is influencing Elizabeth. I see that she feels the same stress. I feel …

 fifteen-year-old student

I love to compete. When my teachers give a bonus or prize for the best exam marks, I win almost all the time. If I don't win, I become very upset. At soccer, I practise a lot. I really want my team to win, and I'm very disappointed when we lose. When I go to bed, I often can't sleep because I worry too much about not winning. Last week …

Self-Evaluate

Is my solution relevant to the topic?

Did I use the conditional form and intensifiers correctly?

Task 2 Doing Your Best

If you have ever won a competition, you know that the feeling of winning is wonderful. Competing is a great experience for many reasons: the thrill of the preparation, the excitement of the competition, the people you meet, the rewards you receive (whether you win or lose) and the life lessons you learn.

1 Read about an achiever.

In the following text, you will read about Lilia, who loves to compete. She enjoys meeting new people at competitions and appreciates the support of her family. Of course, she wants to win, but when she doesn't win, she knows that she did her best.

> Before reading the text on page 11, discuss what competition means to you. Answer these questions with your class:

> ① What are the advantages of competition?

> ② What are the disadvantages?

> ③ Are you a poor loser? How do you react when you lose?

> ④ Do you sometimes do less so that you don't win? Do you feel bad if you win and others don't?

> Read the text on page 11.

> When you have finished reading, answer the questions below in your own words:

> ⑤ Why didn't Lilia compete after the weighing?

> ⑥ Why was she upset?

> ⑦ Why did her teacher talk to her coach?

> ⑧ How did Lilia react when she didn't win?

> ⑨ What is her final goal?

> ⑩ How would your feel if you were Lilia and you lost?

> ⑪ What lesson did you learn from this story?

Plan: Take your time reading.

Take notes on important parts of the text.

Go Further

> Make a list of the words that you didn't understand and write down their definitions. Start your own personal dictionary.

> Invent a story about a competition that you would like to win. Include dialogue and description. Share your story with a partner or a small group of students.

Self-Evaluate

Did I answer all the questions?

Did I take time to answer the questions as best I could?

The Best Day of My Life

Sma^rt
Words
encounter = meet
annoyed = not happy
barely = almost not at all
throw = make an object move through the air

It all began when I was twelve years old and entered, for the first time, the State Selection for tae kwon do in the state of Nuevo León. I was a black belt, and I loved to compete. When this great day, which I had so longed for finally arrived, I woke up early so as not to arrive late. When I arrived at the gymnasium, I **encountered** many people that I didn't know, but I was with a friend from tae kwon do school where I train. She had already been in the Selection and knew many people who were in the competition. My friend introduced me to everyone she knew.

After talking for a while, we went to warm up before the fights began. All of the competitors were weighed. I was placed in the weight range of thirty to thirty-five kilograms in the women's category.

When all of the competitors had been weighed, they posted the names of the competitors and who each would be fighting in her weight class. I found my name all alone. I didn't have anyone against whom to fight! I called my coach to tell him and he said, "How lucky! You don't have to fight!" I was **annoyed** because I like to fight, but it was okay because I knew that I would still qualify for the Selection.

As I had been selected, I learned that I was going to have to be coached three times a week in the city of Monterrey. However, I could not go three times a week because I had other school activities. Then my professor spoke to my coach and it was arranged that I would go on Thursdays and Saturdays for training.

At my first training, I stayed very separate from everyone because I didn't know anyone and I am very serious. I **barely** spoke to anyone and just practised. But when we started doing tests and demonstrations, my companions began to ask me things. Everyone could **throw** me very well, but there was one [sic] could throw me best. Her name was Andrea. During the training sessions we were always put together.

After one month of training, we arrived at the regional event. We managed to pass the regional phase and continue on to the National Olympics! I could not believe it! I was very excited to go to the Olympics!

When the time finally came to go the National Olympics, I was very nervous, but I tried to forget my nervousness and concentrate on my fight. Luckily I was chosen to fight the first day. I entered the battle area with my coach who gave me final instructions. This fight I won in the first half. Then it was time for the second fight, which I unfortunately lost. I did everything I could to win, but sometimes things do not work out so well, and one must know how to lose.

My parents, Mario and Sanjuanita, and my brother were there supporting me the whole time and giving me encouragement. They went with me to all of the competitions. The other person who gave me all of his support was my tae kwon do teacher. That was one of the most important and happiest moments of my life. I met many people and plan to continue to compete until I have won a gold medal, not just the National Olympics, but the international Olympics as well.

Starla Griffin, "Lilia: Nuevo Leon, Mexico," *Girls, 13,* New York, Hylas Publishing, LLC, 2005, pp. 150–151

2 Discuss your tips for success.

Doing well at school isn't always easy. Everyone wants to achieve good grades, but some students have difficulty managing their time. In the following activities, you will learn different tips to help you succeed. First, you will explore the tips that you already know and use.

Take a risk. Name all the tips that you know and use.

> Discuss your tips with a partner and, together, write a list of tips to help you succeed at school.

> Find as many tips as possible in three minutes, for example:
> *Rewrite my class notes at the end of the day.*

> When the time is up, compare your tips with those of your classmates.

> Then write your answers to the questions below individually.

Talk

I think that the best tip is …

What helps me is …

I always …

That's a great idea.

What about you?

❶ Which pair of students found the most tips?

❷ In your opinion, which tips are the best?

❸ Do you use these tips? Why or why not?

Self-Evaluate

Did I share my ideas with my partner?

Did I use Smart Talk to help me?

Facts

Multi-Tasking

Are you a multi-tasker? If you are, you may not be doing your best. Do you work on the computer and talk on the phone at the same time? Do you watch TV and do your homework? Do you clean up your room while eating your lunch? If so, you are a multi-tasker and may feel overworked and stressed. Multi-tasking is the art of doing many things at once. Many people believe that women are better multi-taskers, but several top neuroscientists and cognitive psychologists say there is no proof of female multi-tasking superiority.

People who multi-task have the impression that they are saving time and are being more productive than if they do one task after the other. However, some studies have proven the contrary: multi-taskers can be slower because it is more difficult for the brain to process many activities at once. Multi-tasking also involves certain risks for children and teens, who may not be giving their homework enough time and learning another crucial skill: the ability to focus on one thing at a time.

Businessman in Convertible, 1993, Dave Cutler (1960–)

3 Read about more tips for success.

Now that you have found your own tips for success, read the following text and find out what experts suggest you do to perform your best.

> Read the tips below and identify those that are similar to yours.

Be Smart

Pay attention. Find the tips that are similar to yours.

Compare the text with what you already know.

If You Want to Succeed in School

1. Be present in class and ask the teacher for feedback on your performance.

2. Form a study group with other students. When you help and test each other, you get better **grades**.

3. Set specific and reasonable study goals. For example, say "I'll read ten pages of my **novel** tonight" instead of "I'll read my entire book this weekend." Set yourself up to succeed—not to fail!

4. Take ten-minute breaks while you are studying. If you are feeling sleepy, get up and move around to stimulate your body and mind.

5. Take turns sitting in front of the class—it's the best place to see and learn from your teacher.

6. Ask questions in class. If you are in doubt about something, your partners probably are, too.

7. Take notes that are complete and well-organized. Review your notes and reading every day.

8. Be on time for exams. Bring pens, pencils and erasers so that you don't panic at the last minute.

9. Take a moment to calm down before looking at the test. Close your eyes and remind yourself that you know the answers. Take a deep breath and relax.

10. Attend a tutorial at lunchtime when you need help.

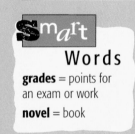

Smart Words

grades = points for an exam or work

novel = book

> Compose a short paragraph answering the questions below. Write at least ten sentences.

1. Are there any tips in the text above that are similar to those that you and your partner thought of? Which ones? When do you use them?

2. Are there tips that aren't useful to you? Which ones? Why?

3. Which two tips are the most useful to you? Why? Name the subjects you will use them in and explain how you will use them.

Self-Evaluate

Did I write a complete paragraph?

Did I explain how I will use the tips in a new context?

TASK 3 The Power of Positive Thinking

There are many ways to achieve your goals, for example, by doing your best every day, surrounding yourself with positive people, setting time aside to work on your dreams, getting enough sleep, … Another way is by using the technique of visualization.

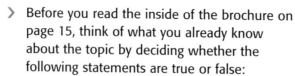

1 Read about visualization.

Athletes use visualization all the time to achieve their goals. They imagine everything about the competition, for example, what will happen throughout the day, how they will feel, whom they will talk to, what they will wear. They imagine their body moving, and of course, they imagine winning! In this activity, you will read a brochure about visualization.

Make guesses based on what you already know.

Scan: Look for specific information in the text.

Read the questions beforehand.

> Before you read the inside of the brochure on page 15, think of what you already know about the topic by deciding whether the following statements are true or false:

❶ Visualization is the ability to use one's imagination.

❷ Negative thoughts attract positive actions.

❸ Visualization can only be done consciously.

❹ Imagination can become reality.

> Read the information from the brochure on page 15 and answer the questions below individually.

❺ Which sentence explains what visualization is?

❻ Name five things that you would like to accomplish with the help of visualization.

❼ Do you believe in the power of visualization? If so, what do you intend to use it for—your marks, your personal life, your love life? If not, why don't you believe in it?

Self-Evaluate

Did I answer the questions correctly?
Did I use all the resources needed to answer as well as I could?

The Power of Visualization

Inside the Brochure

I f you watch Olympic athletes before a competition, you will often see them with their eyes closed. They are imagining their competition. Some athletes claim that they don't even start a practice without visualizing it first. Successful people in all **fields** use visualization both consciously and unconsciously.

Visualization is the process of creating a mental image of what you want to do or feel. It is a very powerful mental training technique, and it is an interesting way to prepare your brain for what you want to happen in your life.

Visualization experts affirm that including all of your senses makes this type of meditation even more effective. Mental programming can be visual (what you see), **kinesthetic** (what you feel), auditory (what you hear), olfactory (what you smell) and gustatory (what you taste).

Margaret, Irish Girl, 1967,
Antonio Ciccone (1939–)

Minds and bodies trained through visualization are able to perform what they have imagined. Visualization is simple to do. The first step is to quiet your mind and relax. This can be **achieved** by closing your eyes, taking a few deep breaths and blocking out the world around you. When you are relaxed, think about positive images or words that reflect what you want to happen.

Did you know that your brain doesn't distinguish whether what you imagine is true or not? It simply remembers the images that you put in it! Try an experiment this week. Every morning, spend five minutes imagining what you want your day at school to be like. Think about the results that you would like to achieve. During the day, keep your visualization firmly in mind and see what happens. Use positive **self-talk** to help you achieve your goal. For example, instead of thinking "Don't fail," put the word "Win" in your mind. You can improve this technique by repeating the images over and over again.

Let's see what happens in your life!

Words

field = area

kinesthetic = related to body movement

achieved = accomplished

self-talk = talking to yourself

How to Make a Brochure

A brochure is a pamphlet containing pictures and information about a product or service. It is short but contains a lot of information. There are many brochure formats. Here are four examples:

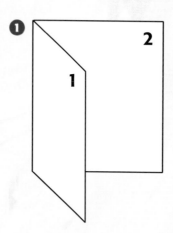

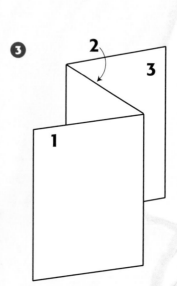

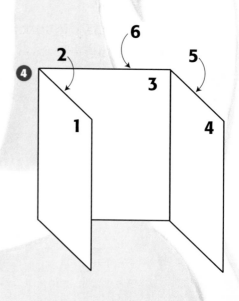

Here is how the information is usually organized on a six-panel brochure as in example 4 above:

Panel 1: On the front cover, there is the title, topic or idea and maybe a logo or something to surprise the reader.

Panels 2, 3, 4: On the three inside panels, there is a lot of information and text.

Panel 5: On the right-side panel, there is a summary of the information found on the three inside panels.

Panel 6: On the back cover, there is information about the author, such as the author's name, address, telephone number and e-mail address, as well as a website address to visit for more information.

2 Write a flyer about ways to relax.

A flyer is a piece of paper, usually distributed by hand, that advertises an event or product. When you feel stressed, it is a good idea to have a reminder of all the little things you can do to relax. One way to remember is to write them down and then keep this list in a place where you can look at it often.

> Write your flyer by following the steps below.

Step 1 **Prepare**

> Think of ways to relax that you have heard of or read about.
> Write down at least ten ideas in note form. For example:

  Take a hot bath.   *Spend time with friends.*

> Explain why these ideas can help you relax.
> Research the Internet for more relaxation and stress-management techniques.

Step 2 **Produce**

> Write short sentences.
> Show the flyer to a partner and ask for feedback.
> Make changes to the text as necessary.
> Check your spelling and verbs.
> Make your final flyer. Add drawings or coloured paper.

Step 3 **Present**

> Show your flyer to your classmates.
> Compare flyers and vote for the best flyer.
> Distribute copies of your flyer in school to help students feel less stress.

Did I do all the steps required in this task?
Did I include ten tips?

Green Dancer, circa 1880, Edgar Degas (1834–1917)

Set goals. Try to make the best-looking flyer!

Encourage yourself. Be proud of the tasks you are doing in English.

Options
Use computer software to make a realistic-looking flyer.

Facts

Stress

Do you have too much stress in your life? Look at how stress can affect you if you don't make a change:

How stress can affect your mind	How stress can make you feel	How stress can affect your body	How stress can affect your behaviour
• memory problems • difficulty making decisions • inability to concentrate • confusion • seeing only the negative • repetitive negative thoughts • poor judgment	• moody and hypersensitive • restless and anxious • depressed • easily irritated • overwhelmed • unconfident • apathetic	• headaches • digestive problems • muscle tension and pain • fatigue • weight gain / loss • skin problems • sweating palms	• eating more / less • sleeping too much / too little • isolating yourself • neglecting responsibilities • nervous habits • grinding your teeth • losing your temper

3 Learn about laughter therapy.

Giving your best performance is easier when you take time to relax and laugh. As you know, laughing feels great and is good for the body. Did you know that children laugh over three hundred times a day? Did you know that teenagers laugh much less frequently, and that adults only laugh about eight times a day? In this activity, you will watch a video on laughter therapy and learn about the effects of laughter on your health and well-being.

> Before watching the video, complete the following paragraph about laughter therapy.

> Use the list of words below.

effect	funny	giggling	hot spots
immune system	overcome	pain-free	problems

Be Smart

Listen carefully.

Take notes. Use word mapping.

Many people are laughing their ⬛⬛⬛ away with a new kind of therapy that involves ⬛⬛⬛ and a great sense of humour. Schools are becoming ⬛⬛⬛ for laughter since it puts students in a good mood and at the same time boosts their ⬛⬛⬛. Laughter has a very serious ⬛⬛⬛. Doctors have discovered that watching ⬛⬛⬛ videos allows people with diseases to sleep ⬛⬛⬛ for a couple of hours and eventually ⬛⬛⬛ their sickness.

> Watch the video and put the information that you hear in a word web. What information is important to you?

For example:

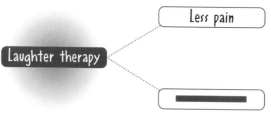

Smart Talk

First of all, I put …
I understand that …
I agree. I have the same notes on …
We did a good job—we spoke English all the time!

> Exchange the information that you have in your word web with a partner.

Self-**E**valuate

Did I share all my ideas with my partner?
Did I speak clearly so that my partner would understand?

Reach Your Goals

We may have different goals and our own methods for accomplishing them, but we all feel the same way when we succeed—good about ourselves!

Explain how you achieve success.

Option A

Write a brochure about ways to achieve your best performance.

Option B

Write a story, journal entry, newspaper article or poem about an event that you are proud of.

Option A

Write a brochure about ways to achieve your best performance.

Step 1 **Prepare**

> Reread this unit. As you read, take notes on information that you think will be helpful to include in a list of tips to achieve your best performance.

> Divide the information for the brochure according to what will go on the front cover, the right-side panel, the three inside panels and the back cover (see the Smart Stop on page 16).

> Think about the pictures that you want to include.

Step 2 **Produce**

> Design your brochure and lay out the pictures.

> Add your written text and include original ideas.

> Use the conditional form and intensifiers.

> Check your spelling in a dictionary.

> Show your brochure to a partner and ask her or him the following questions:

- Is the information in the brochure presented clearly? Is the brochure well-organized?

- Is the information helpful? Is something missing? Are the pages full enough?

> Make the appropriate changes and write your final copy.

Step 3 **Present**

> Hand in your finished copy to the teacher.

> Exchange your brochure with a classmate and read your classmate's brochure.

Option B

Write a story, journal entry, newspaper article or poem about an event that you are proud of.

Step 1 **Prepare**

> Think of an important event. (If you can't think of anything, invent one.)

Ic^T

Options

Use a computer to make your brochure and your story. Add graphics, colours, pictures and special fonts.

> Answer the following questions to complete your story:
> - What was the event? When did it happen? Where did it take place? Why was it important to you?
> - What happened before the event, during the event and after the event?
> - What do you remember most about the event? What lesson did you learn?

Step 2 Write

> Write a draft of your text.
> Include an introduction and a clear conclusion.
> Use the conditional form and intensifiers.
> Add details such as colours, smells and feelings.
> Add dialogue to make the story more interesting.

Step 3 Revise

> Reread your text to make sure that your ideas are clear.
> Ask a classmate to read your text and suggest changes.

Step 4 Edit

> Check your spelling in a dictionary.
> Verify that you used the conditional form and intensifiers correctly.
> Make changes to your text.
> Write your final copy.

Step 5 Publish

> Give your story to the teacher.
> Read your story out loud to a partner or a small group.

Smart Words
REVIEW

1. achieved
2. annoyed
3. at the end of the day
4. barely
5. encounter
6. field
7. flunk
8. grades
9. kinesthetic
10. novel
11. self-talk
12. strength
13. thin
14. throw
15. upset

Self-Evaluate

Did I follow all the steps?
Did I find original and interesting ideas related to the topic?
Did I use the conditional form and intensifiers correctly?
Did I use a dictionary?

Reflection

1. Which activity did you like the most? Why?
2. Which activity was the most challenging for you?
3. Name two strategies that you learned to use in this unit.
4. If you had to do this unit over again, what would you do differently?
5. What are your goals for the next unit? What would you like to improve?

Dying to Be Perfect

Thousands of adolescents dream of becoming sports stars. More and more are deciding to use anabolic steroids to improve their chances. For seventeen-
5 year-old Taylor Hooton, this decision eventually cost him his life.

Taylor Hooton of Texas (U.S.A.) was a popular boy who played on his school baseball team and did well in classes.
10 But Taylor felt pressure to be even better.

"When Taylor was sixteen, his baseball coach told him he needed to get bigger to move up in the team **ranks**," his father, Don Hooton, recounts. The 6'2", one
15 hundred and eighty-pound young man saw only one option.

Taylor started using anabolic steroids in early 2003. His father immediately noticed wild **mood swings** and took him
20 to a psychiatrist. Soon, Taylor admitted to steroid use and promised to stop. Hooton and his wife thought they'd **dodged a bullet**, yet that summer Taylor stole a laptop computer. His parents
25 decided to not allow him to drive his truck or hang out with friends for two weeks as a punishment.

The following morning, Taylor begged his mother not to punish him. "Taylor came
30 in and had a couple tears in his eyes," says Hooton. "But his mother didn't budge."

"So he reached over and squeezed her hand, went upstairs and hanged himself."

35 Pressure to be the best

Taylor is just one of hundreds of thousands of teens who abuse steroids.

Steroids **suppress** the body's ability to produce testosterone. When a user **cycles**
40 **off**, it takes the body a few months to return to normal and severe depression can occur.

There are no exact numbers on adolescent suicides related to steroid
45 **withdrawal**, but Hooton says it is not uncommon. "I've probably talked to two, three dozen parents … the same exact thing that happened in our home happened to them, it's usually violent."

50 According to [Hooton], 500 000 to 600 000 American high schoolers have used steroids. "Nobody takes just one shot of steroids, so when I say a half a million kids, that means those kids have cycled
55 on these drugs," he says.

The use of drugs to improve performance or body image is a serious problem for teens around the globe. Frédéric Donzé of the World Anti-Doping Agency (WADA)
60 notes that while there are no comprehensive international statistics, it is a serious problem. "No sport and no country are immune."

The accessibility of the drugs is also
65 alarming. Dr. Lyle Micheli of Boston's Children's Hospital found that teens obtain steroids at gyms. He says there is an underground black market and finding steroids over the Internet is
70 even easier.

Many teens know that steroids are dangerous. But teens are often motivated to use them by the pressure to excel in sports or to look good. "Parents and
75 coaches are putting too much pressure on young kids—it's overwhelming," Yesalis says.

But it is not so easy. Professional baseball players like Jose Canseco, Jason Giambi
80 and Raphael Palmeiro have used steroids. Hooton reflects, "It's back to role models. I don't care what a professional baseball player is doing … unless my sixteen-year-old kid is looking up to him.
85 [Kids think] 'if it's ok for them, why isn't it ok for me?'"

Michelle Won, *Winning at Any Cost?*, Los Angeles, UNESCO, 2006

Overloaded Adolescents
Teenagers need less stress in their lives

The typical adult notion of layabout teenagers lounging in front of the TV, **yakking** for hours on the phone, their rooms littered with dirty clothes and
5 pizza crusts? All wrong, according to a recent study by Statistics Canada.

The real picture is much more positive, and in fact rather alarming in the other direction: Youngsters headed to
10 adulthood, stressed out about their future, **under the gun** to accomplish more each day than they can, and working as hard as possible to fit everything in.

15 Surprised? Want proof? No problem. There's plenty of proof. Statistics Canada looked at the amount of time teenagers spend on education (either in school or doing homework), paid work and
20 housework.

A typical school day for a Canadian teenager—between the ages of fifteen and nineteen—included school, homework, paid work and housework.
25 They are gainfully occupied in some fashion for 9.5 hours a day, equivalent to a fifty-hour workweek.

In comparison with teenagers from selected other countries, Canadian teens
30 led the way in time spent on unpaid and paid work on school days. Canadians spend eighty minutes more on school activities than **Finnish** teens, for example, and more time on paid work.
35 The Finns did more housework, however.

The study had several useful hints for parents in terms of their children's time

management. Generally, long hours in the paid **workforce**—twenty hours a
40 week or more—are found to be **detrimental** to school performance.

Time spent on homework was strongly influenced by gender and by cultural background. This matters because the
45 good study habits developed by devotion to homework are believed to improve academic performance.

Comparing girls and boys of Canadian-born parents with those of foreign-born
50 parents, the study found boys of Canadian-born parents did less homework than any other category. The children with highly educated parents did significantly more homework than
55 children of less well-educated parents.

Sex stereotyping is **dying out** on the housework front, at least among teenagers of Canadian-born parents, where there was no significant difference
60 in the effort made by girls and boys. Among children of immigrant parents, however, girls did more housework.

Stress seemed a fixture in teens' lives, with many saying they felt under
65 constant pressure to do more than they could handle. Two in three said they cut back on sleep to get everything done.

If the teens you know have lives like these, perhaps it's time to cut them a
70 little slack, or at least understand that they, too, are under stress. Maybe that explains why they need to sleep until past noon on weekends.

Editorial, "Teenagers need less stress in their lives," *The Gazette*, June 4, 2007, p. A16

Smart Words

yak = talk continuously about unimportant things

under the gun = under great pressure

Finnish = people who live in Finland

workforce = people who work in an area

detrimental = causing harm

die out = become less and less

Starting a **Band**

Unit 2

In this unit, you will explore what goes into making a successful band. You will learn about the roles each band member plays, what bands do to stay successful and how to market yourself using video, posters and audio.

HOW DO YOU START A SUCCESSFUL BAND?

Final
TASk

Promote your band.

Option A

Advertise your band or an upcoming show using a poster or a website.

Option B

Create an album cover for your band complete with lyrics.

Option C

Design promotional material for your band. Explain why you chose this design.

Smart Start

It is hard to find anyone in the world who doesn't enjoy music. Your taste in music reflects who you are and where you come from. Music is a universal language that has the power to change the world.

1 Start a band.

Many people have dreamed of becoming a famous musician. Have you?

> Read and answer these questions.

> Share your answers with a partner.

1. What kinds of music do you like best?

2. Name some bands you know. What type of music do they play?

3. What is the best part about being a musician?

4. What is the hardest part about being a musician?

5. Who is usually in a band? Name the important roles.

6. Does everyone who works for a band have to be a good musician? Why or why not?

7. Have you ever wanted to be famous? Why or why not?

8. What do you need to do to become a successful band?

Self-Evaluate

Did I elaborate on my ideas?

Did I speak in English all the time?

2 Take an aptitude quiz.

Maybe you are already a member of a band or you would like to start one. Maybe you have no musical ability at all, but would like to help out your friends in a band in other ways. What role would you be best at? Take this quiz to find out how you could be most useful for your band.

> Before you take the quiz, ask yourself: "What role would I be best at in a band? Would I be a good manager? Would I be good at writing songs? Would I be good at advertising and publicity?"

> Read the quiz and write down your answers.

> Compare your quiz results to the answers you gave before taking the quiz. Were you right about your role?

What's My Tune? Aptitude Quiz

Words

outgoing = friendly and sociable

thoughtful = serious and quiet

reliable = dependable

1 Which of the following sets of adjectives best describes you?

a) Friendly and diplomatic
b) Creative and quiet
c) **Outgoing** and optimistic

2 How do you prefer to work?

a) In a group—I like to encourage others.
b) Alone—I like to work on my own ideas.
c) It doesn't matter—as long as I am the centre of attention!

3 When you have a problem, how do you solve it?

a) I talk to everyone and try to find a solution for all of us.
b) I write out my feelings in a song or a poem.
c) I get angry and then laugh about it quickly.

4 Which sentence best describes your qualities?

a) I am well-organized and get along well with others.
b) I am **thoughtful** and imaginative.
c) I am creative and funny.

5 What is your biggest problem when you work in a team?

a) I make too many compromises— I let everyone tell me what to do.
b) I don't like to listen to others— My ideas are usually better.
c) I am more concerned with appearance than with quality.

6 Which activity do you prefer?

a) Spending time talking with friends
b) Reading or writing by myself
c) Creating a video or poster starring my friends and me

7 How do you feel about rules?

a) Rules should make everything fair.
b) Rules should respect the individual.
c) Rules should be broken if necessary.

8 What is the best project you have ever done?

a) A project I worked on with friends
b) A project I worked on by myself
c) A project that is beautiful

9 What do you usually do in a group?

a) I make sure everyone feels included.
b) I wait until someone asks to hear my ideas.
c) I talk first about my ideas.

10 Which of the following sets of adjectives best describes you?

a) **Reliable** and dependable
b) Creative and unique
c) Successful and distinctive

If your score is mostly A:

You are diplomatic and well-organized, and you listen to everyone's ideas.

You would make a great **MANAGER**. The manager of the band is in charge of organizing gigs (places to play) and making sure that the band members get along.

If your score is mostly B:

You are very creative and good with language. You enjoy writing and working by yourself.

You would make an excellent **SONGWRITER / COMPOSER** for the band. Your original ideas will ensure that your band is unique.

If your score is mostly C:

You are creative and like to be noticed. You are good at creating posters and videos.

You would make an ideal **PUBLICIST**, the person in charge of the band's publicity and advertising. You will make sure that the band's name becomes well-known.

Forming a Band

Members of a band each have their roles. They play different instruments and are responsible for various aspects of the band's success. Even if you have no musical talent at all, there is still a place for you in a band.

Be Smart

Rephrase: Repeat what someone else said to show that you understood it. "So you said that …"

Take your time. You don't have to answer right away—Think about it first! "Just a minute, please."

1 Get together and find a name.

Now that you have a good idea about your role in the band, it is time to find other band members and decide upon a name.

> Write down your role on a piece of paper and give it to your teacher. (Have a second choice ready just in case.)

> Your teacher will write down the roles of everyone on the board.

> Find two other people who don't have the same role as you and sit with them.

> Read the suggestions below to help you think of ideas for a band name.

Options

Look at websites or blogs of popular bands to get a better idea of band names.

Suggestions

• Think about using the word *the* in front of your band name, for example, The Beatles, The Ramones, The Beastie Boys, …

• Use an expression you have heard before, for example, "Plan B."

• Find the nearest book. Go to page 56, paragraph 2, line 3, words 5, 6 and 7—That will be your band name.

• Go to an online encyclopedia and skim through a random article. At any time in the article, stop skimming, close your eyes and point at a word. Select a few words around it (less than five words in total), and that will be your band name.

• Brainstorm together, then narrow down your list. If one of you dislikes a name, don't use it.

• Look around at the labels on items, at the names of different computer fonts, at household objects, for example, "Hi-Fi."

• Open a dictionary or phonebook to any page and look for interesting names or words.

> Use Smart Talk while you discuss what name to choose for your band.

> Once you have decided on a name, write it on a piece of paper with your band members' names and roles.

> When you are finished, hand in the paper to your teacher.

> Ask the publicity person in your band to present your band members and band name to another group.

Go Further

> Design a logo for your band and hand it in next class. Use colour and images to illustrate your band's name and message.

> Be creative! Present your band name as a rap or as another kind of song.

Smart Talk

I think … would be a good name.

I agree / disagree because …

I like … because …

What about …?

What do you think?

First of all, …

Are we finished?

Good job!

Self-Evaluate

Did I contribute to the discussion?

Did I persevere even when I made mistakes?

Smart Facts

Musical History in England

Although it is just a tiny island, England has a long and rich musical history. In the sixteenth century, England was well-known for its Anglican choral music, that is, music that was specifically written to be sung and played at church.

George Frederick Handel, an important classical music composer, wrote most of his best work in London, England in the 1700s. In the late 1800s and early 1900s, the British listened to the new musical style of operatic comedy from Gilbert and Sullivan.

The biggest change in English musical history occurred in 1962 when The Beatles (from Liverpool, England) transformed rock and roll and became the world's most popular musicians of all time. The Beatles' success made it easier for other British bands, such as The Rolling Stones, The Who, Queen, Iron Maiden, Black Sabbath, Led Zeppelin and Pink Floyd, to be better known outside of England. Today, British musicians play many musical styles from ska to pop to reggae to punk to techno.

George Frederick Handel (1685–1759),
18th century, Thomas Hudson (1701–1779)

2 Read tips about starting a band.

One of the simplest and most effective ways to transmit information on how to do something is to create a list of tips. Usually, you will find "Top Ten" tip lists, because ten is an easy number to remember. In this activity, you will compare information from two websites to determine which tips are the same and which are different.

> Before you read, think of three questions you want answered, for example:
>   • Where can we practise?
>   • How can we find other band members to play music with?
>   • Who can we perform for?
>
> Use the numbers to help you understand what the important ideas are.
>
> While you read, try to find the answers to your pre-reading questions.

The Pianist, No. 40, 1957, Pablo Picasso (1881–1973)

Wiki: Starting a Band

You don't have to study music for years to start a band, and you don't have to spend a lot of money on equipment. Starting a band is a great way to have fun with friends while exercising your creativity and your brain.

❶ Get a guitar or piano and learn a few basic chords.

❷ Find a place to play. Most great bands start out in a garage.

❸ Find band members. A three- or four-person group is an excellent way to start. Try advertising or asking around for people who like to play different instruments.

❹ Create a song list. You and your band **mates** will want to agree on songs that you all like and want to play. Have at least five songs you know well before playing in front of people at a **gig**.

❺ Practise! Learn the music and words.

❻ Your band needs a name—Think of names that you all like.

❼ Organize a party with friends and family so that you can perform your songs in front of an audience. Find a talent show or another place that will let you play on stage.

8 Advertise your band. Talk with other people about your band, create posters for your shows and design a simple website.

9 Create publicity for your band. Take pictures with your band in different environments—in an alley, in front of a brick wall or in a field looking off into the distance. Find out if there are any ways to promote your band at your school. A high school talent show is a great way to get people to see your band.

10 Find equipment. Talk to your school's music department about using their practice rooms. They are usually free and include a sound system and a drum kit.

Guide to Starting a Band

1 Learn how to play. Start off with a few lessons on the instrument of your choice. Joining your school band can be a great way to learn.

2 Find people to play with. Talk to your friends (and friends of friends) to discover who else has been playing music or wants to play. Put up a sign at a local music store, coffee shop, bookstore, …

3 Find a place to play. Try somebody's garage, basement or bedroom. There are **rehearsal** studios with equipment, such as **amps**, drums and microphones that you can rent. (In Montréal, it costs about $30 per hour, and there is usually a three-hour minimum.)

4 Have a song to work on together. Maybe a member of your band wrote a song, or maybe you will just play **cover songs** for now. You can download sheet music of published songs off the web.

5 Meet regularly, at least a couple of times per week. Be nice to each other during the process. Bands get along best when they try out new ideas before saying, "No, it won't work."

6 Decide on a band name. Brainstorm together, and then eliminate names from the list. If one of you dislikes a name, don't use it.

7 Record a demo. You should make a rehearsal tape so that people can have an idea of what you sound like. Use your demo to try to get gigs.

8 Look for a venue. Does your school have a talent show? Can you play at a friend's party? Is there a local band that you like? Ask if you can open for them sometime.

9 Choose appropriate clothing. Wear what you are comfortable in and what will make you feel confident. It should match your musical genre. (If you play punk music, dress punk, with a studded belt, wrist cuffs, …)

10 **Chill out**. It doesn't matter where you play—You are going to be nervous. Even if your music isn't very good yet, ask your friends and family to support you.

> Answer these questions in complete sentences.

1. Which tips did the texts have in common?
2. Which tips were different?
3. Do you think any of the tips can be eliminated? Which ones? Why?
4. Can you think of an important tip that could be added? Write your tip.
5. Which text do you think is the most useful? Why?
6. Use what you learned to write down the five most important things a band should do to get started.

Talk

 Go Further

> Exchange your questions with a partner and ask your partner to answer them.
> Imagine that you are interviewing your favourite musician. Add five questions to your list about how she or he got started in music. Do research to find the answers.

Self-Evaluate

Did I answer the questions with complete sentences?

Did I answer all the questions correctly?

Facts

The Meaning of Wiki

"Wiki" is the Hawaiian word for "fast." The word "wiki" entered the English language officially on March 15, 2007 when it first appeared in the *Oxford English Dictionary*.

A wiki is a collaborative website that allows people to add, remove and edit content. There are many encyclopedias, dictionaries and other resources on the Internet that are wikis where the information is supplied and corrected by the public.

In 2006, a popular online wiki-encyclopedia challenged commercial encyclopedias to see who made more mistakes, and it was concluded that the online encyclopedia had fewer mistakes than the professionally published commercial books!

 3 Write a "to do" list.

Now that you have read both texts, share your ideas with your group. One of the texts that you read was a wiki. Here is your chance to rewrite the wiki so that it reflects your group's ideas on how to start a band.

> As a team, find ten things "to do" to get started. Use the list of five things that you already thought of in your answer to question 6 of Activity 2 to help you. You may have to add or eliminate ideas.

> Make sure that one of you writes down your group's "to do" list.

An Interview with Jon Stein

Jon Stein is a musician and music teacher who teaches in Montréal and who puts together bands for a living. One day, Jon had a great idea. He decided to give his students a unique opportunity to show off their skills by forming "garage bands."

 1 Read Jon's bio.

Jon started playing music in high school and he hasn't stopped since. Read Jon's blog to find out what motivated him to start a career in music.

A blog is a "web log." It usually has a title, a profile (the person's name, age, location and interests) and a list of postings or log entries categorized by date.

Look at the questions before you read to scan and find specific information.

Use the title, the picture and the blog features to help you understand.

Blog Entry Title	Blog Entry Date	Profile

From the Garage

Getting Started
January 20, 2008

I started taking guitar lessons when I was in grade three, but I didn't like my teacher, so I stopped. In grade nine, my friend Bruce introduced me to a great guitar teacher named Elliot. Bruce and I both took guitar lessons from Elliot for a few years.

Then, in grade ten, I got together with a few other kids from my school and decided to form a band to play at the school talent show. Bruce played keyboards and I played guitar. We were really into '60s and '70s rock.

We practised hard for that show. The day before, we thought we were great and we were really excited. The show was a disaster. Our first song was terrible. I remember shaking so badly that I could hardly play. I was completely confused because all the notes I was playing sounded wrong, but I had practised them and they were supposed to be right! After the show, we learned that one of the guitarists had tuned the guitars and bass to the wrong key. We actually played through the entire song that way and then played one more song before getting off the stage. We were so inexperienced. I was **crushed**. **Live and learn**, I guess. I was upset for a while, but then I started thinking about next year ...

I didn't give up, but kept on playing in bands. We used to jam in the basement at my parents' house. Most of my neighbours hated the noise so much that they moved!

Since then, I have played in at least twenty bands, toured the country several times, played in Europe, released a dozen or so albums and recorded a few hundred songs.

I started teaching music five years ago and I love it. One of the best things I do is to encourage young musicians to find other people with whom to play in a band. When you have a goal like performing together at a show, it really motivates you to practise a lot and get better.

Teaching music is part of my whole experience with music. Music is my life.

Age: 38
Gender: Male
Occupation: Professor of Stringology*
Location: Montréal, Canada

Words

crushed = feeling terrible because you failed at something

live and learn = discover from your experiences

Interests		Favourite Music			
Teaching guitar and bass	Coaching bands	Rock	Metal	Punk	Ska
Playing and writing songs	Cycling	Funk	Acid jazz	Electro	
Producing and recording music					

*Stringology isn't a real word in English—It is a joke. The suffix -ology means the study of something. For example, psychology is the study of the psyche (or mind). Jon made up this word as a joke because many musical instruments, such as guitars, have strings.

Options

Create your own blog or website that gives your bio and updates on your band.

> Answer the questions below individually using complete sentences.

> Share your answers with a partner.

1 How old was Jon when he started playing music?

2 When did he start playing music again? What instrument did he play?

3 Who was his new music teacher? What did he think about her or him?

4 What went wrong at his first show?

5 Why does he love teaching?

6 Think of three questions you would like to ask Jon about following a career in music or starting a band.

2 Listen to Jon.

We decided to interview Jon and ask him some more in-depth questions about the most important things to know when starting a band.

> Before listening, look at the Smart Words below.

> Listen to the interview carefully.

> Use the word web to help you organize your ideas.

> Review your notes and then answer the questions on page 33 while listening to the interview a second time.

Focus on the information you hear. Don't be distracted!

Look at the questions before listening and think of what the answers could be.

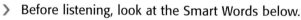

Positive aspects

Being in a band — Strategies for success

Difficulties to expect

Words

dabble = do or be involved in something, but not in a serious way

network = meet and talk to people who may be useful to your work

PA system = equipment that makes someone's voice loud enough to be heard by a group of people (short for "public address" system)

jive = get along

> After listening, answer these questions.

1. What does Jon say is the best part about being in a band?
2. What is the hardest part about being in a band?
3. How did Jon form his first band?
4. How does a band find places to play?
5. Why is a band like a family?
6. How does a band resolve their problems?
7. How often should a band practise together?
8. What advice does Jon give to people who want to start a band? (Give at least one suggestion.)

Go Further

> Listen to the interview again and write down the facts that answer the *wh-* questions (*who, what, where, when, why* and *how*).

> Listen to the interview again. Choose three questions that Jon was asked and change his answers. (You can make them funny or serious answers.) Write the questions and the new answers in a dialogue to perform.

Self-Evaluate

Did I answer all the questions correctly?

Did I choose an effective strategy to help me understand the interview?

Facts

Copyright

A copyright is the legal right to be the only person or company that produces or sells a book, play, film, song, … When you copyright your ideas, you make sure that no one else can sell them without your permission. It is very important to copyright your music so that no one steals your hard work from you!

When you write a cool song, how can you be sure that no one else will hear it and record it before you do? How can you prove that you are the original author? You need a copyright to prove that the song is yours.

One way to copyright your songs is to send yourself a copy of your recorded music (on tape or CD) in the mail. When you get the package, don't open it—Keep it in the sealed, post-marked envelope.

You can also visit your country's copyright office website for instructions on how to register your songs. (You might want to wait until you have produced an entire CD, because each time you register something, it costs about $30.)

3 Write a message to a musician.

Do you think it is a good idea to take music lessons when you want to be part of a band? Is there something that you would like to know? Jon often replies to e-mails and letters from aspiring musicians. Here is your chance to share your ideas with him or another musician of your choice and ask a few questions.

> Write a message to Jon or another musician.

> You can:
>   - Tell him what you thought about his idea to start a music school for bands.
>   - Ask him questions about what he does.
>   - Describe your band to him.
>   - Explain what you do (or would like to do) in your band.
>   - Ask him for advice.

Options

E-mail your message to Jon or another musician and see if you get a response.

Find a blog written by Jon or another musician and post your message as a response to the blog.

Step 1 **Prepare**

> Brainstorm to find questions or ideas you want to include in your message.

> Think about the person to whom you are writing your message. Jon is a professional and an adult. What format will you use—a letter, an e-mail, a response on his blog? How formal should you be? What polite phrases will you include in your message?

Step 2 **Write**

> Write a draft of your message.

Step 3 **Revise**

> Is your text personal? Did you give enough information?

> Read your message again. Does it make sense?

> Ask someone to read your message and comment on your work.

> Make changes.

Step 4 **Edit**

> Check your questions—Are they formed correctly?

> Use a dictionary to check words you aren't sure of.

> Make corrections.

> Write a final copy.

Step 5 **Publish**

> Give your message to your teacher to read.

> Send your message to the musician.

 **S** e l f - **E** v a l u a t e

Did I refer to the ideas in Jon's interview or bio?

Did I make sure that the spelling and grammar in my message were correct?

The Mandolin Player (1914–1915), Marc Chagall (1887–1985)

Structure

Simple Present and Present Progressive Tenses

When you write a message to either Jon or another musician, you will need to use the simple present tense to ask questions and the present progressive tense to explain what your band is doing.

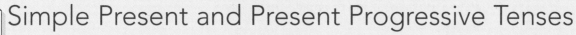

Simple Present Tense
Monday Tuesday Wednesday Thursday Friday Saturday Sunday
I **play** my guitar every day.

Present Progressive Tense
now
I **am playing** my guitar right now.

Simple Present

Use the simple present
- For actions that occur every day or express a routine
  We **have** band practice every Monday.
  He **practises** every day.
- For a general truth
  Amps **are** heavy.
  My father **plays** guitar in a band.
- For likes and dislikes
  I **love** heavy metal music.
  She **doesn't like** jazz.

Rules for the simple present
- Add -s for the third person singular.
- Add -es for words ending in sh, ch, s, x and o.
- Subject + verb + rest of sentence
  He **wants** to be famous.
  She **watches** music videos.
  It **gets** crowded at concerts.

- Pay attention to the verb to be.
  I **am** (I'**m**) happy to perform.
  You **are** (You'**re**) a good singer.
  She/He/It **is** (She'**s**/He'**s**/It'**s**) nice.
  We **are** (We'**re**) good musicians.
  They **are** (They'**re**) very skilled.

Present Progressive

Use the present progressive
- To describe an action taking place right now
  I **am enjoying** the show.
  He **is playing** drums now.
  They **are missing** band practice.
- To describe an action that will take place in the near future
  I **am singing** in a band tonight.
  Mary **is doing** an audition soon.
  Sam **is playing** a guitar solo soon.

Rules for the present progressive
Affirmative
- Subject + verb to be + main verb + ing
  I **am singing**.
  You **are watching** TV.
  She/He **is trying** to perform.
  We/They **are rehearsing** on stage.

Negative
- Subject + verb to be + not + main verb + ing
  I **am not going**.
  You **are not buying** the tickets.
  She/He **is not listening** to the music.
  We/They **are not dancing**.

Key Words:
every day, all the time, usually, sometimes, often, never

Key Words:
now, at this moment, today, tonight, soon, Look! Listen!

Young Québec Musicians

Québec is filled with talented young musicians. You will now discover a few such musicians and learn about the challenges they face in the music industry.

1 Listen to musicians talk about their band.

Be
smart

Pay attention while you listen and watch. Don't panic even if people are speaking quickly. Your teacher will play the video again.

Clément, Éric, Rémy and Milène are a group of young musicians who play together in a band. Listen to what they have to say about their experience with becoming successful in music.

> Before you watch the video, ask yourself these questions:

1. How old do you think the musicians are?

2. What do you think their biggest challenges will be if they want to become successful?

3. What strategies will you use to help you understand this video?

> Watch the video and take notes.

- Write the new words you hear.
- Note the parts of the video that you do not understand.

2 Reflect on the video.

Now that you have watched and listened to the young musicians discuss their experiences, reflect on what you saw.

> Answer these questions individually.

> Share your answers with your group.

1. What surprised you most about the video? What did you learn that was new?

2. What questions do you still have about the musicians or about starting a band?

3. Do you think that you would like to listen to the band's music? Why or why not?

4. What can you do to encourage young Québec musicians?

5. What advice would you give these musicians about their music or about publicizing their band? Think of at least three suggestions together with your group.

Self-Evaluate

Did I answer the questions correctly and give my personal opinion?

Did I choose an appropriate strategy to help me?

Spreading the Word

It is time to promote your band. You will need publicity and advertising so that people will know the name of your band, what kind of music you play and where they can see you or buy your music.

1 Find out what you can do.

Work with your group to decide how to promote your band.

> Read the text below to find ideas for different ways to promote your band.
> Think of three different forms of media that you can use to promote your band.

Be Smart

Ask for help if you don't understand a word, sentence or idea.

Use new words and ideas from this text in the next activity.

How to Promote Your Band

Figuring out how to encourage people to start listening to your music is one of the hardest parts of being a musician. You can be incredibly talented, play amazing music and get along really well with everyone in your band, but if no one has heard of you, they won't buy your music!

5 What can you do to promote your band and start **spreading the word** about your music? Well, one of the first things to do when you are trying to promote your band is to identify your TARGET AUDIENCE (who you think will listen to your band's music). If you know who you want to listen to and buy your music, you will know how to create better advertising. For
10 example, if you are part of a band that plays children's music, your target audience would include parents. Parents read parenting magazines—This would be a great place to put an advertisement for your band.

Once you know who your target audience is, you need to identify what your target audience WANTS or NEEDS. For example, parents want to know that
15 their children will be happy and learn something when they listen to your music, so you need to make that clear by including information about how educational your songs are, or by printing up the **lyrics** to your songs so that parents can read them and sing along with their children.

Think about how your band STANDS OUT from the others—What makes
20 your band different? Unique? Better? For example, is your band an all-girl band? Is it a band that promotes a cause, like one against racism? Make sure that you tell people all about why you are different!

Be creative when it comes to finding DIFFERENT MEDIA to promote your band. For example, think about creating posters, videos, a website or band
25 blog, T-shirts, hats or other articles for your fans to buy and wear. Start posting your music on the Internet. Make **links** from your website to other bands with similar musical styles and encourage other bands to make links to your website in exchange.

Where are the BEST PLACES to talk about your band? For example, if your
30 target audience is other teens, where do they go to listen to music—all-ages clubs, talent shows at schools? Do they listen to a certain radio station?

Smart Words

spread the word = pass on a message
lyrics = words in a song
link = connection to another website

Do they go on specific websites? Once you figure out where your fans are, get a gig at that club, play at their schools, call up radio stations and ask them to play your songs, make sure your songs are posted on that website.

35 Ask people who like your band's music to pass on the message for you. This is called **GRASSROOTS** because the message comes from the people who listen to your music, not from the people promoting it. Encourage your friends and fans to write about your band on their websites, and to wear T-shirts or other articles of clothing to promote your band.

Go **Further**

> Test what you understood by writing your own definitions or examples for the words in CAPITALS in the text. For fun, quiz a friend—Cover up the words in capitals and ask a partner to try to match your definitions to the words in capitals in the text.

> Find out more about marketing. Use the Internet or ask people you know who are involved in marketing as part of their job to give you information. Present what you find out to your group or class.

2 Plan your strategy.

Now that you know more about how to promote your band, it is time to put your ideas into action.

Take your time and think about what you want to say before speaking.

> Sit with your group members.

> Answer the questions below together as a team.

> Decide what task each group member will do to promote your band.

> Write down your plan together as a team.

1. What are the five best marketing suggestions in the text? Why are they the best?

2. Who is the target audience for your band?

3. What is your target audience interested in?

4. What different forms of media will you use to promote your band?

5. Where will you promote your band?

6. How will you make your band stand out from other bands?

Sm**a**rt

Talk

Our group needs to … if we want to promote our band.

We can use … to help us.

Do we all agree?

What do you think?

Why don't we try …?

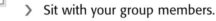

S e l f - **E** v a l u a t e

Did I use Smart Talk to help me?

Did I ask for help from others when I needed it?

3 Attract attention to your band.

One of the best ways to grab someone's attention is through visuals. Think of the number of times that you have seen posters or commercials for a band, an album or a concert. Which ones attracted your attention?

> Look at these two posters.

> What do you notice about each poster?

> Answer the questions below individually and then with a partner. Use the information on the features of a poster in Smart Stop (page 40) to help you.

❶ What information do the posters give you?

❷ Is the language complicated or simple? Do the posters use complete sentences?

❸ What colours do the posters use? Do you think that they are effective? Why or why not?

❹ Which visuals on the posters do you like better? Why?

❺ What are the posters trying to tell you? What is their purpose?

❻ Who do you think the posters are talking to—adults, teens, children? What are the people reading the posters interested in?

❼ Do the posters catch your attention? Why or why not?

❽ Do you think the posters would attract more people's attention if they were written in both French and English?

❾ If you had to choose between these two posters to advertise your show, which one would you choose? Why?

❿ Where would these posters be most effectively placed: in front of a school, in a grocery store, on a lamppost, near a certain bus stop or metro? Explain your answer.

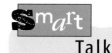

ADAM TO ZOE

with special guests
THE FRONT WHEEL

Friday, March 12 @ 9 p.m.
Tickets in advance: $7;
$10 at the door

The Main House,
12345 Main St.

For more info:
222-222-2222

60 Watt Bulb,
Stony and friends

present
The Food Bank Benefit Concert

Saturday, February 18

Doors open at 8 p.m.

Tickets: $12 at the door;
$10 with a can of food

Legion Hall Café, 873 Greenwood

A Moore Musick Production

Features of a Poster

Headline

The **headline** is noticed by 30 percent of the people who see the poster. It reinforces the poster's message.

Tips and tricks: Make it short (fewer than five words). Play on emotion: Make people laugh, feel angry or think.

Visual

The **visual** part of a poster is the picture or photograph. It is noticed by 70 percent of the people who see it. It is the most important part because it establishes the message of your poster.

Tips and tricks: Use photographs because people are more attracted to realistic images. Choose the colours in your images carefully to attract people.

Body / Text

The **body / text** is noticed by only 5 percent of the people who see the poster. For this reason, there isn't always text on a poster. When there is text, it comes under the headline. The sentences making the point of the poster and giving arguments appear here.

Tips and tricks: Keep the text short and simple. Use facts and statistics if you can.

Signature

The **signature** is noticed by 15 percent of the people who see the poster. It refers to the brand name, the logo or the name of the organization, company or creator.

Tips and tricks: Use bright or contrasting colours to make the signature stand out.

60 Watt Bulb, Stony and friends

present

The Food Bank Benefit Concert

Saturday, February 18

Doors open at 8 p.m.

Tickets: $12 at the door; $10 with a can of food

Legion Hall Café, 873 Greenwood

A Moore Musick Production

Internal Features	External Features
Things to include in a poster	**Things to think about before making a poster**
• An interesting visual • A clear topic / idea • Simple language • A clear headline • Important information	• Who is looking at the poster • What they need to know • What colours will attract attention • Where to put the poster so that it will be seen

Presenting Your Band

It is time to put your plan into action. With your team, you decided how each member would promote the band. Now you will present a media package containing different items to promote your band. You will explain why you chose to create each item and how it will encourage people to listen to your music.

Promote your band.

> Each person in your band should choose one of the following options to create a media text.

> Make sure that everyone does something different for the band. For example, if two people make two posters, one poster should promote a show and the other should promote the band in general.

Option A

Advertise your band or an upcoming show using a poster or a website.

Option B

Create an album cover for your band complete with lyrics.

Option C

Design promotional material for your band. Explain why you chose this design.

Options A, B and C

Step 1 Prepare

> Work with your band members and review your plan from Task 4. Which media text will each group member be designing? What is the goal of each text? For example, what will the website say about your band?

> Brainstorm for ideas. Who is the target audience for your band? What kind of music does the band play? Why will people want to buy your band's music?

> Do you have a variety of media texts—posters, videos, audio clips, Internet ads, …?

> Research. Use the Internet, look in magazines, talk to musicians, find other interesting ways to promote your band.

> Start by writing a plan or sketch of what you will do.

Options

Use musical instruments or digital equipment and software to record an audio demo. Edit it with software.

Use graphic software to create a poster for your band.

Take pictures of your band and use the images in your poster.

Film your scene using digital video. Edit it using computer software (cut and paste and add titles and sound).

The Musicians, 1924, Emmanuel Bellini (1904–1989)

Step 2 Produce

> Each person in the group should create her or his own media text.
> Include details such as colour, text size, relevant information, ...
> Ask a member of your group to take a look at your media text and give you suggestions.
> Revise: Is your message clear? What could you add or remove to make it better?
> Edit: Check your language. Are the spelling and grammar in your texts correct? Did you make sure that you used the simple present and present progressive tenses correctly?
> Make changes.
> Create the final version of your media text.

Step 3 Present

> Present your media text to the class as a group.
> Each person should present her or his media text individually.
> The publicity person should start the presentation by introducing the individual group members and explaining why you chose to promote your band in this way. For example: *"Our group is called Electric Goats. We are a band that writes children's songs, but we use only electronic instruments. We decided to create a poster, a website and an audio demo of our music. Pierre will start by presenting his poster ..."*
> Ask for feedback from other groups.
> Give feedback to other groups.
> Reflect on the audience's reaction and cooperation within your group.

Self-Evaluate

Did I follow all the steps?

Did I use the simple present and present progressive tenses correctly?

Did I use what I learned in the unit to help me make an effective media text?

Did I use different resources?

Reflection

1. Which activity did you like the most? Why?
2. Which activity was the most challenging for you?
3. Name two strategies that you learned to use in this unit.
4. If you had to do this unit over again, what would you do differently?
5. What are your goals for the next unit? What would you like to improve?

The Death of the Album

If you want the latest song from your favourite musical artist or group, chances are you will go directly to your computer and not to the local music store. When
5 you find the song you are looking for, you will download it and add it to a bank of music that you have spinning on your MP3 player. You will probably never see the album cover.

10 An album is a collection of songs by the same artist or a group of artists. An album consists of the cover art, the liner notes, the CD and the case it comes in. Opening and looking at the album cover
15 used to be as important as listening to the music.

Not so long ago, music companies had teams of people who would help design the cover of the album. They would
20 carefully choose the artwork and the title to complement the band. The liner notes included the lyrics, a list of the names of all the people who worked on producing the album, and messages from the
25 artists to their fans. It was a way of connecting with the people who would buy the music.

Today, people interact and enjoy music very differently. Digital music has caused
30 this change. People like to select songs they love and control the order in which they will listen to them. With companies offering a small price for downloading a single song, people are less likely to buy
35 an album for twenty times or more the price of a song, especially when they really only know one song.

Artists also have web pages filled with all the information that fans could possibly

40 want. Lyrics, artwork, videos, tracks or songs, concert information; the list is endless. Some artists even have blogs on their websites as a way of communicating with their fans. More and more artists are
45 offering mini-albums of four or five songs. These cost less than full-length albums and usually contain enough music to get an idea of the artist's style.

Some record companies are holding on
50 to the album, at least in CD format. These companies are trying to encourage people to buy CD albums by cutting the sales prices. Some labels have also started including video games with the
55 album as well. Bands like Metallica and Red Hot Chili Peppers have also said no to online downloading services. They feel their albums should not be sold as individual songs because it takes away
60 creative control.

Some people argue that the benefits of a new format are too numerous. No one complained when the CD was introduced. You no longer had to get out
65 of your chair and turn the record over. A CD played all the songs, one after another, and you could also put it on repeat and hear the whole album over and over again.

70 Changes to the way we physically store music have had a great impact on both the music industry and the artists. These changes, from the CD to the MP3 and the **dawn** of downloading, have taken the
75 **dust**-collecting album and reduced it to something that fits in the palm of your hand. So the question remains: Can we stop the death of the album?

Words

dawn = creation

dust = very small amount of dirt

Writing Set Lists

By Jonathan Stein

A **set** list is the order in which a band plays their songs at a show. The order in which a band performs their songs on stage is an extremely important part of their show. Here are a few tips on how to write a good set list.

If your band has an opening **slot**, this means that you are playing before a more popular band. This type of set is shorter than if you are the main or headlining band. Being an opening band can sometimes be difficult. You should prepare a short, tight set of approximately thirty minutes in length. If you are the headliner, your set can be longer, usually between an hour and an hour and a half. In general, it's best to have a set that is a bit shorter than longer; that way, you always leave the audience wanting more.

If your band plays covers, you will probably need to prepare two to three sets of forty-five minutes to an hour. In this case, you need to place your best songs carefully so that they will have maximum impact. At most clubs, the first set is usually a warm-up set. The second set is the main set because that is the point in the night when the most people are likely to be there. Sometimes you need to be flexible and change things **on the fly**.

The first song

The first song is probably the most important song of the entire show. As the saying goes, "You only have one chance to make a first impression." This is so true when you are performing. If you don't catch the audience's attention with the first song, you are probably in for a rough ride. When you are performing on stage and the audience is into your show, it's an amazing feeling. When the audience is not paying attention, it's a horrible feeling. You should always start off with a very strong song and have your lead singer say a few opening words to welcome your audience.

The last song

The last song is also extremely important. This is the final memory the audience will have of you. You should always end with a very strong song; that way, the audience will leave with a strong impression of you.

Dynamics

If you play every song at the same dynamic level, the audience will become bored and lose interest. If the set starts out loud and fast, it should get slower and/or quieter a little later on. If you want to end the show with a bang, the songs right before the last one must be a little less intense. Imagine you are taking the audience on a **journey**. You know that feeling. It's the same feeling we have when we listen to music, when we hear our favourite song.

Finally, a good set comes down to how well you know your songs. As you get to really know your songs, you will also get to know which songs are the strongest and which songs the band plays best. You should rehearse your sets well before the day of a show and record them so you can hear if they are sounding good. Listen to or watch live performances by your favourite bands to see how they do it.

Smart Words

set = performance by a singer, band or DJ

slot = short period of time allowed for a particular event

on the fly = quickly, while doing something else

journey = travelling from one place to another

You Are **Beautiful**

Unit 3

In this unit, you will discuss definitions of beauty and self-image. You will learn about body transformations and tattoos, beauty standards and how advertisements are changing to reflect real people.

WHAT DOES BEAUTY MEAN TO YOU?

Final
Task

Talk about real beauty.

Option A

Create a magazine ad promoting a positive body image.

Option B

Prepare a quiz related to beauty.

Smart Start

Do you compare yourself to the pictures of teens that you see on TV and in magazines? Do you like to follow fashion trends? Who is beautiful to you? Do you think there is more pressure for girls or boys to fit in with "the look"? Beauty is an interesting and complex issue.

C1 1 Discuss your definition of beauty.

The media influences our definitions of beauty, but our standards of beauty are also very personal. For example, you may think that tattoos make someone look fashionable, but your friend may think the opposite.

> Sit with two classmates. Choose a speaking card each.

> Read the questions on your card out loud. All three students in the team must answer the questions.

> Share your group's response with the class by reporting the team members' answers to the questions on your card.

Be Smart

Use gestures. Your hands and face speak too!

Ask for help if you don't understand a question.

Smart Talk

Beauty is …
I think …
In my opinion, …
I don't agree with you …
It depends …

Speaking Card 1

1. Do the images you see in magazines and on TV influence the way you see yourself?

2. What are the physical traits that you admire in your closest friends?

3. Do you consider muscular people to be attractive? Why?

4. What attracts more attention—blue eyes or brown eyes? Blond hair or dark hair?

Speaking Card 2

5. Which image sells more products—a picture of a young woman or of an old woman? Why?

6. Find five adjectives to describe the women you usually see in magazines and movies. Find five adjectives to describe the men.

7. Why is it hard to look like models?

8. If you had slightly **crooked** teeth, **freckles** or curly hair, would you try to change the way you look? Why?

Smart Words

crooked = not straight

freckles = small patches of light brown colour on the skin

Speaking Card 3

9 Name a movie star, athlete or musician you consider to be beautiful and explain why you feel this way.

10 If you are a girl, do you feel better when you are wearing makeup? If you are a guy, do you feel better when you are wearing fashionable shoes and your favourite T-shirt?

11 Do you know girls who look like the models in fashion shows?

12 Think of your family and friends. Do they look like the people you see in the media?

Portrait of a Young Woman in a Lace Hat, 1891, Pierre Auguste Renoir (1841–1919)

Self-**E**valuate

Did I answer all the questions?

Did my team members understand me?

 2 Explain what is beautiful.

Beauty is often a combination of inner beauty, which includes personality, intelligence, grace and charm, and outer beauty, which is defined by health, youthfulness, symmetry and **complexion**. However, sometimes beauty is defined by other criteria that can be quite surprising, proving that beauty really does come in many forms, shapes, colours and sizes.

⟩ Look at these pictures and think about why each one is beautiful.

⟩ Discuss your ideas with your classmates.

Words

complexion = colour, texture and appearance of a person's skin

T^sk A ① Under Pressure around the World

Many women struggle to meet an unrealistic body image that is portrayed in the media. Men also feel unhappy about their bodies. The pressure to look better has caused many people to turn to new and dangerous body transformation techniques.

"I think that weightlifting is a good idea to build muscles, but training every day is ..."

C1 **1** Try the speaking competition.

All over the world, people have found ways to change their bodies in order to make themselves look better. What do you know about these techniques? The aim of this activity is to say at least four sentences related to the topic. The partner who speaks the longest wins.

> With a partner, take turns talking about the topics below.

> Time your partner to see who speaks the longest.

> Discuss the topics as a class. What do you know about them and what would you like to know?

Be Smart

Take a risk. Say everything you know about the topics.

Topics for Student A

Getting implants
Piercing the body
Injecting chemicals into the face
Having surgery

Smart Talk

O.K., let me see, getting a tattoo is ...

I think that ...

I believe that ...

It is my opinion that ...

I mean ...

Topics for Student B

Weightlifting
Getting a tattoo
Putting on makeup
Dyeing your hair a different colour

Lipstick, 1908, Frantisek Kupka (1871–1957)

Self-**E**valuate

Did I try to speak as long as possible?

Did I stay on topic?

Structure

Gerunds

Did you notice that the verbs in the previous activity all end in *ing*? *Weightlifting, getting, putting,* … are gerunds. In English, a verb can be used as a noun by putting *ing* at the end.

For example: ***transform*** *your body* → ***transforming*** *your body*

Gerunds
Gerunds are verbs (verb + *ing*) that have the same function as a noun.
A gerund can be the subject of a sentence. ***Swimming*** *transforms your body.*
A gerund can be the object of a sentence. *Katherine is always* ***dieting***.
Certain verbs are followed by a gerund, for example: *admit, appreciate, avoid, consider, enjoy, finish, imagine, practise, risk, suggest* *I imagine* ***changing*** *my body.*
Some verbs are followed by the infinitive, for example: *agree, appear, ask, choose, decide, expect, hope, learn, promise, wish* *I decided* ***to stay*** *the way I am.*
Be careful—Some verbs can be followed by either a gerund or an infinitive, for example: *begin, continue, forget, hate, like, love, prefer, remember, start, try* *Andrew hates* ***to see*** *his friend sad.* *Andrew hates* ***seeing*** *his friend sad.*

Rules for Forming Gerunds
If the verb ends in *e*, drop the *e* and add *ing*. *phone* → ***phoning***
If the verb ends with a single consonant, double this final consonant. *plan* → ***planning***
If you use the negative form, put *not* before the gerund. *We talked about* ***not getting*** *a tattoo this year.*

> **Write sentences using the following verbs as gerunds.**

1. weightlift
2. decide
3. talk
4. change
5. lose
6. transform
7. eat
8. exercise

> **Finish the following sentences with a gerund or an infinitive.**

1. I enjoy …
2. She hates …
3. He agrees …
4. They finished …
5. We tried …
6. My friend wishes …
7. Our teacher asked us …
8. I appreciate …

2 Read about body transformations.

Throughout history, people have modified their bodies by piercing their skin with bone or metal, stretching their ear lobes and lower lips, squeezing their waists with corsets, twisting their hair into dreadlocks, … Recently, people are finding new ways to change their bodies.

> Before you read, think about the following questions:

   ❶ Is being tall necessary to look beautiful? Do you think you need to be tall to find a good job?

   ❷ Would you take the risk of spending hours under anaesthesia in order to look better? Explain your answer.

   ❸ How much would you be ready to spend on your body? How much money is too much?

> Read about three kinds of body transformations below.

> While you read, think about whether you would be willing to undergo one of the surgeries.

Be Smart

Continue reading even if you don't understand every word.

Ask your teacher when you aren't sure about a sentence.

Leg Stretching

Many Chinese teenage girls want to have longer legs, but unlike most girls, Kim Ying actually did something about it.

She had an operation, carried out with only local anaesthetic, in which her leg bones—just below the knees—were sliced apart and metal rods were put
5 into the bones.

She thinks that being taller—she was five foot one (1,5 metres) and is now five foot four (1,6 metres)—will bring her more job opportunities if she moves to the United States.

Four times a day, she used a **wrench** to adjust bolts on **callipers** connected
10 to the **rods** inserted into her legs to stimulate growth in the bone marrow, and slowly she stretched her legs.

She was ready to pay 70 000 yuan (approximately $9000) to have the leg-stretching operation performed at a Beijing clinic.

Recently, clinics have received many inquiries from overseas, and they have
15 already stretched the legs of a number of foreigners, including Japanese, Americans and Canadians, who pay double the Chinese price.

Note: In 2006, China decided to ban leg stretching for cosmetic purposes. This medical procedure is still performed around the world for patients who have different leg lengths due to a birth defect, injury or disease.

Smart Words

wrench = tool used for turning a bolt

calliper = metal support for the leg

rod = straight metal bar

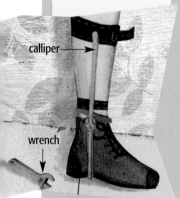
calliper
wrench

Extreme Makeovers

20 Complete physical makeovers are extremely popular in Hollywood, and both men and women feel the pressure to change almost every body part in order to achieve the look that they see in the media. Mouths, eyes, cheeks, teeth, stomachs and breasts are all going under the knife.

These complete transformations involve an enormous team of professionals:
25 **surgeons**, doctors and cosmetic dentists. To obtain that perfect look, men and women also get the help of hair and makeup artists, stylists and personal trainers. These people are ready to spend all the money they have—and even go into debt—in order to look beautiful. They are also ready to suffer the physical pain and health risks that come with all these changes. They say
30 that their new looks have given them confidence and that their lives have changed for the better thanks to their good looks.

Note: Medical procedures in extreme makeovers can help severely burned patients or children born with facial problems such as a cleft palate.

Options
Find visual examples related to these texts on the Internet. Try to find "before and after" pictures.

Eyelid Surgery

Choosing to have cosmetic surgery is an intensely personal decision, and
35 each person has different motivations that are multiple and complex. Double eyelid surgery is the most popular cosmetic operation within Asia and the Asian population of the United States. The only difference between Asian patients and Occidentals is that the average age of Asian patients is significantly lower.

40 Asian people born without a **crease**, or with a very low or weak crease in their eyelids, are asking for double eyelid surgery. They also say that they want fuller eyelids in order to be able to apply makeup. A defined crease makes the eye appear bigger, and bigger eyes are a universal sign of youth and energy.

Words
surgeon = doctor who operates
crease = line in the eyelid

45 **Note:** Your heredity and ethnic background determine your features. Some people will try drastic procedures to attain western beauty standards.

> Fill out each section of this graphic organizer.

> Share your answers with your classmates.

What words did you learn?	What surprised you?	How would you change your body?

Swans Reflecting Elephants, 1937, Salvador Dali
(1904–1989)

3 Find the problem.

Four teens sent letters explaining how they or someone they knew felt about their bodies. Their letters explained the problems and the difficulties they face each day.

> Read the advice we gave each teenager.

> From the response, determine what the person's problem was.

> Write the original letter or e-mail stating the problem.

> Write at least four sentences. Use the Writing Process on page 297 of the Smart Reference section for help.

Example:

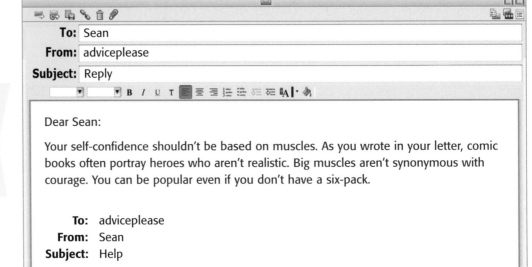

To: Sean
From: adviceplease
Subject: Reply

Dear Sean:

Your self-confidence shouldn't be based on muscles. As you wrote in your letter, comic books often portray heroes who aren't realistic. Big muscles aren't synonymous with courage. You can be popular even if you don't have a six-pack.

To: adviceplease
From: Sean
Subject: Help

When I was young, I read many comic books. Most of the stories described heroes who were strong, courageous and loved by everyone. I believed that I had to have all these qualities if I wanted to become a great person. Whenever I see another person who is more muscular than I am, I lose my self-confidence. How can I change my attitude?

Response 1

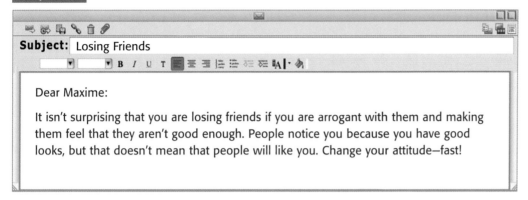

Subject: Losing Friends

Dear Maxime:

It isn't surprising that you are losing friends if you are arrogant with them and making them feel that they aren't good enough. People notice you because you have good looks, but that doesn't mean that people will like you. Change your attitude—fast!

> What did Maxime's letter say?

Response 2

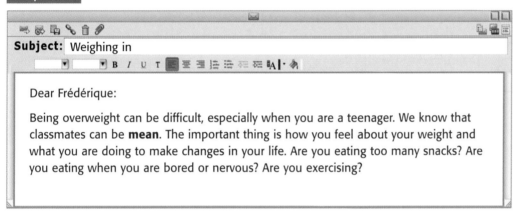

Subject: Weighing in

Dear Frédérique:

Being overweight can be difficult, especially when you are a teenager. We know that classmates can be **mean**. The important thing is how you feel about your weight and what you are doing to make changes in your life. Are you eating too many snacks? Are you eating when you are bored or nervous? Are you exercising?

> What did Frédérique's letter say?

Response 3

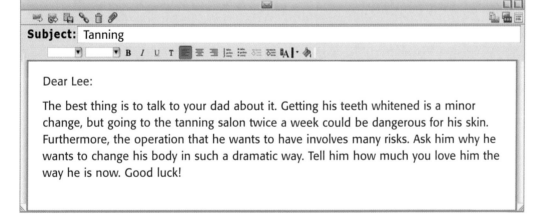

Subject: Tanning

Dear Lee:

The best thing is to talk to your dad about it. Getting his teeth whitened is a minor change, but going to the tanning salon twice a week could be dangerous for his skin. Furthermore, the operation that he wants to have involves many risks. Ask him why he wants to change his body in such a dramatic way. Tell him how much you love him the way he is now. Good luck!

> What did Lee's letter say?

Self-Evaluate

Did I use the correct verb tenses?

Did I use the dictionary to check the words I wasn't sure of?

How to Find the Main Idea

When you read a text, it is important to be able to identify its message. Are you able to find the main idea, or do you remember only the details?

Imagine that your friend asks you about the movie you saw last night. Can you tell your friend the main message of the movie in one sentence?

The main idea in a text is normally found in the introductory paragraph. In a paragraph, the main idea is usually the first sentence.

How to Write a Paragraph

Paragraphs usually include three types of sentences:

1 The topic sentence describes the main idea.

2 The supporting sentences provide more information and prove, explain and give examples about the topic sentence. These sentences often start with:

First, Second, Third, …

3 The closing sentence repeats the main idea of the paragraph in different words.

A tattoo is a fashionable thing to have. (Topic sentence with the main idea)

Teenagers all over the world are getting them done. (Supporting sentence)

They can choose from thousands of designs. (Supporting sentence)

A tattoo costs about … (Supporting sentence)

In my class, five students have tattoos because tattoos are fashionable. (Closing sentence)

Example:

Tattoos Are In

Tattoos are a fashionable thing to have. Teenagers all over the world are getting them. If you visit a tattoo shop, you can choose from thousands of designs, suited to every taste. The demand for tattoos has increased dramatically in the last few years and so have the prices. You should know that the price of a tattoo depends on its size. I interviewed all the students in my class—Five students have one. They decided to get a tattoo because it was a fashionable thing to do.

> Practise writing paragraphs using the topic sentences below.

> Include three supporting sentences and a closing sentence.

1 Losing weight is a serious concern for teenage girls.

2 Ads portray young people much more than old people.

3 Men start taking steroids to become muscular more quickly.

4 Stars in the media are defining our looks.

The Art of Tattoos

The adult body has about 1,4 to 1,9 square metres of skin. Tattoo artists call the skin a "canvas" because like a canvas, it can be a surface on which to create art.

 1 Discuss your opinion of tattoos.

How many people in your class have tattoos? An estimated one in six teenagers has a tattoo. Do you like tattoos? If you have a tattoo, does it make you feel more confident? Is a tattoo a work of art?

Part A React to a picture.

People react differently to tattoos.

> What do you think of the person in the picture?

> Answer these questions individually.

❶ Do you like the way the person in the photo looks? Why or why not?

❷ Would you like your parents to look like this? Why or why not?

❸ Do you think that having so many tattoos affects the kind of jobs this person can do? Why or why not?

❹ Do you think that this person is proud of having so many tattoos? Explain your answer.

Part B Give your opinion.

Some people think that tattoos are beautiful and make a person look hip, while others think they are vulgar and will quickly go out of style. What is your opinion?

> Read the following statements.

> Decide whether you agree or disagree with each statement and explain why.

❶ Tattoos are ugly, especially on the arms.

❷ Tattoos are a way of expressing who you are.

❸ You should choose a tattoo that is meaningful to you.

❹ It shouldn't be legal for minors to get tattoos.

❺ People have tattoos only because they want to look "cool."

❻ Once a person has a first tattoo, chances are they will get another one.

Share ideas with your classmates.

If you don't know a word, try a synonym.

Talk

Tattoos are …

I agree / disagree with you because …

I understand your point of view.

It is difficult to answer because …

Do you really think that?

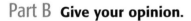

Self-**E**valuate

Did I participate actively?

Did I use Smart Talk to help me?

2 Watch a video about tattoos.

 The word *tattoo* comes from the Tahitian word *tatau*, meaning "to mark." You will watch a video explaining why people get tattoos and why people want to remove them. You will learn about the history of tattoos and why the tattoo culture in Borneo is disappearing.

> Before you watch the video, write down what you know and what you would like to know about tattoos.

> Try to think of at least three statements or questions for each column.

	What do you know about tattoos?		What would you like to know about tattoos?
1	They are permanent.	1	How much do they cost?
2	▬▬▬▬▬▬	2	▬▬▬▬▬▬

Read the questions beforehand to know what information to listen for.

Ask your teacher for help if necessary.

> Watch the video twice. The second time you watch, answer these questions.

1 What tattoo does John Irving have? Why did he choose this tattoo?

2 How do they give tattoos in Borneo?

3 What is the difference between men and women regarding the reasons they get tattoos?

4 What is one thing you shouldn't do when you get a tattoo? Do you agree with this rule?

5 How much does it cost to have a tattoo removed?

6 How many tattoo shops are there in Vancouver? Are you surprised by this number?

7 What is the main idea of the video? (See Smart Stop on page 54 of this unit.)

8 Do you have a different opinion about tattoos now that you have seen this video? What surprises you most about tattoos? Explain your point of view.

Self-**E**valuate

Did I answer the questions correctly?

Did I write complete sentences to give my personal opinion?

Portrait of a New Zealand Man, circa 1768–1780

3 Read an interview with a Maori tribesman.

The Maori are the native people of New Zealand. For Maoris, facial tattoos, called *moko*, are very significant. In ancient Maori culture, most **high-ranking** Maori people received a *moko*, and people who didn't have them were considered less important.

You will read an interview with George Tamihana Nuku, a Maori tribesman, to learn why this ancient tradition is becoming popular in our Western society.

> Before you read the text, answer these questions:

1 What do you think of facial tattoos?

2 Would you like to have a tattoo on your face?

3 Would you treat or think of someone differently if they had a facial tattoo? Explain.

Maori man with *moko*

An Interview with George Tamihana Nuku

What would you like to tell people about yourself and about the Maori and the *moko*?

I'm very interested in talking about *moko* and explaining about why we have the art of *moko* and what it means to us now in this time. I'm interested
5 also in the relationship with *moko* from the past and how it has formed the basis of our culture and like I said, how it applies in today's context.

Is it appropriate for people to ask you about the *moko* and your culture? How does that make you feel?

I'm glad people stare because it's something that's meant to be looked at.
10 I'm sure people are curious about *moko*. I would be. If I didn't know anything about it and I saw someone who looked like me, I'd want to ask something and I'd want to stare. I find that the children are the ones who don't have a problem with that. They come straight up to me and ask: "What's that on your face?" And they stare.

15 **What kind of reaction have you had from folks here in the States?**

There's the whole spectrum of reactions. Some people are, I guess, quite blasé about it, like maybe they have seen it before. Some people, they haven't seen it before.

Can you talk a little more about how *moko* represents connections between
20 **the past and the future, and connections between generations?**

The **practitioners** of today are doing a fantastic job of creating a *moko* for the twenty-first century that is relevant to our needs and our aspirations of now and our lifestyle. For example, we are using modern technology in the creation of *moko*. We are using sterilizing machines and rubber **gloves** and

Words
high-ranking = very important
practitioner = person who practises a tradition
glove = covering for the hand

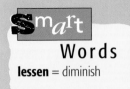
Words
lessen = diminish

25 electric needles. We say this is a very traditional practice to use the best things available to you to create your story.

I think our ancestors would be proud of us for adopting this approach of utilizing the best to maintain our standard, to **lessen** the likelihood of degeneration of the art form. I know that in the next generation time, the 30 *moko* will be an exciting art form. It will be something that will reflect their times.

Elements of *moko* have been adopted by certain parts of Western popular culture. I'm curious what you would say to a young American teenager who has a tattoo with elements of the *moko* in it. What would you want 35 **him or her to know?**

Young people are going to seek something that's exciting and intoxicating like *moko* and the connotations that go with it. They're also going to look for some form of identity and something that makes them distinctive in the global morass. This has been a subject of long and bitter discussion at home 40 amongst the peoples, where people have advocated that we shut the door and don't allow people access to our *moko*.

The practitioners are saying quite the opposite. They're saying we must go and engage and we must take our art form to the world because then at least we have a say in the quality of the art form.

45 **How would you respond to non-natives who wear some of the designs that are similar to the *moko*?**

If you don't live the things that go with it, then it's only a design. It's not a *moko*. First and foremost, it comes from your lineage. It defines who your parents and grandparents [were] from the beginning of time. That's number 50 one. Number two is that the *moko* is reinforced and validated by your commitment to the group. And the group owns you. You are the group and the group is you. If you don't have those things, then it's not a *moko*.

Ryan Mitchell, "Maori Chief on Facial Tattoos and Tribal Pride," *National Geographic News*, October 14, 2003

> Answer these questions and write the line number where you found the answer.

1 How does George Tamihana Nuku feel when people stare?

2 Name two different reactions he gets from people when they see his *moko*.

3 What kinds of modern technology are tattoo artists using?

4 Why do some teens want a *moko*?

5 Is a facial tattoo considered a *moko* if you aren't native? Why or why not?

6 What does a *moko* tell you about someone?

Self-**E**valuate

Did I answer the questions correctly?
Did I ask for help when I didn't understand?

Changing Beauty Standards

Beauty standards are always changing. Can you name some of these changes?
What are the differences between your parents' tastes and your tastes?

 1 Read about skinny models.

If you have ever watched a fashion show, you know that the main characteristic of models is that they are very skinny. Some models (women and men) develop eating disorders to remain thin.

You will read about why skinny models are creating a problem in the fashion world.

> Before reading the text, look at the title to help you understand it better.

> After reading the text, find five true or false statements related to the text.

> Quiz your partner to find out how well she/he understood the text.

Look at the Smart Words
before reading the text.

Take notes while
reading.

Skinny Models Banned from Catwalk

Madrid, Spain—The world's first **ban** on overly thin models at a top-level fashion show in Madrid has caused **outrage** among modelling agencies.

Madrid's fashion week has turned away underweight models after protests that girls and young women were trying to copy their **rail-thin** looks and
5 developing eating disorders.

Organizers say they want to project an image of beauty and health, rather than a **waif-like** or "heroin-chic" look.

But Cathy Gould, of New York's Elite modelling agency, said the fashion industry was being used as a **scapegoat** for illnesses like anorexia and
10 bulimia.

"I think it's outrageous. I understand they want to set this tone of healthy beautiful women, but what about discrimination against the model, and what about the freedom of the designer?" said Gould, Elite's North America director, adding that the move could harm careers of naturally "gazelle-like"
15 models.

Madrid's regional government, which sponsors the show and imposed restrictions, said it did not blame designers and models for anorexia. It said the fashion industry had a responsibility to portray healthy body images.

"Fashion is a mirror and many teenagers imitate what they see on the
20 catwalk," said regional official Concha Guerra.

The mayor of Milan, Italy, Letizia Moratti, told an Italian newspaper this week she would seek a similar ban for her city's show unless it could find a solution to "sick-looking" models.

The Madrid show is using the body mass index or BMI—based on weight
25 and height—to measure models. It has turned away 30 percent of women

Words

ban = prohibition

outrage = strong reaction

rail-thin = very thin

waif-like = very skinny

scapegoat = someone blamed for the mistakes or faults of another

who took part in the previous event. Medics will be on hand at the September 18 to 22 shows to check models.

"The restrictions could be quite a shock to the fashion world at the
30 beginning, but I'm sure it's important as far as health is concerned," said Leonor Perez Pita, director of Madrid's show.

"Skinny models banned from catwalk," Madrid, Spain, Reuters, September 13, 2006

 2 Write and act out a sketch.

What is your opinion of the ban discussed in the previous activity? Should skinny models, both men and women, be excluded from fashion shows? Why or why not?

> Read the two situations below and write sketches.

 Situation A

You are a naturally skinny model and the organizers think you are too thin. You want to convince them to let you stay in the fashion show. What will you tell them?

 Situation B

You are the mother or father of an anorexic teenager. What will you tell the organizers to convince them to maintain the ban?

Use gestures. It will help you express your message.

Step 1 **Prepare**

> Read the two situations.
> Work with a partner and choose your roles for both situations.
> Don't forget that the model can be a man or a woman.
> Take a few minutes to think of arguments.

Step 2 **Produce**

> Write a six-sentence dialogue for each situation.
> Read your texts again. Did you include arguments?
> What can you add to make them more interesting? Can you add details and humour?
> Can you write longer or shorter sentences to make them clearer?
> Did you verify words in a dictionary?
> Make changes and write a final copy.

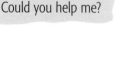

Talk

I regret to tell you …
I feel that …
I would prefer …
Is it all right?
Could you help me?

Step 3 **Present**

> Practise your dialogues with your partner.
> Present them to another group or to the class.
> Vote on the best team.

Self-Evaluate

Were my sentences clear?

Did I make my arguments convincing?

3 Talk about what is attractive to you.

In this activity, you will discuss interior and exterior beauty. What do you like in other people?

> Sit with a partner.
> Choose to be either the boy, Matteo, or the girl, Elia.
> Read through the cartoon together.
> Whom do you identify with most—Elia or Matteo? Why?
> Discuss these questions with your partner:

1. Think about two famous people whom you find attractive (one woman and one man) and explain why you think they are attractive.

2. Describe these people using two categories: their exterior beauty (physical traits, body shape, clothes, hair, sense of style, …) and their interior beauty (sense of humour, intelligence, creativity, youthfulness, …).

3. Which is more important to you in a girlfriend / boyfriend—interior or exterior qualities? Why?

4. Do you think people appreciate you more for your interior or exterior qualities? Why?

Use what you learned in the unit to give your opinion.

Talk

He is attractive because …

She's good-looking because …

Interior / exterior beauty is more important …

It depends on …

What I like is …

People think I'm …

Did I try my best?

Did I pronounce the words properly?

T^as^k 4 Real Beauty

Advertising companies are now showing that beauty comes in different shapes and sizes. An important beauty criterion is looking healthy. Ads are starting to use "real" people to sell their products.

1 Learn about a new type of ad.

Learn how advertising is starting to reflect changes in our standards of beauty.

> **Listen to the text and answer these questions:**

1. What is the main idea of the text? Write it in your own words. (See the Smart Stop on page 54.)

2. Can you name companies that are using "real" people in their ads?

3. Are you positively influenced by these types of ads? Do you buy these products?

4. What is your opinion about the changes that have been made to the beauty industry?

5. What strategy did you use to understand the text better?

 Further

> Create a collage of the "perfect" body and face according to what is proposed in the media. Cut out pictures of different body parts from a magazine. Explain what the "problem" with this picture is.

> A marketing company wants to launch a new product for teens with a slogan that says: "Please Read Me Instead of Judging My Cover." What could this product be? Write the rest of the text that will accompany the ad.

Words

lucrative = that pays well

billboard = large sign used for advertising

nowadays = today

 S e l f - **E** v a l u a t e

Did I answer the questions correctly?

Did I give my personal opinion?

Facts

Reality Check

You might have read this many times, but it is important to remember that the images you see in magazines have been changed with computer techniques. The shapes and sizes have been altered—the nose, the breasts, the thighs, the hands, the cheeks—everything has been changed to fit the look of the day. Freckles, wrinkles and skin folds have been removed. Nobody in real life looks this perfect—not even the models! The problem with this trend is that advertisers are sending you the message that if you look perfect, you will be happy and successful.

Be Smart

Listen attentively.

Plan. Look at the Smart Words before listening.

Take a risk. Write the word even if you aren't sure how to spell it.

2 Analyze a new type of ad.

You just learned that companies are changing their ads to show "real" people. Here is an example of an advertisement for teens.

> **Look at the ad carefully.**

Your Beauty, Your Way

Dermatologists know that makeup can **harbour** acne-causing bacteria. That moisturizers can **clog** your pores, causing nasty blackheads and whiteheads. That many cosmetics contain allergens like lanolin (grease secreted by sheep) and carmine (made from crushed beetles) that can give you rashy, blotchy skin.

So why does the beauty industry insist that you need their products to be pretty? Do they make more money when you're happy and confident? Or when you're **plagued** by "imperfections" that they just happen to be able to "fix"?

Luckily, it's easy to take care of your skin without buying into the game. Wash it gently.

Get plenty of sleep. Drink water. Exercise. Eat lots of fruits and vegetables. Don't overdo it in the sun. Easy, inexpensive and natural.

Why let the beauty industry tell you how to feel about yourself?

It's your beauty. Do it your way.

Smart Words

harbour = contain
clog = block
plagued = irritated

AdBusters Media Foundation, Vancouver, British Columbia, Canada

Guess the answers
when you aren't sure.

Walking Male, 1960,
Alberto Giacometti
(1901–1966)

> Answer these questions individually to help you understand the ad on page 63 better.

> Then discuss your answers with your classmates.

1 What is the ad trying to sell? What is interesting about it?

2 Who is the "model"?

3 Who is the target audience: males or females, adults or teens?

4 What are the biggest letters in the ad? Why do you think they are written bigger?

5 Ads often have very short texts, but in this case, we see the contrary. Why do you think the ad's message is long?

6 Do you agree with this sentence from the ad: "Why let the beauty industry tell you how to feel about yourself?" Why or why not?

7 What is the purpose of the ad: to express feelings, to inform, to influence you?

8 Give your opinion by completing the following sentences:

I learned that …

My favourite part of the ad is …

I disagree with …

If I made an ad, I would …

I think people should …

If we want to change the advertising industry, we have to …

Self-Evaluate

Did I answer the questions correctly?

Did I give my personal opinion?

C2 3 What do you like about you?

Having a healthy body image means that you feel good about the way you look. It also means that you take care of yourself. You eat well, you exercise, you take time to see your friends, you do fun things and you get enough sleep. Feeling beautiful is about feeling energetic and resisting the pressure to have the perfect look.

> Make a list of twenty things you like about yourself: ten things related to your body and ten things related to your personality and accomplishments. For example:

I like my hair and my sense of humour.

> Ask your friends what they like about you. You may be surprised to hear what they have to say!

Final Task

The Beauty Expert

You have explored the meaning of beauty in different contexts. Now is your chance to be the beauty expert.

Talk about real beauty.

Option A

Create a magazine ad promoting a positive body image.

Option B

Prepare a quiz related to beauty.

Option A

Create a magazine ad promoting a positive body image.

Step 1 **Prepare**

> Choose the product you want to sell, for example, a type of cream, soap, clothes, …
> Brainstorm. Who is the target audience for your product: men or women? How old are the people for whom you are advertising?
> Research. Look at magazines to find interesting and different ways to show the body. Do you want to show various kinds of beauty?
> Decide on the message you wish to send to your audience. Do you want to encourage them to feel happy or confident?
> Write notes about how you will present the product.
> Take pictures of the product or find pictures from ads.

Step 2 **Produce**

> Create your ad. Write your text.
> Use ideas from the ad on page 63.
> Glue or draw pictures that show a positive and realistic body image.
> Reread your text. Do you see any mistakes? Are the spelling and grammar correct?
> Ask someone to look at your work and comment on it.
> Make changes to the ad and produce a final copy.

Step 3 **Present**

> Display all the ads on the class walls.
> Make a chart to vote for the best ad. Which ad is the most effective? The most realistic? The most eye-catching?

Option B

Prepare a quiz related to beauty.

Step 1 **Prepare**

> Review the unit.
> Research the Internet and magazines to find information on topics such as body image, weightlifting, tattoos and advertising.

Options

Do research on the Internet.

Use your camera to take pictures for the ad.

Use a scanner to scan images. Then use software to modify the images.

Use software to create the quiz.

Put your quiz online.

> Write down a few ideas. What questions would you like to include in the quiz?
> Decide for whom you are writing the quiz: your friends, your parents, children?
> What is the purpose of your quiz: to inform, to influence, to express your opinion?

Step 2 Write

> Write a minimum of ten questions. They can be true-or-false or multiple-choice questions.
> Include questions related to the surveys you did.
> Include questions related to websites.
> Include questions related to the positive and negative aspects of pictures from magazines.

Step 3 Revise

> Verify that you have included enough questions.
> Make sure that you have prepared the answers to the quiz so that you can check your friend's results.
> Ask a friend to try out the quiz to determine whether the questions are clear.

Step 4 Edit

> Review question formation in the Smart Reference section (page 272).
> Check that you have used the correct verb tenses.
> Verify the spelling of words you aren't sure of in a dictionary.
> Make changes and write a final copy.

Step 5 Publish

> Give your quiz to your teacher.
> Your teacher will distribute the best quizzes for you to try.

Words
REVIEW

1. ban
2. clog
3. complexion
4. crease
5. crooked
6. freckles
7. glove
8. harbour
9. high-ranking
10. lessen
11. mean
12. outrage
13. plagued
14. practitioner
15. rail-thin
16. rod
17. scapegoat
18. surgeon
19. waif-like
20. wrench

Self-Evaluate

Did I follow all the steps or adapt them for my project?

Did I include ideas that I learned in an original way?

Did I check that the spelling and grammar were correct?

Did I use different resources?

Reflection

1. Which activity did you like the most? Why?
2. Which activity was the most challenging for you?
3. Name two strategies that you learned to use in this unit.
4. If you had to do this unit over again, what would you do differently?
5. What are your goals for the next unit? What would you like to improve?

Bound by Beauty

People have always done strange things to be beautiful. Today we spend thousands of dollars on surgery to alter the shapes of our bodies. For almost a
5 thousand years, Chinese women also altered their bodies—but not with surgery. They practised a form of mutilation called "foot binding." To do this, women would break and tie up their
10 feet in order to make them smaller. Small, three-to four-inch feet were considered beautiful and meant access to a world of privilege and wealth. Today, there are only a **handful** of survivors
15 from the foot-binding era in China. Soon, people around the world will remember these women, who paid a high price for fashion, only through photos and the three or four-inch silk **slippers** they wore.

20 Binding was practised in China from the tenth century to the beginning of the twentieth century. The earliest record of foot binding dates back to the Tang Dynasty (618–907). Tang Dancers
25 wrapped their feet with long strips of cloth to make their feet smaller, helping them take the small, light steps needed to dance. Some legends say that women's feet were also bound to
30 impress the emperor.

Foot binding was very painful and resulted in severely disfigured feet. Families started binding their daughters' feet when the girls were as young as five
35 years old. Binding started so young because the bones were very soft and easy to break. In the first year of the foot being bound, the four small toes would usually break. The toes were wrapped
40 very tightly and then pulled towards the **heel** of the foot. The arch of the foot became very bent because the toes were pulled as close to the heel as possible.

The bandages were tightened every day,
45 which was usually more painful than the broken bones.

There were other problems that occurred because of binding. Toenails would grow into the skin of the foot, causing
50 infections, and the infected feet had a strong odour. Women were often sick with fever because of the pain caused by binding and several died from infections. Also, because their feet were so
55 unnaturally small, it was difficult for women to keep their balance. Sometimes they would fall and break their **hip bone**.

There was a lot of pressure on young girls to have their feet bound. Men only
60 wanted to marry women with tiny feet, and some girls had no choice but to give in to the pressure. With bound feet, these women were considered beautiful, gained status in the community and
65 maybe even had the chance to marry into a wealthy family.

The practice was officially banned in 1912, but parents still continued to bind their girls' feet in secret. Women hid
70 their bound feet from government officials because they and their families would be punished for continuing the practice. After binding was banned, these women were forced to work on their feet
75 doing jobs like digging **ditches** and farming. These jobs were considered difficult even for women who didn't have deformed feet.

The last of these women who had their
80 feet bound as little girls still live in areas across China today. They have endured a life of pain as a result of their feet. Some estimate that about two billion women in China had their feet bound and
85 broken before the practice was stopped.

Smart Words

handful = very small number or amount

slippers = light shoes worn in the home

heel = back part of the foot

hip bone = bone at the top of the leg

ditch = long hole at the side of a road

Permanent Pigment: Future Regrets
You're on the losing side of the tattoo battle

Words

forthcoming = willing to give information

addicting = creating a desire for more

forearm = lower part of the arm above the hand

get rid of = remove

Here's one of the frustrating realities about the psychology of tattoos: Future possibilities just don't enter into the equation.

5 No question, that's a parent's number one worry when it comes to tattoos: that their child will go out and get this permanent thing on her or his body with no thought to the future.

10 Yet suddenly everybody has a tattoo—or at least it seems that way. So what should parents do?

To get some answers, I conducted a number of brief, informal, unscientific 15 interviews. Basically, I went up to people—in a supermarket, an electronics store, a bookstore, a coffee shop—and asked them about their tattoos.

With no exceptions, the people I spoke to 20 were immediately and enthusiastically **forthcoming**.

Here's what I found.

Most had multiple tattoos. The first person I spoke with, a man in his early 25 twenties, had both arms covered. After he got his first one he wanted another. If there was an open space it pleaded to him for a tattoo. "It's **addicting**," he said. ("Addicting" was a word I would hear a 30 number of times.)

People's first tattoos in particular often had special personal meaning. One young woman said her first was her name on her back.

35 Another's first was a sun on his **forearm** that he and his high-school band had agreed to get together—but he had backed out. When one of the band members died, he got his first tattoo at 40 twenty as a memorial to his dead friend.

People didn't necessarily regret their choices. One woman explained she would no longer choose what she had picked for her first tattoos, but she would 45 not **get rid of** them because they were part of who she had been—her personal history drawn out on her skin.

I asked a group of young workers with bare arms why they chose not to have 50 tattoos. Each one, in fact, did have a tattoo—they just weren't visible. When asked why, they answered in unison, "Jobs." They did not want to do something that would get in the way of 55 their white-collar career plans.

So what does it all mean?

First, tattoos are not going away any time soon. Second, you may not like the look of tattoos, but they are not all bad. There 60 seems to be something self-affirming for people who choose to get tattoos— they're proud of them. They're a personal statement.

Also, getting a tattoo is not as impulsive 65 an act as many think. People give much thought to their tattoos—what they mean, where they are going to put them, the possible consequences—though they do not always take the conservative route.

70 What does this mean for parents? Many teenagers under the age of eighteen want tattoos. But at this stage parents have real control. For one thing, at many places you have to be eighteen or have a 75 parent's consent to get a tattoo.

Also, they do hear your words. So tell them what you think.

"At least wait until you are older. You may regret your choice now and it's 80 something you will have to live with."

Or: "As long as you live under this roof you will not get a tattoo." (Which is a bit of a bluff.)

Your kids will hear you. In fact, all except 85 one of the people I talked to got their first tattoo after they were eighteen. Why not before? The most common answer: "Because my parents would kill me."

Anthony E. Wolf, "Permanent Pigment: Future Regrets," *The Globe and Mail* website, October 16, 2007

Buy **Nothing**

In this unit, you will explore the influence of marketing and consumerism in our lives. You will think about the amount of advertising in your environment and discuss ways to make life simpler and more meaningful. Finally, you will learn about Buy Nothing Day and experience a day without consuming.

HOW CAN WE PRACTISE SIMPLICITY IN OUR SOCIETY?

Final
T**A**sk

Find ways to promote Buy Nothing Day or voluntary simplicity.

Option A

Design a media text publicizing Buy Nothing Day or voluntary simplicity.

Option B

Write a letter to a newspaper describing your experiences on Buy Nothing Day.

Smart Start

Are you affected by advertising? Do you love to shop? You may not believe it, but advertising really does influence people to buy things. Take a look around you. Think about how many ads there are and how much they encourage you to buy things.

1 Name that brand.

Do you think you aren't affected by advertising? Try this simple experiment.

Use your dictionary to help you.

> Copy the chart below onto a piece of paper.

> When your teacher gives you the signal, write down as many brand names as you can think of in two minutes under the heading "Brand Names."

> Then, on your teacher's signal, write down as many names of trees and flowers as you can think of in two minutes under the heading "Names of Trees and Flowers." These pictures will help you get started.

	Brand Names	Names of Trees and Flowers
1	▬▬▬▬	pine tree
2	▬▬▬▬	water lily
3	▬▬▬▬	▬▬▬▬

> Look at your lists and compare them with a partner.

> Discuss the following questions with your partner.

　① Which list is longer: the one under the heading "Brand Names" or the one under "Names of Trees and Flowers?"

　② Do the results surprise you? Why or why not?

　③ Was it hard to find names of trees and flowers? Even in French?

　④ Why do we know more brand names than names of trees and flowers?

　⑤ Do you think the results of this experiment would be the same if someone tried it a hundred years ago? Why or why not?

　⑥ Do you or your friends buy and wear items with brand names? Which ones?

2 Calculate your "screen time."

What would you do if the electricity was cut in your neighbourhood for over twenty-four hours? Would you be able to survive? Would you be bored? We all spend time looking at screens of electronic devices, for example, computers, televisions and cellphones. Try this activity to calculate your "screen time."

> With a partner or a small group, think of as many "electronic" activities as you can in five minutes.

> Write your answers down on a piece of paper.

> Calculate the number of hours you spend doing each activity.

> How much time do you spend looking at a screen in a week, a month, a year? How much time do you think you will spend looking at a screen in your lifetime?

> Use Smart Talk to share what you discover with your classmates.

S e l f - **E** v a l u a t e

Was my message on topic?

Did I speak without hesitating?

Facts

Canadian Broadcasting Corporation

Today, people around the world love to watch TV. By one estimate, typical North Americans will have watched almost ten years of TV by their seventieth birthday!

Can you imagine a time when there wasn't a TV in almost every home? One of Canada's pioneers in television is the Canadian Broadcasting Corporation (CBC). CBC / Radio Canada first broadcasted radio programs in 1927 and started broadcasting TV programs in Montréal and Toronto in 1952. Televisions were a luxury item back then, so not everyone had one. It wasn't until the 1960s that you could watch TV in colour. Now many families own multiple TVs. People buy the latest-model TV even if their TVs are working properly!

Marketing to Teens

Where do you see brands? Advertisers are smart; they make sure that you see brands everywhere! Advertisers also make sure that they send a clear message to the people they want to buy their products, especially teenagers and young adults.

C1 1 Talk of brand names you see.

How many ads do you see, hear or watch each day? Think about what you see while watching TV, surfing the Internet, riding the bus or driving on the highway. Advertising is everywhere!

Smart Talk

I saw … ads / logos.

In the vending machines at school, there are …

I think that schools should / shouldn't advertise, because …

We could talk to … about the issue.

> Look around your classroom (at clothes, computers, books, …) to find ads or logos.

> Read these questions individually and then discuss the answers with a partner:

1. How many ads or logos did you find in your classroom?

2. Think about your school cafeteria. What do the vending machines contain: soft drinks, candy, …? What logos do you remember seeing there?

3. Can you think of any other advertising in the school? Where is it?

4. Should schools be free of advertising? Why or why not?

5. What can you do to protest the amount of advertising in your school? Who can you talk to about it? What reasons can you give to convince this person?

6. Write down as many places as you can think of where you might find advertisements.

Self-Evaluate

Did I speak without hesitating?

Did I use Smart Talk to help me?

C2 2 Learn how students at one school fought back.

Should schools be free of advertising? That was the opinion of students at a school in Mississauga, Ontario, when their school agreed to let a company present twelve minutes of "teen news" every day in exchange for free audiovisual equipment. Watch the video to find out how the students protested to the school administration—and what the results were!

> Before you watch the video, think about these questions:

1. Is it a good idea for schools to allow companies to advertise their products in exchange for free equipment?

2. Does your school display any advertisements? If so, where are the ads displayed? What do they promote?

3. Are there any ads in this textbook? Do you think there should be? Why or why not?

> Read the questions below and then watch the video.

> Use Be Smart and the Smart Stop on page 74 to help you.

> After watching the video, answer the questions.

> Discuss your answers in a small group or as a class.

4. What is YNN? Why did the school want it?

5. How did the students protest YNN? Give at least one example.

6. What happened when the students protested YNN? Give at least one example.

7. Was the students' protest successful? Why or why not?

8. What is the main message of the video?

9. How would you react if you were a student at this school? What would you do?

10. Do you know of any similar advertising problems at your school? How can you make teachers, administrators and students aware of these problems?

11. Look at the Smart Stop on page 74. In the video, what kind of camera shots did the filmmakers use to show the interviews, the board meeting and the band's performance on stage?

Pay attention–Don't be distracted!

Go Further

> Watch the video again. Use a character web to keep track of the people you see in the video and the ideas in which they believe.

> How would you change the lighting, sound and camera angles to make the school principal look better? Discuss your answers in a small group and then write a paragraph summarizing your ideas.

Self-Evaluate

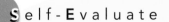

Did I answer the questions correctly?

Did I make a connection between the video and my community?

How to Explore Video Media

Video media combines images with sound and movement to make a very powerful medium.

Camera Shot: The camera shot dictates what you will and will not see.

	Close-up	Medium Shot	Long Shot
Shot:	• Usually focuses on a person's face	• Shows a person from the waist up	• Shows an entire scene (several people, a room, …)
Effect:	• Used for interviews • Shows the emotions and expressions displayed on someone's face	• Used for interviews • Shows a person in her/his surroundings	• Shows the context of what is happening
Example:	• The interview with a student at the protest in *YNN*	• The introductions of the students in their bedrooms in *YNN*	• The shots of the school board meeting or the scenes showing the band's performance in *YNN*

Tilted Angle, Close-up Shot   High Angle, Medium Shot   Low Angle, Long Shot

Camera Angle: The camera angle is the direction and height from which the camera shoots the scene.

	Tilted	High	Low
Angle:	• The camera is looking at the person or object being filmed from at least a forty-five degree angle	• The camera is above the person or object being filmed	• The camera is beneath the person or object being filmed
Effect:	• Makes a banal shot look more interesting	• Makes the person or object being filmed look less important	• Makes the person or object being filmed look important or even threatening
Example:	• The shots of the classroom desks and the television in *YNN*	• Looking at someone from the sky	• The shot of the principal's legs as he walks down the hall in *YNN*

Voluntary Simplicity

With each new piece of technology that humans invent, for example, the computer, companies promise us a better, easier life. However, many people find that they receive just the opposite! We seem to have less and less time. Some people react to the stresses of modern living by rejecting modern inventions. "Voluntary simplicity" refers to the practice of choosing ways to simplify our lives.

1 Find out about voluntary simplicity.

What is voluntary simplicity? How do we practise it? Why would we want to do this? In the following activity, you will listen to information about voluntary simplicity.

> Before you listen, think about how you could make your life simpler.

> Answer the following questions while you listen to the text.

  ① Name three ways people communicated in the past and three ways people communicate today.

  ② Define voluntary simplicity.

  ③ Find two ways of celebrating the holiday season for people who practise voluntary simplicity.

  ④ Who is responsible for encouraging us to buy things?

> After listening, discuss these questions with your classmates.

  ⑤ Do you think that practising voluntary simplicity is a good idea? Why or why not?

  ⑥ Name one way you could simplify your life. How would this change impact you? Explain your answer.

  ⑦ Which is more to blame for encouraging people to buy things they don't really need: the advertising or the people themselves? Why do you believe this?

Go Further

> As you work through the unit, write down the words that are new to you. Use this list to create a crossword puzzle with clues for a partner.

> Find out more about someone who is known for advocating voluntary simplicity. Do research and present interesting facts about the person to your classmates.

Use a dictionary as you listen.

Reflect: What will you do next time to help you understand even better?

Words

consumerism = buying things

meaningful = significant

advocate = support

Self-Evaluate

Did I persevere and maintain a positive attitude?

Did I think about which strategies to use to understand the text before I started listening?

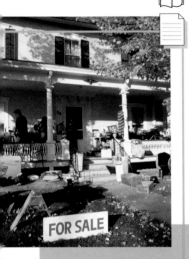

FOR SALE

2 Learn ten ways to simplify your life.

The text that you are about to read was written by Linda Breen Pierce. Linda once lived the so-called **American dream**. However, she and her husband gave up their fancy home and their extravagant vacations to simplify their lives and focus on the things that really mattered to them. Linda started a research project called "The Pierce Simplicity Study," in which she studied the lives of over two hundred people who had made the decision to live simply.

> ❯ Before you read the text, think of at least three reasons why people would simplify their lives by giving up fancy homes and extravagant vacations.

Predict what the text will be about.

Take notes while you read.

Words

American dream = belief that success and prosperity are available to everyone

purchase = buy

cozy = warm and comfortable

leisurely = in a slow and relaxed way

commute = travel to and from a job each day

foreign = relating to a country that isn't your own

Recipe for Simplicity

We work hard and play hard, filling nearly every moment with activity. Most families believe they need two incomes to pay for a standard of living that has doubled in the last fifty years. But do we? Based on my three-year study of over two hundred people who have simplified their lives, I found that we can work less, want less and spend less, and be happier and more fulfilled in the process. Here are ten suggestions to simplify your life.

❶ Don't let any material thing come into your home unless you absolutely love it and want to keep it until it is beyond repair. Too much stuff—It's suffocating us. **Purchasing**, maintaining, insuring, storing and eventually disposing of our stuff sucks up our precious life energy.

❷ Live in a home with only those rooms that you or someone in your family use every day. Create a **cozy** home environment that fits your family. You will find this is much more satisfying than living in a museum designed to impress your friends.

❸ Limit your work (outside of the home) to thirty hours a week, twenty if you are a parent. To live a balanced life, we need "down" time—time to daydream, to relax, to prepare a **leisurely** meal, to take a walk. If we surround our structured activities with empty spaces, those activities will become more productive and meaningful.

❹ Select a home and place of employment no more than thirty minutes away from each other. **Commuting** time is dead time. Preserve your energy and money for more rewarding life experiences.

❺ Limit your children's extracurricular activities to one to three a week, depending on age. Otherwise, you will exhaust yourself, and your children will grow up addicted to constant stimulation.

❻ Take three to four months off every few years and go live in a **foreign** country. Living in a different culture fascinates, excites and vitalizes us. It teaches us to live in the present, a core practice of simple living. We gain perspective when we experience a foreign culture. We learn how much we have to be grateful for.

7 Spend at least an hour a week in a natural setting, away from crowds of people, traffic and buildings. Three to four hours of nature time each week is even better. There is nothing more basic, more simple, than the natural world.

8 Do whatever you need to do to connect with a sense of spirit in your life, whether it be prayer, religious services, journal writing, meditation or spiritually-related reading. Simplicity leads to spirituality; spirituality leads to simplicity. Cultivate a practice of silence and solitude, even for fifteen to thirty minutes a day.

9 Seek the support of others who want to simplify their lives. Join or start a simplicity circle if you enjoy group interaction.

10 Practise saying "no." Say "no" to those things that don't bring you inner peace and fulfillment, whether it be more material things, greater career responsibility or added social activities. Live consciously and deliberately.

Linda Breen Pierce, "Recipe for Simplicity," *The Simplicity Resource Guide* website, Carmel, California, Gallagher Press, 2003

> Match the examples given below with the numbers of the corresponding suggestions from the text above.

a) Enrolling in a yoga class to improve your mental and physical health.
   Suggestion: 8

b) Reducing the amount of time you spend going to and from work by living closer to your place of employment.

c) Not purchasing a new computer every time a new version is available.

d) Hiking, camping or walking in the forest.

e) Choosing a smaller home in which to live.

f) Travelling to and living in another country for a short period of time.

g) Carefully selecting how you spend your time.

h) Socializing with other people who live simple lives.

> Answer the following questions individually.

1 What surprised you about the article?

2 Do you think this article is more relevant to parents or teens? Why?

3 Do you think that the tips for simple living are realistic? Choose three suggestions that you could follow to simplify your life and three that you couldn't follow. Give reasons why you could or couldn't apply these suggestions to your life.

Self-**E**valuate

Did I answer the questions correctly?

Did I write complete sentences giving my personal opinion?

3 Write about making your life simpler.

If you had to give up something in your life in order to make your life simpler, what would it be? Would you go a day without watching television? Would you walk to a friend's house and have a conversation face-to-face instead of calling? How would doing these things make your life better?

A Stroll in the Woods, 1886–90, Henri Rousseau (1844–1910)

> Write a plan of what you would do in a week to practise voluntary simplicity.

Step 1 **Prepare**

> Brainstorm to find different ways to make your life simpler and reasons for or against voluntary simplicity.

> Organize your thoughts into an outline: Monday, Tuesday, Wednesday, …

> Give reasons why the activities are good ideas to try. For example, spending less time watching television means spending more time reading or talking with your friends and family.

Step 2 **Write**

> Use your outline to write your first draft.

Step 3 **Revise**

> Read your plan out loud. Do your ideas make sense?

> Ask someone to read the plan and give you feedback.

> Make changes.

Step 4 **Edit**

> Circle all the words in your plan of which you are unsure, then check the spelling in a dictionary.

> Verify your count and non-count nouns. Use the Smart Structure on the next page to help you.

> Write a final copy.

Step 5 **Publish**

> Give your plan to your teacher.

> Post your plan in your locker or on your fridge as a reminder.

Ic**T**

Options

Add images to your plan.

Post the plan on your blog or personal web page.

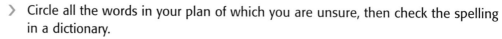

Self-Evaluate

Will my suggestions help someone who is interested in voluntary simplicity?

Did I use count and non-count nouns correctly?

Structure

Count and Non-Count Nouns

When you are talking about what you will or will not buy, or what you will or will not do to simplify your life, you need to use nouns. As a general rule, if you can count the item, it is a count noun. If you can't count the item, it is a non-count noun.

Count Nouns (Nouns That Can Be Counted)
There is a singular and a plural form of count nouns.   A **gift** / two **gifts**   An **hour** / two **hours**   Use *there is* when a singular noun follows.   **There is** one gift on the table.   Use *there are* when a plural noun follows.   **There are** two gifts on the table.   To indicate a small quantity, use *a few*, or *many* in the negative form.   There are **a few** posters.   There are**n't many** posters.   To indicate a large quantity, use *many* or *a lot of*.   There are **many** gifts under the tree.   There are **a lot of** presents given at Christmas.

Non-Count Nouns (Nouns That Can't Be Counted)

Groups of objects	**Masses**
Equipment, furniture, hair	Rice, sand, sugar
Fluids	**Abstract ideas**
Milk, gasoline, water	Happiness, love, sadness

Usually non-count nouns have no plural form.
I need **sunshine** *in my garden.* (not *sunshines*)

Non-count nouns don't take articles (*a*, *an*, *the*).
I need to do **homework** *tonight.* (not *a homework*)

To indicate a small quantity, use *a little* or *much* in the negative form.
There is **a little** *ice cream left.*
*There is***n't much** *ice cream left.*

To indicate a large quantity, use *much* or *a lot of*.
Will it take **much** *time?*
There is **a lot of** *money in my wallet.*

Expressions of Quantity (Used with Both Count and Non-Count Nouns)

Some
There are **some** *cookies in the jar.* (count noun)
I hope there is **some** *sunshine this afternoon.*
(non-count noun)

Any
Do you have **any** *presents for me?* (count noun)
Is there **any** *coffee left?* (non-count noun)

Enough
I don't have **enough** *potatoes to make the soup.*
(count noun)
We have **enough** *money to buy a car.* (non-count noun)

Plenty of
There are **plenty of** *mountains in Switzerland.*
(count noun)
She has **plenty of** *money in the bank.* (non-count noun)

No
There were **no** *squirrels in the park today.* (count noun)
We have **no** *time left to finish the project.*
(non-count noun)

A piece of
I had **a piece of** *apple and a muffin for a snack.*
Julia has **a piece of** *furniture for sale that would look great in your room.*

> Practise writing sentences using the nouns and expressions from the word bank below, for example:
>
> *An ant has many feet.*

Nouns:	Expressions:
Foot, photo, gasoline, fish, makeup, baby, tooth, meat	Few, little, much, a lot, any, enough, some, many

Buy Nothing Day

You may have noticed that there are certain months of the year when we really feel the urge to buy something. Think about the month of February: Have you ever bought a present for Valentine's Day? What about November and December: Do you feel like you need to buy presents for the holidays? Holidays are supposed to be about spending time with family and friends. Now, for many, they're all about shopping.

Christmas in London, 1907,
Maurice Toussaint (1882–1974)

1 Discuss your holiday habits.

Take time to reflect on what the holidays mean to you.

> Make a list of the activities you do during the holidays in December. For example: *bake cookies, go shopping, …*

> On the same piece of paper, write down two presents that you would like to receive and two presents that you will probably give to other people.

> Do a survey of your classmates to find out about their holiday habits, including students who:
> * Do the same activities as you.
> * Have made a gift before.
> * Will buy fewer gifts this year.

Find Classmates Who:	Students' Names
Do my number one holiday activity.	▬▬▬▬▬▬
Have made a gift before.	▬▬▬▬▬▬
Will buy fewer gifts this year.	▬▬▬▬▬▬

> When you finish your survey, discuss the following questions with your classmates:

> 1 How many of the activities on your list do you do alone, with friends, with your family?

> 2 Is giving and receiving presents an important part of your holiday? Why or why not?

> 3 What do you usually do with gifts you receive that you don't like?

> 4 Have you ever made a gift for someone? What was it?

Self-Evaluate

Did I take a risk and try using new expressions?

Did I use Smart Talk to help me?

Facts

Mahatma Gandhi

Mahatma Gandhi was born in 1869 and died in 1948. He was a major political and spiritual leader in India. He believed in simple living. When he was alive, he made his own clothes and followed a vegetarian diet. He believed very strongly that in order to be happy we must give up possession of anything that can't be owned and shared by everyone around us. He believed that possessing items causes jealousy and stress (we are always afraid that someone will take the item away from us) and that once we possess a thing, we are always hungry for something better. The solution is to give up everything that isn't necessary for our basic survival and to take pleasure in sharing what we have with those around us.

Do you know anyone in your community who practises a simple lifestyle?

Mahatma Gandhi, 1968, Fredda Brilliant (1903–1999), London, England

2 Learn about Buy Nothing Day.

Think about everything that you buy in a day—gum, lunch, chips, drinks, bus tickets, … Would it be easy for you to stop buying these things for a day, a week, a month?

One group decided to encourage people to think about how much they buy during the holiday season by starting a worldwide movement called Buy Nothing Day. On Buy Nothing Day, people try to go the whole day without spending any money.

In order to inform others about Buy Nothing Day and involve as many people in the event as possible, the organizers needed publicity. One of the ways they decided to promote their message was by creating poster ads.

> Take a look at the ad on page 82 promoting Buy Nothing Day.

> Think about the features of an ad or poster. (See the Smart Reference section on page 282.)

> Answer these questions about the ad:

   1 Who does the ad target? What age group? What culture?

   2 What is the ad's main message?

   3 What symbol does the ad use to represent the idea of shopping? Is this an effective symbol? Why or why not?

   4 Does the ad encourage you to participate in Buy Nothing Day? Why or why not?

   5 Do you want to follow any of the suggestions presented in the ad? Why or why not?

   6 Which vocabulary words were difficult for you in the ad?

   7 Where might you see this ad posted?

   8 Can you think of another image that could be used to promote Buy Nothing Day? Explain or draw your idea and share it with a partner.

Ask your partner or teacher for help.

Use what you learned about posters to analyze the next ad you see.

ᴱᔅᑕᴧᑫᴱ ᑕᴧᴧᔭᔑ1/1ᔑᔑ

BUY NOTHING DAY

As the planet starts heating up, maybe it's time to finally **go cold turkey**. Lock up your
5 debit card, your credit cards, your money clip, and see what it feels like to opt out of consumer culture
10 completely, even if only for 24 hours.

With global warming **on the tips of everyone's tongues**,
15 what better time to point out real alternatives to **unbridled** consumption than by
20 taking your BND celebrations to the street? Put up some posters, offer a credit-card cutup, do the
25 Buddha walk up and down your local mall—anything that will get people talking.

Dreading the holiday
30 season? The to-do lists and sales hype? This year, **gather** your loved ones and do things the old
35 fashioned way. Forget the **heaps** of presents—Give out gift exemption **vouchers** instead.
40 Focus on food and family and fun, not spiritless hours trapped in **lineups**. 'Tis the season to
45 be **frugal**.

AdBusters Media Foundation, January / February 2007 issue 69, vol. 15, no. 1, Vancouver, British Columbia, Canada

3 Learn about the "Buddha Walk."

People who participate in Buy Nothing Day and voluntary simplicity find unique and interesting ways to draw attention to their cause. One activity that is frequently organized is called the "credit card cut-up," where a group of people stand in a mall with scissors and offer to cut up shoppers' credit cards. These activities are peaceful protests aimed at educating the public. If authorities ask the organizers to leave, they always comply. You will read about one group's experience in the following text.

> Before you read the text, think of all the ways you have learned to participate in Buy Nothing Day or voluntary simplicity.

> Make a list of the different ways to participate.

> Read the text out loud with your classmates.

Walk Like the Buddha— The Art of Slow Protest

The "Buddha Walk" has its origins in a documentary movie in a scene where a monk is moving ever so slowly and peacefully through a busy New York City street. The idea was adapted for Buy Nothing Day in a large shopping mall—one of the world's largest—in Edmonton, Canada.

5 Four of us started moving in super-slow-motion, one behind the other, as the busy **mall patrons** passed us by.

The action worked—Shopper after shopper stopped to watch as we made our way from the **ground floor** to the main floor. People gathered, and many of them wondered out loud what we were doing and why we were there.
10 Some of them thought we were part of the local **fringe theatre** festival. Others remarked that we were simply strange; one person even suggested that we might steal something.

Eventually a mall security officer arrived to engage us in a conversation as we continued our slow progression through the mall.

15 *Security:* You'll have to stop that or I'll have to remove you.

Us: Stop what?

Security: What you are doing.

Us: What are we doing?

Security: You are creating a spectacle.

20 *Us:* How are we creating a spectacle?

Security: Well ... uh ... you are walking very slowly.

Sm**a**r**t**
Words
flustered = confused
jeer = make fun of
sense of catharsis =
feeling of relief

Us: [slowly pointing to an elderly person moving across the mall very slowly] Well, what about her? She's moving very slowly.

Security: No, she's moving at the normal speed.

25 **Us:** Can you show us what is the normal speed? I mean, how slowly can we walk and still remain in the mall?

Security: [getting **flustered**] No, you simply have to leave the mall. Leave the mall or I will call the police to remove you.

At that point, we left the mall. We didn't feel the need to press the issue
30 with the police department. But as we walked off, a strange thing happened. The crowd that had gathered started clapping for us and **jeering** at the security officials. These shoppers—primarily middle-aged people— were now applauding, partly because of the absurdity of the situation and partly, perhaps, because we all have a desire to stand up to authority and
35 we get a certain **sense of catharsis** when we do.

We live in a time when we all seem to be out of breath most of the time, running from place to place. The Buddha Walk lets you take a much-needed breath. At the same time, the action breaks people out of their routines, which is one of the first steps to change.

40 And besides, it's one of the best actions for any old lazy day when you want just a little something to do.

AdBusters Media Foundation, January / February 2007 issue 69, vol. 15, no. 1, Vancouver, British Columbia, Canada

> Reflect on what you read.

> Answer these questions in a paragraph:

1. What would happen to you and your friends if you did the Buddha Walk in your neighbourhood?

2. What would be the most ideal place to attract attention with the Buddha Walk?

3. How do you think people would react?

4. Do you think it is a good idea to try doing the Buddha Walk? Why or why not?

5. Do you think that doing the Buddha Walk is a criminal act or a legitimate form of expression? Why do you think this?

6. What is another form of peaceful protest that this group could do to draw attention to their cause?

Self-**E**valuate

Did I write complete sentences giving my detailed, personal opinion?

Did I use what I learned to help me imagine a protest in my community?

Different Ways of Living

Now that you know about Buy Nothing Day and voluntary simplicity, it is time to give them a try! Experiment with the suggestions presented in this unit or find your own ideas.

Find ways to promote Buy Nothing Day or voluntary simplicity.

Option A

Design a media text publicizing Buy Nothing Day or voluntary simplicity.

Option B

Write a letter to a newspaper describing your experiences on Buy Nothing Day.

Option A

Design a media text publicizing Buy Nothing Day or voluntary simplicity.

Step 1 **Prepare**

> Brainstorm: Think of ideas you want to include in your media text.

> Define the audience and the purpose of the text, for example:

> *I want to promote voluntary simplicity in my family by explaining five ways our family can live more simply.*

Arbutus, 1922, Emily Carr (1871–1945)

> Determine a format for the text. Will it be a poster, a banner, a video ad or a public service announcement?

> Determine what images or techniques you will use to make the text effective. Think about colour, format, text size and important information to include.

Step 2 **Produce**

> Create a draft of your media text.

> Use count and non-count nouns.

> Show your media text to someone. Ask the person for feedback, suggestions, ideas, …

> Make changes and write a final copy.

Step 3 **Present**

> Post or display the media text. Where will it be most effective: at school, in your neighbourhood, on the Internet?

> Think about the text's effectiveness: Did your strategies work? Did people understand your message? What was their reaction? What would you do differently next time?

Options

Do research on the Internet to find different ideas for your text.

Use your digital camcorder, camera or cellphone to make clips or take still pictures.

Use computer software to include, modify and edit the clips, images, titles and text.

Post the letter on the Internet, on your personal web page or in your blog.

Write a letter to a newspaper describing your experiences on Buy Nothing Day.

Step 1 Prepare

> Define your purpose: Why are you writing this letter?
> To whom are you writing the letter: other students, adults?
> Organize your ideas into a plan. Include an introduction, the main body of the letter (with your ideas in order) and a conclusion.

Step 2 Write

> Use your plan to write a draft of your letter.
> Include count and non-count nouns.

Step 3 Revise

> Read through the letter again. Does it make sense?
> Ask someone to read the letter and give you feedback.
> Make changes.

Step 4 Edit

> Check the spelling of words in a dictionary.
> Verify count and non-count nouns using the Smart Structure on page 79 and your grammar using the Smart Reference section or another resource.
> Correct your mistakes and write a final copy.

Step 5 Publish

> Give the letter to your teacher or to the school newspaper.
> Mail the letter to an activist organization.

Smart Words
REVIEW

1. commute
2. cozy
3. dread
4. flustered
5. foreign
6. frugal
7. gather
8. go cold turkey
9. ground floor
10. heap
11. leisurely
12. lineup
13. mall patron
14. purchase
15. voucher

Self-Evaluate

Did I follow the steps?

Did I present the ideas in my text in a logical order with a clear message?

Did I use count and non-count nouns correctly?

Did I use a dictionary or other resources to help me?

Reflection

1. Which activity did you like the most? Why?
2. Which activity was the most challenging for you?
3. Name two strategies that you learned to use in this unit.
4. If you had to do this unit over again, what would you do differently?
5. What are your goals for the next unit? What would you like to improve?

Anti-Consumption Activists

Naomi Klein

It's hard to believe that Naomi Klein was obsessed with brand names and what she could buy as a teen. It's also difficult to imagine this anti-corporate activist
5 working her weekends at the mall. Born and raised in Montréal, Québec, Naomi Klein is a Canadian journalist, activist and the author of several books, including No Logo. This book has become
10 the **manifesto** of the anti-globalization movement worldwide.

Ms. Klein's writings are among the first to expose major corporations' manufacturing practices in some of the
15 poorest countries in the world. She has visited **sweatshops** that have rules against talking and smiling, and places where the toilets are **padlocked** except during two fifteen minute breaks each
20 day, forcing workers who sew clothes for western stores to urinate in plastic bags under their machines. Klein brings world attention to women like Carmelita Alonzo, a seamstress for a popular
25 western brand clothing company who died after being denied time off for pneumonia.

Because of Klein's writings, people in the west are now demanding to know
30 whether the companies whose clothes they choose to wear are following ethical labour standards. These big businesses are being forced to answer tough questions from the people they target to
35 buy their products, and it's working! Klein is also informing those workers who are paid only $2 for a shoe that sells in Canada for over $100 of the truth of their situation, in the hope that change
40 will happen on both sides. Consumers' behaviour has a global impact, so think about how you want to affect the world next time you go shopping!

Kalle Lasn

Kalle Lasn was born in Estonia and
45 immigrated to Canada in the '70s. He is the Chief Executive Officer of Blackspot Anticorporation, the founder of Adbusters, an author and filmmaker, and a leading Canadian activist in the anti-
50 consumption movement.

For fifteen years, Lasn's documentaries and commercials have been broadcast on PBS and CBC, as well as around the world. He has won fifteen international
55 awards for his work in film. His activist work began after he made a thirty second ad on the **disappearing** old-growth forests of the Pacific Northwest. No one would sell him **airtime** to
60 broadcast his commercial.

Lasn created the Adbusters Media Foundation and Powershift Advertising Agency to fight for the rights of citizens and activists to access airwaves. In 1992,
65 he helped launch Buy Nothing day. To this day, he has never been successful in buying airtime on major networks to broadcast his commercials. He believes this is because major networks fear they
70 will lose support from major corporations that want us to keep consuming.

Lasn's work is aimed at educating the public. He believes over-consumption is
75 having major consequences on quality of life and the state of the environment. Everything that consumers buy impacts the planet in some way, from the packaging that is thrown in landfills to
80 the sweatshops where goods are manufactured. Lasn is also quick to remind people that the wealthiest nations, like Canada and the U.S., consume 86 percent of the goods on the
85 world market, leaving only 14 percent for the rest of the world.

Words

manifesto = written statement of beliefs and practices

sweatshop = factory where people work in poor conditions for little pay

padlocked = locked with a detachable lock hung on a hook

disappearing = stopping to exist

airtime = time given to an advertisement on radio or TV

Free-Lunch Foragers

"Freegans" are a growing subculture that has opted out of capitalism by cutting spending habits and living off consumer waste.

5 For lunch in her modest apartment, Madeline Nelson tossed a salad made with shaved carrots and lettuce she **dug out** of a Whole Foods **dumpster**. She flavored the dressing with miso powder 10 she found in a trash bag on a **curb** in Chinatown. She baked bread made with **yeast** plucked from the garbage of a Middle Eastern grocery store.

Nelson is a former corporate executive 15 who can afford to dine at four-star restaurants. But she prefers turning garbage into gourmet meals without spending a cent.

On this afternoon, she **thawed** a slab of 20 pâté that she found three days before its expiration date in a dumpster outside a health food store. She made buttery chicken soup from another health food store's hot buffet leftovers, which she 25 **salvaged** before they were tossed into the garbage.

Nelson, fifty-one, once earned a six-figure income as director of communications at Barnes and Noble. Tired of representing a 30 multimillion dollar company, she quit in 2005 and became a "freegan"—the word combining "vegan" and "free"—a growing subculture of people who have reduced their spending habits and live off 35 consumer waste. Though many of its pioneers are vegans, people who neither eat nor use any animal-based products, the concept has caught on with Nelson and other meat-eaters who do not want 40 to depend on businesses that they believe waste resources, harm the environment or allow unfair labour practices.

"We're doing something that is really socially unacceptable," Nelson said. "Not 45 everyone is going to do it, but we hope it leads people to push their own limits and quit spending."

Nelson used to spend more than $100 000 a year for her food, clothes, books, 50 transportation and a mortgage on a two-bedroom co-op in Greenwich Village. Now, she lives off savings, volunteers instead of works, and **forages** for groceries.

She garnishes her salad with tangy 55 weeds picked from neighbors' yards. She freezes bagels and soup from the trash to make them last longer. She sold her co-op and bought a one-bedroom apartment in Flatbush, Brooklyn, about an hour 60 from Manhattan by bike. Her annual expenditures now total about $25 000.

Freeganism was born out of environmental justice and anti-globalization movements dating to the 65 1980s. The concept was inspired in part by groups like "Food Not Bombs," an international organization that feeds the homeless with surplus food that's often donated by businesses.

70 Freegans are often college-educated people from middle-class families.

Freegans troll curbsides for discarded clothes and ratty or broken furniture, which they repair to furnish their homes. 75 They trade goods at flea markets. Some live as squatters in abandoned buildings, or in low-rent apartments on the edges of the city, or with family and friends.

In recent years, Internet sites have posted 80 announcements for trash tours in Seattle, Houston and Los Angeles and throughout England. Some teach people how to dumpster-dive for food, increasing the movement's popularity. At least 14 000 85 have taken the trash tour for groceries over the last two years in New York. Another site offers lessons for cooking meals from food found in dumpsters, such as spaghetti squash salad.

90 Though recycling clothes and furniture doesn't strike most people as unusual, **combing** through heaps of trash for food can be unthinkable to many.

Erika Hayasaki, "Free-Lunch Foragers," *Los Angeles Times*, September 11, 2007, col. 1

Smart Words

dig out = remove, pull out

dumpster = large metal garbage container

curb = corner

yeast = type of fungus used to make bread rise

thaw = let frozen food become warmer

salvage = save from being thrown out

forage = search for food or other things

comb = search thoroughly

Peace Now

In this unit, you will explore the meaning of peace and violence and learn about teens who were victims of bullying and hazing. You will think about the kinds of violence that surround you and analyze your reactions to conflict. Finally, you will brainstorm to find peaceful solutions to violence and ways to promote peace in your school and community.

HOW CAN WE PROMOTE PEACE IN OUR SCHOOLS?

Final Task

Encourage peace in your school and community.

Option A

Write an article for your community newspaper.

Option B

Create a class mural displaying poems, letters and posters that promote peace.

Smart Start

Everybody wants peace in the world and yet there is violence everywhere. Peace and violence are complex issues. In this task, you will reflect on how peace and violence relate to our immediate lives. How can we bring more peace into our lives and reduce the violence around us?

1 Define peace and violence.

Peace is usually defined as a state where there is no war, or as quiet and tranquillity. Violence is described as behaviour intending to hurt people. In your private life and in school, the words *peace* and *violence* can mean many different things. What comes to mind when you think of these opposites? Find your own definitions and examples of these important concepts.

> Write as many words as you can think of related to peace and violence using the letters of the alphabet. To help you, think about the feelings associated with words such as *angry, happy, understanding, …*

> Share your answers with your classmates.

> Complete your own list with the answers given by other students.

Take your time to think of the words.

Plan. Use a dictionary to check your spelling.

Peace and Violence							
A	*aid*	**C**	*calm*	**E**	
B	*brave*	**D**	*danger*	**F**	

2 Keep a journal.

Keeping a journal of your impressions and thoughts will help you to monitor and remember what you are learning. Take notes and write your thoughts as you work through this unit.

> Divide the journal page into two columns and start taking notes about the previous activity.

> Continue filling in your journal during the unit in order to help you with the Final Task.

> At the end of the unit, compare your journal with a partner's and complete your notes.

General Notes—
Questions—Highlights

Personal Thoughts
and Comments

3 Find examples of violence.

Depending on where you live, what school you go to, what your family and close friends are like, you may have different impressions of violence. Where do you see violence? Do you see violence only on TV? Or do you also see it in your community? There are many different forms of violence:

- family violence
- relationship violence
- racial violence
- political violence
- criminal violence
- school violence
- sports violence
- violence in the media

> Think about your personal experiences, the films that you have seen, the books that you have read, …

> Find two examples for each category of violence using a word organizer (see sports violence example below).

> Discuss the examples with your classmates.

The Scream, 1893, Edvard Munch (1863–1944)

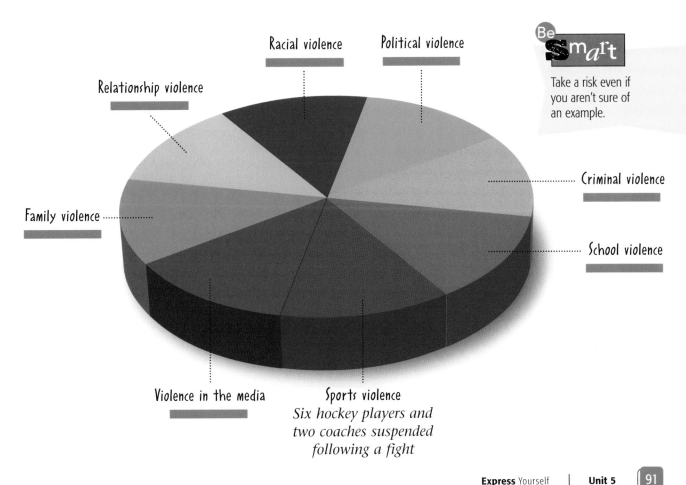

Racial violence

Political violence

Relationship violence

Family violence

Violence in the media

Sports violence
Six hockey players and two coaches suspended following a fight

Criminal violence

School violence

Be **Smart**

Take a risk even if you aren't sure of an example.

^TA^{sk} 1 Learning from Violence

Bullying is probably a new word to you. To bully is to intimidate another person. A bully is a person who uses strength or power to harm or intimidate a person who is seen as being weaker. Bullying can have devastating effects on its victims. Is bullying a problem at your school?

Be
Smart

Listen attentively. Don't be distracted.

Don't panic even if people speak fast in the film clips. Your teacher will play the DVD again.

Use a dictionary to help you answer the questions.

1 Watch film clips about bullying.

Bullying has physical and psychological effects. Being bullied never feels good. In these short testimonies, you will hear young people talk about bullying in their lives. Have you ever felt scared to go to school? Who did you turn to for help?

> Before watching the film clips, look at the following emotion words.

> Choose the words that you associate with being the victim of bullying. How would you feel if someone bullied you?

angry	comfortable	embarrassed	happy	humiliated
hurt	in charge	lonely	loved	nervous
relaxed	sad	stressed	strong	worried

> Watch the film clips and answer the following questions in your own words.

 Pushed to the Limit

❶ What do the students in the school do to the boy?

❷ Why does the boy choose not to tell an adult about the bullying?

❸ Why doesn't he like going to school?

 Nothing to Joke about

❹ Do you use the word *gay* to describe something that is stupid?

❺ In your school, is the word *gay* used in the same way as described by the boy?

❻ Why is it a problem to use the word *gay* out of context?

 Standing Up

❼ What does it mean to "stand up" for someone? Look up the phrase in your dictionary.

❽ Have you ever stood up for someone who was being bullied? Why or why not?

 **Solutions**

❾ Name two solutions presented in the clip.

❿ In your opinion, what is the best solution for bullying?

Go Further

> Make a list of bullying incidents you have seen in your school. Have you ever protected someone who was being bullied? Have you ever been bullied by someone yourself?

> Make a list of the negative effects of bullying. Try to imagine what a victim of bullying has to go through every day at school. What do you think this person writes in her/his journal? Describe a typical day for such a victim.

Self-Evaluate

Did I understand the testimonies given by the youngsters?

Did I make personal connections?

2 Analyze situations of peace and conflict.

Conflict is a natural part of life. Situations of conflict arise in class, in the cafeteria, in the schoolyard, on the bus, at home, with your friends, with people you don't know. It is important to be able to resolve these situations without using violence. How do you react to conflict? What can you do to change a situation of conflict into a situation of peace?

> Name three situations of conflict in your life.

> Identify your reactions to the situations. Do you feel angry? Do you feel helpless? Do you want to scream? Do you want to cry? Do you simply ignore the situation?

> Think about what the ideal reactions to the situations would be (even if you in fact react differently).

> Name three situations of peace in your life.

> Identify why you think each situation is peaceful.

Example 1

Situation of peace—*In the student council, I often work on projects with the same girl. We work very well together because we complement each other.*

Reason—*I really respect the girl. I listen to what she has to say.*

Example 2

Situation of conflict—*I often disturb the class by speaking to a classmate while the teacher is explaining something. Of course, the teacher warns me.*

Reaction—*I ignore the teacher, which makes him very angry and gets me into trouble.*

Ideal reaction—*The next time the teacher warns me, I will listen to him and stop speaking while he is giving the lesson.*

> Discuss your answers with your classmates.

3 Think about how you can help a friend.

The best way to resolve a difficult situation is to talk about it. Ignoring a problem won't make it go away—It may only become worse. How would you help a friend with a problem?

> Read the problem situations below.

> Answer the questions about each problem with a partner.

Think about what you would do if you were in these situations.

Situation 1

A friend comes to school with bruises on his arms. You ask him what happened and he tells you that his mother did it because he hadn't cleaned his room. When you tell him that wouldn't happen in your house, he replies, "It's no big deal—My mom is rough only when she's drunk."

1. How would you feel about your friend being hurt by his own mother?

2. Is it normal for parents to hurt their children?

3. What could you do to help your friend?

Talk

I would / should / could …

It isn't normal …

A teacher could help by …

My friend should …

Situation 2

Your teacher is talking about violence and says that she is glad it doesn't happen to anyone in the class, because you live in such a nice community. However, you know differently. One of your friends recently confided in you about being bullied violently by someone in the class. Your friend has only told you about the situation.

1. Would you report the bully? Why or why not?

2. Would you confront the bully? Why or why not?

3. How can a teacher help?

Situation 3

A guy you know is always teasing your friend. He blocks her in the corner of the hall and asks her to give him kisses. She is a very shy girl and doesn't like the attention. He doesn't have a crush on her, but he knows that she will turn beet red from his advances. The other boys think that it is funny and they all laugh when he does it.

1. Would you talk to the guy? What would you say?

2. Would you tell a teacher you trust?

3. What could your friend do to avoid the situation?

Self-Evaluate

Did I take time to understand each situation?

Did I find solutions that would be effective?

The Kiss, 1907–1908, Gustav Klimt (1862–1918)

Gangs for Social Justice

In the media, we hear about street gangs causing violence in communities and disturbing the climate of peace. However, there are also good gangs who have fun together and help one another.

1 Read about LOVE.

Leave **O**ut **V**iolenc**E** (LOVE) is a youth violence prevention organization that started in Montréal. LOVE helps youth end violence in their lives and become community leaders for violence prevention. Through specialized programs, they develop the skills and motivations to help break the cycle of violence. LOVE's leaders understand violence because they have been personally challenged by gangs, weapons, domestic violence, racism, drugs and bullying.

> Before reading the article, decide if the following ideas from the text are facts or opinions.

  ❶ The participants are special people.

  ❷ LOVE organizes a photojournalism project.

  ❸ According to the organization, LOVE is the best solution to violence.

  ❹ The photographs can be seen in different exhibits.

  ❺ The project is funded by very generous people.

> Read the article.

Ask for help if you don't understand a word, sentence or idea.

Plan. Before reading the text, read the comprehension questions.

Leave Out ViolencE (LOVE)

They meet after school in the windowless basement of a Montréal college, surrounded by spotlights and floodlights, reflectors and **backdrops**, platforms and wires, and much chaos.

They are the Leave Out Violence (LOVE) kids, twenty-four teenagers between
5 the ages of fourteen and eighteen. Some have been the victims of violence, a few have been **perpetrators**, but all have decided that they want to do something, as one says, "to inform people that violence never was, never is and never will be the solution."

And they're working hard to meet a **deadline**, because this summer they
10 plan to publish their own book of photographs and writings on the issue of violence, its causes, its prevention and its impact on their lives.

So far, their work is **mind-blowing**, as far from typical "kids' stuff" as it could possibly be. The 250 people who saw LOVE's first exhibit of mounted photographs, poems and narratives last June were amazed at their power.

15 The show **prodded** nerve endings and provoked tears. "Peace and love may be dead, but there is always hope," says a caption underneath a photo of a small child doing homework in a dark kitchen. A narrow stream of dazzling sunshine has found its way into the sombre room, creating a path of light across the little girl's book. A **bleak** landscape, viewed through the black bars

Words

backdrop = painted cloth hung at the back of a stage

perpetrator = person who does something illegal

deadline = date by which something should be done

mind-blowing = amazing

prod = push quickly

bleak = cold and without comfort

20 of an iron fence, is captioned, "Not even love should make her stay." Another photo shows a teen **huddled** in darkness on a cold bathroom floor. The caption reads, "My idea of hell: alone in darkness and in total despair." A **jarring** photo of blood splashed in a sink has the caption: "The pain is going all over …"

The purpose of the LOVE photojournalism project is to help teenagers, most 25 of whom have been defined as at risk in some way, to develop a critical awareness of the issues surrounding violence in society today. By bringing them together to teach them the practical, marketable skills of photography and writing, LOVE hopes to improve their self-esteem and show them that they can make a contribution to the community. As one seventeen-year-old 30 says, "Finally, someone sees that I am worth something." Another says, "Someone has to take a stand."

Several aspects of the program are particularly engaging for the kids. First of all, their instructors are a professional journalist and a photographer technician who impose real-world standards on their work. The kids are 35 turned on because they know that they are producing material that will be seen and read by the public. Already, their photographs have been included in exhibits, one of which is now touring Québec.

The project is funded by the Leave Out Violence organization, which is made up of a diverse group of Montrealers, including doctors, writers, police officers, 40 judges, businesspeople, teachers and students, who believe that violence prevention is everybody's responsibility. They are so-called ordinary citizens who believe the African saying that it takes a whole village to raise a child.

Brenda Zosky Proulx, "Leave Out Violence (LOVE)," *Vis-à-vis* (A National Newsletter on Family Violence from the Canadian Council on Social Development), Spring 1996, Vol. 13, No. 2, p. 6

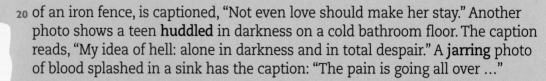

> Answer the following questions individually.
> Then discuss your answers with your classmates.

1 Name two characteristics of the teens described in the text.

2 Why do they want to do something about violence?

3 Why are they working so hard?

4 Do you agree with the statement: "Peace and love may be dead"? Why or why not?

5 What is the purpose of the photojournalism project?

6 What does LOVE hope to improve?

7 Who funds the project?

8 Explain the African expression: "It takes a whole village to raise a child."

9 In your opinion, why is the project effective? Why is LOVE a great idea?

10 In your opinion, what other projects and ideas could LOVE use to appeal to teenagers?

Facts

Another Gang Making a Difference: Big Brothers

The Big Brothers program is known throughout the world. It started with a group of men who were concerned about young boys who were getting into trouble. The men decided to help the young boys by spending time with them: playing sports, going to movies or simply helping them with their school work. The focus of the program is the same as when it was first created: to encourage men and boys to spend time together. A Big Brother's role is to provide a youngster with friendship, trust and encouragement. The Big Brothers of Montréal have helped more than 4000 teens. Do you know anyone who would be a great Big Brother: your uncle, your coach, a friend's dad, your dad, your dad's friend? If so, you should tell him about the program.

You may be wondering if there is a Big Sisters program. Of course, there is! The objective of the program is the same as the Big Brothers program, but activities shared with a Big Sister are slightly different. For example, Big Sisters focus on topics such as balanced eating, feeling good about yourself, relating to your parents, staying active, school issues, …

If you would like to have a Big Brother or Big Sister, look for more information on the Internet. It is a free service.

 ## 2 Learn how to get out of a gang.

Some members of LOVE used to be gang members. They say it was very difficult leaving the gang although it was a harmful environment. Members often stay in the gang, not because they like it, but because they have self-esteem, money and drug problems. Furthermore, other gang members will even use violence to keep them in the gang. However, with the support of their family and friends, it is possible for teens to leave a gang when they want to regain control of their lives. The Edmonton Police Service compiled a list of tips for parents and teens on how to get out of a gang.

Talk

I think the most effective tip is …

I think the next most effective tip is …

The least effective tip is …

I agree / disagree …

> Before reading the text on page 98, think of tips the list will include. Try to guess at least two of them.

> Read the list and decide which tips you find the most effective.

> Rank the tips from the most to the least effective.

> Discuss your ranking with a partner.

Getting Out of a Gang

When a gang member learns that he or she can meet their needs in other ways, the gang may lose its **appeal**. It may be time for them to walk away from gang life. When your child decides they want to leave, here are a few simple steps to help ease the transition:

❶ Believe in your power to change. Gangs are a **dead-end street**. No matter who you are, what you have done or where you live, you deserve better.

❷ Begin spending your time doing other things. Instead of **hanging out** with your gang friends, find something else to do during that time. There are possibilities everywhere: sports, recreation centres, arts programs, drama, school activities—even spending time with your family.

❸ Try to stop looking like a gangster. As you begin to believe in yourself, you will find that you don't need to make other people feel afraid of you in order to feel good about yourself.

❹ Find other things to say, other things to do, and other people to do them with. Stop hanging out with gang members, talking like a gang member, and acting like a gang member.

❺ Get good at making excuses. Some former gang members have said that they stopped taking phone calls from their gang friends or had their family members tell friends from the gang that they were busy or involved in some other activity.

❻ Find people who support you and believe in you. Find people, especially adults, who think that you are special and will keep telling you that. Think of a supportive adult wherever you go that you can **touch base** with if you have a problem or need to talk.

"Getting Out of a Gang" from the Edmonton Police Service website

Self-Evaluate

Did I pronounce clearly so that my partner could understand?

Did I use the text to help me express my opinion?

The Barbarians, 1937, Max Ernst (1891–1976)

Structure

Simple Past, Past Progressive and Present Perfect Tenses

The simple past, past progressive and present perfect verb tenses are used to describe situations that occurred in the past.

Simple Past and Past Progressive Tenses

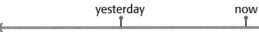

yesterday   now

*Yesterday I **talked** to my teacher about LOVE.* (simple past; action completed)
*Yesterday I **was talking** to my teacher when a journalist came into the classroom.* (past progressive; action in progress)

Simple Past	Past Progressive
Use the simple past	**Use the past progressive**
• For actions that began and ended in the past I **talked** to a friend yesterday. He **did not use** his car last week. **Did** she **send** her poem in November? Remember that there are two categories of verbs: regular and irregular. Regular verbs end in *ed*. I **explained** the situation. Irregular verbs vary (see page 270 of the Smart Reference section). I **understood** the problem.	• To describe an action that took place in the past during a specific time frame *Yesterday, I **was playing** hockey between 4:30 and 6:30 p.m.* I **wasn't trying** to be rude during the meeting. **Were** you **crying** at the end of the movie? • To describe a longer action that was taking place in the past when it was interrupted by a shorter action I **was speaking** to my mom when my dad came into the room. Remember to form the past progressive with: the verb *to be* in the past + the main verb + *ing*. I **was helping** my mom in the kitchen.
Key Words: last night, yesterday, two minutes ago, today, last month	**Key Words:** between … and …, during, when, while

---

Present Perfect Tense

now

January February March April May June

*I **have met** with my teacher many times this year.*

Present Perfect
Use the present perfect
• When an action happened at an unspecified time   He **has** already **been** to Japan. • When an action started in the past and continues in the present   I **have** only **lived** here for a year. • When several actions occurred in the past at different times   Gangsters **have disturbed** us many times over the years. Remember to form the present perfect with the auxiliary *to have* in the present + the past participle (see the irregular verb chart on page 270 of the Smart Reference section).   I **have thought** about it.
Key Words: already, for the past few days, once, twice, yet, many times, before, since

Task 3 Team Spirit

Many schools and sports teams organize initiation rituals at the beginning of the school year to greet new students. Initiation games are usually created for fun and to build team spirit. However, some initiation rituals can become degrading and even dangerous. When this happens, it is called hazing. What can we do to make sure that initiation rituals are fun and safe?

Be Smart

Think of examples from your personal experience.

Smart Talk

I remember …

That is really fun …

I don't think it's a good idea.

I think it's too mean.

1 Think about initiation rituals.

A common initiation ritual is getting new members of a group to dress in silly costumes. What other initiation rituals have you seen in your school or sports group?

> **Answer these questions individually and then share your answers with a classmate:**

   1 Write a list of five initiation ideas. Make sure that they aren't dangerous!

   2 Who do you think has more fun at an initiation party—the people organizing the party or the participants? Explain.

   3 Would you support the following initiation rituals or would you find them cruel?

     • Forcing a person to drink more than fifteen sodas

     • Dressing them up in clothing of the opposite sex

     • Making them walk around naked on campus

     • Tying them down and shaving their head

     • Getting them to sing in front of everyone

College Freshman Initiation, 1938, San Juan, Puerto Rico

Self-Evaluate

Did I listen to my partner?

Did I think about the topic before giving my opinion?

2 Read about a mother trying to stop hazing.

Hazing often takes place at the beginning of a school year or sports season. It occurs in situations where there is no adult supervision. You will read about a mother trying to prevent hazing from happening in schools after her son's bad experience.

> Before reading the text, think about the following question:
> Who should speak to students about the dangers of hazing: parents, coaches, teachers, other students who have had bad experiences with hazing?

> Read the text on the next page.

> While reading, take notes so that you can retell the text to a partner.

No More School Hazing

If Vickie Jahel continues the work she is doing now, every school in Québec will implement anti-hazing policies. Anti-hazing information will be distributed to students and they will learn safe and healthy initiation practices. Jahel is hoping to accomplish this mission through the creation of
5 an organization devoted to eliminating hazing.

Jahel's passionate anti-hazing campaign started after an incident that left her entire family searching for ways to prevent other students from experiencing the abuse that her son endured. Gabriel's fellow football players started by putting a dog collar around his neck and making him
10 walk the field like a dog. Then they made him stay in a freezing shower until he was almost blue.

Jahel's interest in hazing began in September 2007 when she discovered that her son—then a Secondary 4 student—had been hazed on his birthday.

Jahel held a press conference last week to announce the creation of
15 No More School Hazing. Jahel said that the organization's mission is to "eliminate hazing, bullying and abusive acts toward our children." Jahel said that she decided to start the organization after her research discovered that little information was available for families in the same situation.

She believes that our school system failed because it is the responsibility of
20 coaches and other teachers to implement safe rules for all students. Gabriel quit the football team during the **trial** of the three students who were responsible, but returned to the field last season. "My son has proved to victims that you don't have to hide," she said.

Hazing at the high school level is particularly troubling. A major part of the
25 problem is that the general population and schools don't always see hazing as dangerous. Hazing in high schools is often **overlooked** and dangerous rituals are seen as traditions to keep because students, parents, teachers, coaches and principals don't understand the definition of hazing. She said hazing is always premeditated and not accidental.

30 Jahel said that it is time to change what we define as being acceptable behaviour, and stop excusing abuse subjected to a child by saying that "boys will be boys." Jahel has made a commitment to work on the insurance of the **well-being** of everyone's children and grandchildren in our school system. Jahel said that she
35 received many telephone calls of support—some from perfect strangers—that have helped in the **healing** process.

"Hazing is an act of power and control over others," she said. "Hazing is abusive, degrading and often life-threatening. Some people believe that hazing teaches respect. Victims of hazing
40 rarely report having respect for those who hazed them."

Jahel said that she isn't naive enough to believe that she can put an end to hazing, but she hopes to provide information and education so that teens will know that alternative forms of initiation exist, and that hazing is a serious and dangerous crime.

Focus on the words you understand instead of the difficult words.

Words

trial = examination of evidence by a judge and/or jury to decide guilt

overlook = ignore

well-being = feeling of being healthy and happy

heal = become healthy again

Talk

> Retell the text from page 101 to a partner in your own words using your notes.

> Introduce the issue, name the people involved, recount the important events, summarize the solutions and restate the ending of the text.

> Use Smart Talk and the past tenses from the Smart Structure on page 99.

> Ask your partner questions about the text.

Self-Evaluate

Did I include the important parts of the text?

Did my partner understand me?

3 Write a dialogue for a cartoon strip.

Imagine that every high school, CEGEP and university receives information about the dangers of hazing. Do you think this will change what people do during initiation rituals?

> Look at the six-frame cartoon strip.

> Invent dialogue for the cartoon strip and describe each frame.

> Note that there are five characters in the story: two male students, a teacher, a new female student and a principal.

> Follow this outline:

Frame 1 Introduce the story and the two initial characters.

Frame 2 Explain the idea further and introduce the third character.

Frame 3 Explain the problem.

Frame 4 Add details to the problem and add the fourth character.

Frame 5 Find a solution to the problem.

Frame 6 Continue the story and add the final character.

1 Cesar and Jack had a great idea for next week's initiation party. They had the idea of forming groups …

Step 1 **Prepare**

> Write your ideas for each frame following the outline on page 102. Don't forget that old and new students are organizing the initiation party.

> What type of story would you like to write? Which characteristics do you want the characters to have?

Step 2 **Produce**

> Write the descriptions of the frames and speech bubbles.

> Are you on topic?

> Ask a partner to read your cartoon strip. How can it be improved?

> Make changes.

> Use a dictionary to verify your spelling.

> Make sure the verb tenses are correct using the Smart Structure on page 99 and the Smart Reference section.

> Write a final copy.

Step 3 **Present**

> Give your completed cartoon strip to your teacher.

> Display the cartoon strips on the classroom walls. Vote for the best one.

Go Further

> Photocopy a page of your favourite comic strip, erase the speech bubbles and invent new dialogue.

> Illustrate a story that you like using the comic strip style. Use computer software to design your own cartoon strip.

Self-Evaluate

Did I use the correct verb tenses?

Did I use a dictionary?

TASK 4 Solutions for Peace

Schools are implementing programs that aim to make the world a more peaceful place. Teachers are talking about the problem of violence. Parents are trying to protect their children from bullying. Student committees are starting programs to help break the cycle of violence. Recognizing that we have a problem is the first step in finding solutions. Making peace a priority requires individual and societal changes.

1 Brainstorm solutions for peace.

What can you do to make a change? What would you like to accomplish in your class, school, home and community? One of Gandhi's famous quotes is: "Be the change you want to see in the world." How can you contribute to peace?

Part A Create a word web.

Making a word web can help you think of ways to promote peace.

> Create a word web with a partner. Find a minimum of five ideas.

> Share your ideas with the class.

Part B Accept others as they are.

In your word web, did you write: "Accept others as they are?" Putting the emphasis on our similarities instead of our differences is one way to bring more peace to the world. It is true that we are all different, but it is also true that we are more alike than we are different!

> Work with a partner you don't know very well.

> Try to find five things that you have in common.

> Ask each other as many questions as you can until you have found five similarities, for example:

What is your favourite sport?
Where were you born?
What kind of job would you like to have in a few years?

> Share the things that you and your partner have in common with the rest of the class.

Be Smart

Take your time when doing the activities.

Smart Talk

What did you write?

What about you?

Can you explain why you chose this word?

Oh, that's a good idea!

Self-Evaluate

Did I listen to my partner?

Did I use Smart Talk to help me?

Smile.

Be a role model.

Promote peace.

2 Help your teacher.

Solving the problem of violence in school is important. The challenge is to find solutions that will be effective. What programs exist in your school? In this next activity, a teacher and her colleagues wish to create a peace program. They would like your ideas before starting to work on their plan. Do you think they will need other people to help them? When should they start? What materials will they require?

> Before listening to the audio segment, write three questions that you think the teacher will ask, for example:

> *When should we start the program?*
> *Who should be involved?*

> Then listen to the audio segment and answer the teacher's ten questions.

> Use the same verb tense as in the question.

> Use the sentence starters below to help you.

> Write complete sentences.

Sentence Starters

1. I see the most violence …

2. I think … are more violent because …

3. Violence can be explained …

4. Teens can be protected …

5. Parents should be contacted …

6. A negative leader can change … if / when / because …

7. Parents are important, because …

8. Psychological help …

9. It is important to change the climate of the school …

10. In my opinion, …

If you don't understand a question, skip it and answer it later.

Take time to write the best answer you can.

Have a dictionary ready when you write your answers.

Go Further

> Put up posters with peace messages in your school. Find famous peace quotes on the Internet. Ask your art teacher to help you with this project.

> Write a message or a short letter to the student council. Explain your ideas to encourage peace in your school.

Self-Evaluate

Did I answer all the questions?

Did I use the same verb tenses as in the questions?

Poetry

Poets around the world write words to heal and touch our hearts after deadly conflicts. They use words to communicate their ideas and feelings. People have very personal reactions to poetry and enjoy it for various reasons. Here are examples of different types of poems.

Haiku

Haiku is a form of Japanese poetry that follows a strict structure of three lines. The first line has five syllables, the second line, seven syllables and the third line, five syllables.

It's cold—and I wait
For someone to shelter me
And take me from here.

Limericks

Limericks are five-line poems with a strict rhyming structure. This type of poetry is usually humorous.

There was an old man from Peru
Who dreamed he was eating his shoe
He awoke in the night
With a terrible fright
To discover it was totally true.

Lyrical Poems

Lyrical poems express feelings and have the musical quality of a song.

A Little While, A Little While
by Emily Brontë (1818–1848)

A little while, a little while
The noisy crowd are barred away;
And I can sing and smile
A little while I've holiday! ...

Lyre Guitar, 19th century

Narrative Poems

Narrative poems tell a story. This type of poetry may be long or short, simple or complex.

Robot Boy
by Tim Burton (1958–)

Mr. and Mrs. Smith had a
wonderful life.
They were a normal, happy
husband and wife.
One day they got news that
made Mr. Smith glad.
Mrs. Smith would be a mom
which would make him the dad!
But something was wrong with
their bundle of joy.
It wasn't human at all,
it was a robot boy! ...

Free Verse Poems

Free verse poems allow you to express how you feel by playing with words more freely. This type of poetry may or may not include rhymes and punctuation, and may be laid artistically on the page.

rain
    falling
        down

I Dream'd in a Dream
by Walt Whitman (1819–1892)

I dream'd in a dream I saw a city invincible to the attacks of the whole of the rest of the earth,
I dream'd that was the new city of Friends,
Nothing was greater there than the quality of robust love, it led the rest ...

3 Read peace poems.

Poems express feelings. They touch us in a special way because they put images in our minds. The following poems contain messages of hope to inspire us.
The first one was written by a victim of bullying who won the Turn Off the Violence Contest by writing about her experience. The second poem was written by Mattie J.T. Stepanek, a young poet and peace activist.

> Read the two poems.
> While reading the poems, think about their messages. What did the poets want to express?
> Identify the type of poem with the help of the Smart Stop on page 106.
> Practise reading the poems out loud with a partner.
> Express your emotions while reading the poems.

Helpless

There I lie, as still as stone
It was growing dark and I was all alone
I tried to recall what happened that day
I remembered some mean things those people did say
5 They kicked me and shoved me
And did things that weren't nice
They pushed me around like they were rolling a dice
I told them to stop
But no one seemed to care
10 And soon tears were pouring out
And spilling everywhere
Then they left me helpless and **weak**
I was too tired to stand up or even speak
Now I am lying here
15 Wishing I could die
What was the point of living
If your life was one big lie
I know I had no one to call my friend
No one to stick with me until the end
20 And maybe I wasn't one of the most popular girls in school
But something I do know is that bullying is not cool
Just when I thought it was the end
A miracle happened and God gave me a friend
This friend was a true friend as best as can be
25 And I don't know what should have happened to me if she hadn't saved me
But still it **puzzles** me as I see it today
Kids teasing kids and calling names
We are all people and are all the same
So we should start **sticking up for** everyone and stop calling them names!

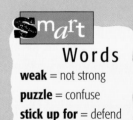

Sm**a**r**t**
Words
weak = not strong
puzzle = confuse
stick up for = defend

Helpless, Turn Off the Violence Contest Winner, Grade 8, Wilma Hansen School, Calgary, Alberta

Recipe for Peace

Peace is possible.
Make peace an attitude.
Want it.
Make a habit of it.
5 Live it.
Make peace a reality.
Share it.
Peace is possible.
Make peace matter.
10 Our matter.
Make peace a priority.
Our priority.
Make peace a choice.
Our choice.
15 Peace is possible.
We must
Think gently,

Speak gently,
Live gently.
20 Peace is possible.
Be happy with who you are.
Be happy with who others are.
Be happy that we are.
Peace is possible.
25 Role model acceptance.
Love others.
Role model **forgiveness**.
Encourage others.
Role model tolerance.
30 Treasure others.
Peace is possible.
Peace is possible.
Peace is possible.

Smart Words

forgiveness = when someone stops being angry with another person

Mattie J.T. Stepanek, "Recipe for Peace," *Reflection of a Peacemaker—A Portrait Through Heartsongs*, Kansas City, Andrews McMeel Publishing, 2005, p. 177

> Answer these questions as a class.

1. Which poem is your favourite? Why?

2. How was the problem in the first poem solved?

3. Give an example from the second poem of how peace is possible.

4. What message would you share in your own poem?

Go Further

> Practise your English with a partner. Rewrite the poems in your notebook as a dictation exercise.

> Find poems on the Internet and choose your favourite one. As a personal challenge, learn one of the poems by heart and recite it to the class.

Smart Facts

Sending Words of Peace to Soldiers

A radio host in Edmonton launched a letter-writing campaign that challenged listeners to write letters to deployed soldiers. The radio station hoped to send a letter to every Canadian serving on an overseas mission, and in the end, they more than tripled their goal, receiving well over 12 000 letters from more than 270 schools. The positive impact of the campaign extended beyond the soldiers who received the letters. The letters expressed to the entire military community the country's thoughts and opinions about the missions and gave the soldiers thoughtful support. Do you know someone in the army? If so, send them a letter.

Say "Yes" to Peace

Now is your chance to speak out for peace. Use what you have learned in this unit to make a difference.

Encourage peace in your school and community.

Option A

Write an article for your community newspaper.

Option B

Create a class mural displaying poems, letters and posters that promote peace.

Option A

Write an article for your community newspaper.

Step 1 **Prepare**

> Choose what you would like to talk about: a local project or a project to be done in another city or country? Who are you writing the article for: teens or adults?

> Do research to find details to support your opinion.

> Add arguments.

> Think of pictures you can include in your text.

Step 2 **Write**

> Write a first draft.

> Make sure to include your opinions and emotions.

> Here are a few writing tips: Avoid long paragraphs, end your text with a punch, and write at least three arguments.

Step 3 **Revise**

> Are your ideas clear? Reread your article out loud to make sure.

> Ask someone to read your article and suggest changes.

> Make the necessary corrections.

Step 4 **Edit**

> Did you use verb tenses correctly?

> Check your spelling in a dictionary.

> Make changes.

> Write a final copy.

Step 5 **Publish**

> Hand in your article to your teacher.

> Send your article to your principal to start making a difference in your school.

War and Peace, 1952, Pablo Picasso (1881–1973)

IC**T**

Options

Create a class or school blog and post the articles written by you and your classmates.

Encourage people to comment on the articles online, or add a message board where they can discuss ideas for promoting peace in schools.

Option B

Create a class mural displaying poems, letters and posters that promote peace.

Step 1 Prepare

> Brainstorm to find ideas to include in your poem, letter or poster.
> For whom are you creating the poem, letter or poster: the students in your class, the next generation of students, your parents?
> If you are writing a poem, look at the Smart Stop on page 106 for ideas.

Step 2 Produce

> Create a draft of your text. Write your ideas, thoughts and feelings.
> Read it out loud. Does the text sound good?
> Is your message clear? What could you add or remove to make it better?
> Did you express what you wanted to say?
> Are you on topic?
> Ask someone to look at your draft and give you feedback.
> Check your spelling in a dictionary.
> Did you use verb tenses correctly?
> Make changes.
> Decorate your text and create a final copy.

Step 3 Present

> Pin your text on the wall alongside your classmates' texts to create a class mural.
> Take time to read the messages of your classmates' texts.
> Vote for the five best texts.

Ic**T**

Options

Take pictures using a digital camera or scan images to include in your poem, letter or poster.

Smart Words
REVIEW

1 appeal
2 backdrop
3 bleak
4 dead-end street
5 deadline
6 forgiveness
7 hang out
8 heal
9 huddle
10 jarring
11 mind-blowing
12 overlook
13 perpetrator
14 prod
15 puzzle
16 stick up for
17 touch base
18 trial
19 weak
20 well-being

Self-Evaluate

Did I follow all the steps suggested?
Did I use verb tenses correctly?
Did I use ideas from the unit to help me?
Did I use different resources, such as a dictionary, the Smart Reference section, a partner?

Reflection

1 Which activity did you like the most? Why?
2 Which activity was the most challenging for you?
3 Name two strategies that you learned to use in this unit.
4 If you had to do this unit over again, what would you do differently?
5 What are your goals for the next unit? What would you like to improve?

Intolerance Still a Problem in High Schools

People always say that high school is the worst place to be if you are gay. They say this because it is true. Nowadays, **derogatory** jokes are often a normal part of a teenager's day-to-day conversations.

We, as **westerners**, like to think that we are **progressive**, but this is an issue that
5 continues to be a problem for our society. Tolerance toward homosexuals is unfortunately still an issue facing young people today.

Although hate toward homosexuals of both sexes is a problem, often gay men are the ones who are discriminated against most often. This reveals a new element of sexism in our culture. For the most part, women are allowed to be masculine nowadays. We are
10 allowed to seek jobs in male-dominated fields, and we are always on the lookout for cases of discrimination. That **battle** has been won.

However, the struggle against the **gender roles** assigned to men has not been as successful. The pressure to be masculine by the media and one's community can often be **overbearing**. Feminism and gender equality is about being whoever you want to be.
15 It is about acting masculine or feminine, no matter what gender you are. This is a message that has yet to get across to students.

In my high school, the word 'fag' could be heard on almost a daily basis. School is a place where all students should feel safe, but I was never free from hateful comments within its walls. I heard the word 'fag' used at least once a week, often in the presence
20 of a teacher who did nothing. This was always something that **bothered** me. I am not gay, but this word hurts my friends who are. And when my friends were hurting, I was hurting too.

Many (if not most) people use the word 'fag' as a joke. Usually, they do not mean to promote hate and ignorance. They often argue that nobody they know is gay, and
25 therefore they are not hurting anyone. However, this is virtually impossible to know in high school. Approximately one out of every ten people is gay, so it is highly likely that someone you know is questioning their sexuality. It does not matter what the context is. Stating a hateful word is still hate, and it is never funny.

If you are in high school, and you are being discriminated against in this way, do not
30 hesitate to talk to someone. Call Kid's Help Phone, or go to a teacher or guidance counselor. Also, keep in mind that high school is not forever. It is only a short period of time in your life, and as you get older, people become more tolerant.

The word 'fag,' and other derogatory terms, hurts people. It makes them hide, and it makes them pretend to be someone that they are not. In my opinion, this is the worst
35 thing that you can do to a person.

Erin Wilson is eighteen and lives in Kingston, Ontario.

Erin Wilson, "Intolerance still a problem in high schools," Young People's Press website, April 23, 2007

S**m**a**r**t Words

derogatory = insulting

westerner = person from the western part of the world

progressive = having modern ideas and methods

battle = fight between groups of people

gender role = expected behaviour based on a person's sex (male or female)

overbearing = overpowering

fag = very offensive word for a homosexual

bother = worry and upset

Just Say No to Hate
(An excerpt from Stephen J. Toope's convocation address to Dawson College grads)

I hope that you are here tonight because somewhere in your academic career you have been inspired. Someone has excited you—a teacher or a fellow student.
5 Something you have read has fired your imagination. Something said in a class has given you an idea about the future. You know that the world, as hard as it can be, is also filled with promise. I think
10 that you share the moral universe of the wonderful Nigerian novelist and poet, Ben Okri, who writes:

We are the miracles that God made
To taste the bitter fruit of Time.
15 *We are precious.*
And one day our suffering
Will turn into the wonders of the earth.

I began to learn that lesson fully only in my 30s. Until then, my life had been
20 relatively uneventful, and I had been encouraged to believe in a beneficent universe. I had been raised in a loving family. I had been blessed with incredible educational opportunities. I had a great
25 job as dean of law at McGill University, a wonderful wife, a lovely little daughter, and a son who had just arrived. Then one day, during a meeting, I was given an urgent phone message. I could never
30 have imagined the consequences: I learned later that night that my parents had been brutally murdered in their quiet Beaconsfield home.

Within a couple of days the perpetrators
35 had been caught—three teenage boys, who had no real motive, who had killed for fun. The **senselessness** of the attack was **devastating**. I imagine that for those of you who lived through the shootings
40 at Dawson, and especially for the family of Anastasia De Sousa, that same shocking and grotesque **purposelessness** must have caused deep **heartache**.

How does one react to senseless violence
45 that rips at the core of our world? There is no single answer. People must be allowed to react in their own ways. I can only tell you how I reacted—and the reaction was almost immediate. I said
50 no. No, you pathetic boys are not going to destroy the memory of my parents, who lived rich and gentle lives. No, you are not going to define my existence or that of my family. No, you will not turn me
55 into a fearful person. No, you will not teach me to hate.

In his majestic novel, *Tess of the D'Urbervilles*, Thomas Hardy writes one of the most evocative and frightening lines
60 in all of English literature. He foretells the inevitability of suffering: "Once victim, always victim."

I stand here today to **refute** Hardy, to proclaim that victimization is as much
65 an attitude as a condition, and to argue that it is possible to confront and address the effects of violence in our own lives. Dealing with the effects of violence is, nevertheless, painful, for
70 individuals, for cities and for societies— It does not allow escape, only confrontation; not triumph, only modest gains. But to be a victim of violence is not to lose control over one's destiny. Our
75 reactions are not programmed, not inevitable.

You took to heart Rev. Sokolowski's words at Anastasia De Sousa's funeral: "The book of her life was closed so
80 suddenly; it was such a short life. But the books of our life are still open, so we all have a chance to do something with our life, to change our life, to do something really good."

Stephen J. Toope is president and vice-chancellor of the University of British Columbia. (This is an edited excerpt from the notes of his convocation address to Dawson College grads June 21, 2007.)

Words

senselessness = absence of meaning or reason

devastating = shocking and extremely sad

purposelessness = absence of a clear goal or reason

heartache = feeling of great sadness

refute = prove that something is not correct

Words Review

Read over the vocabulary selection from each unit and try to remember what each word means.

Unit 1	Unit 2	Unit 3	Unit 4	Unit 5
achieve	amp	ban	commute	appeal
encounter	cover song	clog	cozy	deadline
field	gig	complexion	dread	forgiveness
flunk	link	crooked	foreign	hang out
grades	lyrics	freckles	frugal	heal
novel	mate	glove	gather	puzzle
strength	outgoing	high-ranking	leisurely	stick up for
thin	rehearsal	lessen	lineup	trial
throw	reliable	mean	purchase	weak
upset	thoughtful	surgeon	voucher	well-being

Here are three ways to help you remember the words.

1 Play a warm-up memory game.

> Look at the words for two minutes. Then close your book and write down all the words that you can remember on a separate sheet of paper. How many can you remember?

2 Write sentences.

> Write a sentence using each word. Make sure that the sentences are complete and specific enough to explain the meanings of the words.

Stephen King's novel was filled with suspense. (Correct: The sentence explains what a novel is.)

I love novels. (Incorrect: The sentence doesn't explain what a novel is.)

3 Complete a word web.

> Choose ten words from the above list and complete a word web for each word.

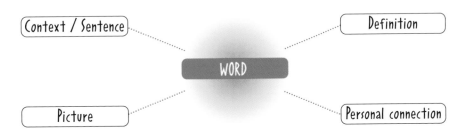

Structure Review

Review the Smart Structures in each unit.

Unit 1	Unit 2	Unit 3	Unit 4	Unit 5
Conditional Form I **would** rather play hockey. I **wouldn't** change the script. **Could** you help me? **Intensifiers** He is **really** busy today. She is **very** happy.	**Simple Present Tense** He **practises** every day. She **doesn't like** jazz. **Does** he **play** in a band? **Present Progressive Tense** She **is singing** right now. He **isn't playing** drums tonight. **Are** they **playing** their guitars?	**Gerunds** **Swimming** is good exercise. Kate likes **playing** music. We finished **planning** the dance.	**Count Nouns** Plural form: Two **gifts** Three **hours** A few **posters** Many **shoppers** **Non-Count Nouns** No plural form: A little **ice cream** A lot of **money** Much **happiness** Any **sunshine**	**Simple Past Tense** I **talked** to my teacher. They **sent** the letter. (irregular verb) **Past Progressive Tense** I **was playing** badminton. **Present Perfect Tense** She **has lived** here a long time. You **haven't gone** home yet. (irregular verb)

Your Turn to Practise!

> **Complete the following exercise.**

1. You ▮▮▮▮ (could / should) eat less junk food if you want to lose weight. (conditional form)

2. My dad ▮▮▮▮ (should / would) help you if he had the time.

3. Find the intensifiers in this sentence:
   We were really excited when they gave us a very big trophy.

4. Write a complete sentence using an intensifier.

5. Simple present or present progressive tense:
   a) Every Friday, we ▮▮▮▮ (eat) pizza before we practise.
   b) ▮▮▮▮ you ▮▮▮▮? (sleep)

6. Write the gerund: ▮▮▮▮ (remove) a tattoo is very expensive.

7. Correct the mistakes (count versus non-count nouns):
   a) There are much presents under the tree.
   b) There are a lot of sugar in the cake.

8. Write two sentences in the simple past tense:
   a) Use a regular verb.
   b) Use an irregular verb.

9. Write a sentence using the past progressive tense.

10. Write a sentence using the present perfect tense.

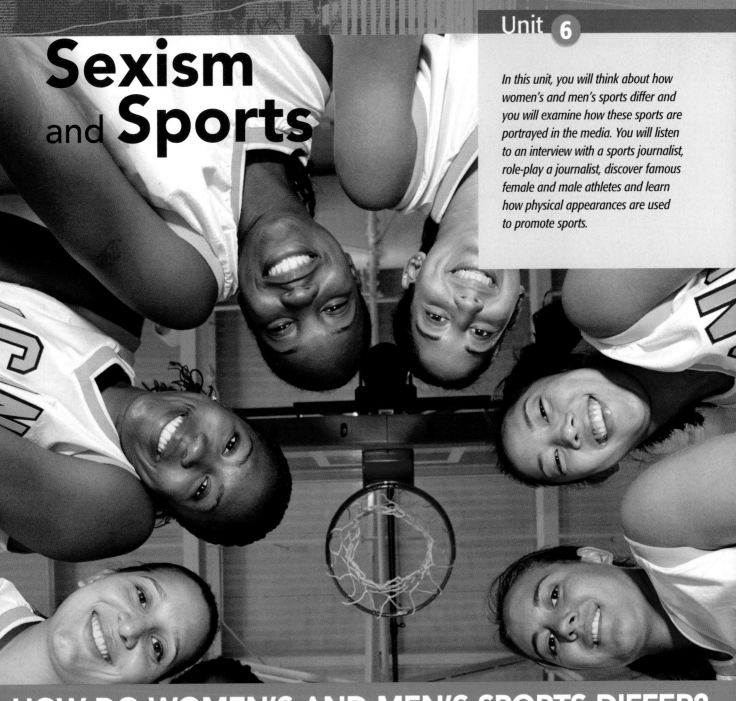

Sexism and Sports

In this unit, you will think about how women's and men's sports differ and you will examine how these sports are portrayed in the media. You will listen to an interview with a sports journalist, role-play a journalist, discover famous female and male athletes and learn how physical appearances are used to promote sports.

HOW DO WOMEN'S AND MEN'S SPORTS DIFFER?

Final Task

Write about a sporting event.

Option A

Write an article on sports and sexism.

Option B

Publicize a sporting event in your community.

Smart Start

Do you play any sports? Do you have a favourite sports team? People in our society love sports, but some sports are more popular than others. Which sports are you familiar with?

1 Play the sports charades game.

Be Smart

Use gestures to express your message.

Encourage your partner while you play the game.

Smart Talk

You go first …

I don't understand that action.

Can you do that again, please?

Is the sport …?

Yes, you guessed correctly!

How many sports can you name? Are these sports played in Canada? What about sports played in other countries? Try this game with a partner.

> Take a few minutes to list all the sports you can think of.
> Share your list with your classmates.
> Sit with a partner and look at the class list of sports.
> Take turns choosing a sport and acting it out. Your partner will try to guess the sport you are demonstrating. Note that you must only answer "yes" or "no" to your partner's guesses and not give away any clues.
> See how many sports you can act out with your partner in ten minutes.

Self-Evaluate

Did I keep trying even if it was difficult?

Did I use gestures to communicate my message?

2 Decide whether a sport is considered to be a women's or a men's sport.

It is time to take a closer look at the sports you listed in the previous activity. Are these sports played more often by women or by men, or equally by both?

> Copy the chart on the following page.
> Look at the list of sports from the previous activity.
> Decide which sports are women's sports, which are men's sports, and which sports are played by both women and men.

> When you have completed the chart, answer the questions below individually.

> Then share your answers with your classmates.

Women's Sports	Men's Sports	Women's and Men's Sports
Synchronized swimming	Rugby	Basketball
▬▬▬▬▬▬	▬▬▬▬▬▬	▬▬▬▬▬▬

smart Talk

I think that … is a sport for … because …

Do you think that … know how to …?

More … play / watch this sport, so we can say it is …

Do you agree that … is a female / male sport?

I think this sport is both a female and a male sport, because …

❶ Which list is longer: the women's sports, the men's sports, or the sports played by both sexes?

❷ What criteria did you use to determine which sports are women's sports: the number of women participating in the sport or the number of women watching it?

❸ What criteria did you use to determine which sports are men's sports? Are they the same as the criteria you used to determine which sports are women's sports? Why or why not?

❹ Look at the sports that are played by both women and men. Which version of the sport usually attracts more attention in the media: the women's or the men's version? Why do you think this is the case?

❺ Which sports would you like to see more women playing? More men playing? Explain your answer.

Self-Evaluate

Did I show a positive attitude while speaking English?

Did I pronounce the words clearly?

Task 1 Media Coverage

Think about how popular women's and men's sporting events are covered in the newspapers or on TV. Is it easier to find sporting events about women or men?

1 Read about gender equity.

In Canada, there is an organization whose goal is to promote women's sports. In the following article, you will read about the issues concerning women's sports.

> Before you read the text below, think of three reasons why women don't participate in sports as often as men do.

> In schools, are girls encouraged to play sports as much as boys? Why or why not?

Italian Race-Car Driver Lella Lombardi at Brands Hatch, March 1974, Kent, England

Plan. Read the questions before reading the text.

Words

slanted = prejudiced

gimmick = trick to attract attention

lack (noun) = not enough

Gender Equity—Real Girls Do Play Sports

*Times have changed since the days when women's participation in sports was limited to applauding men. But as Hattie Klotz reports, many female sports administrators say the playing field is still **slanted** in favour of men.*

At the first Women's World Hockey Championship in Ottawa in 1990,
5 tournament organizers felt they needed a **gimmick** to attract spectators. They dressed the female Canadian hockey players in pink. The pretty-in-pink Canadian women suffered their uniforms, but won the tournament.

At least, they were allowed to play. During the Olympic Games in ancient Greece, women who watched men were thrown from a cliff-top. In 1896,
10 the founder of the modern Olympic Games said that women did have a role this time: applauding men.

Times have changed for women, but not enough, say representatives from the Canadian sport community. The first-ever "Women in Sport" symposium identified three key issues:

15 ❶ **lack** of media coverage of female sporting heroes;

❷ a need for quality daily physical education programs for young girls at school;

❸ a need for increased levels of corporate funding for female athletes.

The way children are socialized is a basic problem, said Ms. McGregor. Girls
20 are given dolls to play with; boys get baseballs and hockey sticks.

"When parents go out to buy bikes for their children, the girl's one is pink and has tassels hanging from the handlebars, with a name like 'Little Miss Sassy,' and the boy's bike is called 'The Boss,'" said Ms. McGregor.

"We hear from parents who take their girls to tournaments and they win
25 trophies. The trophies have a male player on them."

"It is still an insult to say to people 'You throw like a girl,'" Ms. McGregor said.

Words

drop out = leave

counterpart = someone with an equivalent job

lack (verb) = miss, need

Research shows that girls and boys participate in sport at about an equal rate up until the age of six. It then begins to fall off for girls. The numbers, however, drop dramatically for girls at the high school age, when they **drop out** of sports in big numbers.

At that age, girls make up about 30 percent of participants, Ms. McGregor said.

Cassie Campbell, twenty-five, who plays for the Canadian women's national ice hockey team, recollects, "Hockey is a sport that real girls just didn't play. My parents always allowed me to do as I wanted, but in subtle ways tried to convince me to do other things like tennis. But women's hockey is becoming more acceptable."

Figures released by the Canadian Hockey Association show that hockey has exploded among women in the last ten years. In 1988 to 1989, the association had 7100 registered female players, and by 1998, that number had risen to 38 000.

On a national team level, at least, there is equality. The female players are paid the same amount as their male **counterparts** while in training, and have comparable facilities.

But at the professional level, "People just don't want to hear talk of a women's hockey league," said Ms. Campbell.

Another problem women face in sport is low visibility compared to their male counterparts. Because of the low visibility of female athletes, girls **lack** female athlete heroes or role models, Ms. McGregor said.

In women's volleyball, athletes are forced to wear minuscule bikinis. At the last world championships, several teams were fined $3000 (US) for not complying with the dress code. And at the Atlanta Olympics, beach volleyball players were not allowed to wear their national team jackets to receive their medals.

"They had to be little sex objects on the podium," said Ms. McGregor.

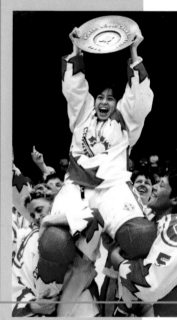

The Canadian team at the Women's World Hockey Championship, Ottawa, March 25, 1990

Hattie Klotz, "Gender Equity—Real Girls Do Play Sports," Canadian Association for the Advancement of Women and Sport and Physical Activity website, June 16, 1999

> Answer the following questions.

1. What trick (or gimmick) did the organizers of the Women's World Hockey Championship use to attract spectators? Do you think it was a good idea to use this trick? Why or why not?

2. Which three issues for women did the "Women in Sport" symposium identify?

3. How are girls and boys socialized differently towards sports? Give two examples from the article.

4. How is hockey equal for women and men on a national level? How is it unequal at the professional level?

5. Can you think of a solution to encourage women to play sports?

Marie-Josée Turcotte,
sports journalist

2 Listen to a sports journalist's opinion.

During the 2006 Winter Olympics in Turin, Italy, the Canadian women's hockey team won the gold medal for the second year in a row, but the media preferred to talk about another event instead: how the men's Olympic hockey team failed to win a medal at all! Marie-Josée Turcotte, a well-known sports journalist, was frustrated by the media's lack of attention towards women's hockey and women's sports in general. Listen to what she has to say in an interview.

> Before you listen to the interview, think about these questions: What do you already know about sexism in the media? How are women's sports covered differently from men's sports? Write this information in the first column of the chart (What I **K**now).

> Think about what you would like to learn about this topic and write it in the second column of the chart (What I **W**ant to Know).

> Choose a strategy you will use while listening to the interview.

> When you have finished listening to the interview, write what you learned in the last column of the chart (What I **L**earned).

Focus on
the information
you hear. Don't be
distracted.

Interview with Marie-Josée Turcotte		
What I Know	**What I Want to Know**	**What I Learned**
• Men's sports have more coverage.	Why?	▬▬▬▬▬▬▬

> Listen to the interview again. Check the last column of your chart. Write down the examples Ms. Turcotte gives to support her opinions.

> Then choose one of the titles below:
>   • *No Media Coverage for Women's Sports!*
>   • *Canadian Women Take Gold! Did You Know?*

> Use your notes from the chart to write a short informative paragraph on one of the above topics for your school newspaper. Include examples and facts from the interview or from previous activities. See Smart Stop in Unit 3 (page 54) for help in writing a paragraph.

Smart Words

defeat = failure to win

coverage = attention given to a story in the media

opponent = person or team you are playing against

deserve = merit

Self-**E**valuate

Did I complete each section of the chart?
Did I include examples in my paragraph?

3 Be the journalist.

Now that you have heard what a real journalist has to say about sexism and sports, it is your turn to become a journalist. In this role-playing activity, you will interview a female athlete and then a male athlete about their views on sexism in sports.

> As a class, make a list of different types of magazines, newspapers and television stations that feature interviews with athletes. Then decide for which media company you would like to be a reporter.

> Prepare your interview questions. Below are eight questions to help you get started. Add five more questions to the list before you begin your interview.

1 Do you think that the media gives your sport enough publicity?

2 Do women's and men's sports have the same exposure? Why or why not?

3 Do you feel pressure to use your looks to promote yourself? Why or why not?

4 What kind of an image do you want portrayed in the media?

5 What does your image say about who you are, about your values and beliefs?

6 Do you think that dressing in revealing clothes is an effective way for athletes to obtain exposure?

7 How do you feel when you see your picture in a magazine or newspaper?

8 What can the media do to better promote sporting events and in particular, women's sporting events?

> Sit with a partner. Together you will role-play an interview with a female athlete and then an interview with a male athlete, alternating roles. For each interview, one student will role-play the reporter and the other student will role-play the athlete being interviewed.

> Use the list of eight questions from the Student Book and the five questions you prepared to carry out the interview.

> Start your role play. For the first interview, the reporter will ask the questions and the female athlete will respond. When you have completed this interview with your partner, switch roles and begin the second interview with the male athlete.

> Use Smart Talk to help you.

Be Smart

Take your time and think about what you will say.

If you don't know a word, use other words to explain your message.

This is a fun activity— Don't worry if you make mistakes!

 Talk

I'm from … magazine.
Can you tell me …
What do you think about …?
I believe that …
I think that …

Self-Evaluate

Did I take a risk and keep trying even when I made mistakes?

Did I use Smart Talk to help me?

Olympic Sports

The most prestigious world sports competition is the Olympic Games. You will learn about Olympic athletes and find out why women can't compete against men in the Olympic sport of wrestling.

1 Discover female and male athletes.

Downhiller, 1984, Ken Danby (1940–2007)

Have you ever heard of the following famous Canadian Olympic athletes?

> Read the descriptions of the athletes individually.
> Match the descriptions with the athletes on the next page.
> Sit with a partner and compare your answers.

1 This athlete was born on June 8, 1985 in Montréal, Québec. He is the current world champion in the one- and three-metre **springboard** competition. He is also the first diver to become world champion in all three categories (one- and three-metre springboard and ten-metre platform).

2 This athlete was born on December 23, 1970. She is a Canadian speed skater and a double Olympic champion in the five hundred-metre event. She became famous when she won the gold medal at the 1998 Winter Olympics and then again at the 2002 Winter Olympics.

3 This champion alpine skier was born on May 11, 1943 in Ottawa. In 1967, she became the first North American skier to win the World Cup. In 1968, she won a gold medal in the giant slalom and a silver medal in the slalom.

4 This two-time Olympic silver medallist in men's figure skating was named after a very famous singer. He was born on March 22, 1972 and grew up in Richmond Hill, Ontario. He was the first man to ever land a quadruple jump in figure skating. He won many medals during his skating career, but never made the Olympic gold.

5 This athlete was born on April 21, 1977 in Calgary, Alberta. At the age of sixteen, she was the youngest member of the Olympic team. In 2002, she won a gold medal in pairs figure skating with her partner, David Pelletier.

6 This athlete surprised the world by winning a gold medal at the 2006 Winter Olympics. Born on November 19, 1983 in Canmore, Alberta, her specialty is women's cross-country skiing (1,1 kilometre sprint).

7 This famous Canadian swimmer was born on February 7, 1968 in Calgary, Alberta. He won three Olympic medals: a silver medal in 1988 and gold and bronze medals in 1992. He is in the Canadian Olympic Hall of Fame.

8 This Canadian athlete was born on December 16, 1967 in Manchester, Jamaica. He emigrated from Jamaica to Canada at the age of thirteen. He won two gold medals at the 1996 Olympics, setting a world record of 9,84 seconds in the one hundred-metre sprint.

Famous Female Canadian Olympic Athletes	Famous Male Canadian Olympic Athletes
 **Nancy Greene** Nancy Greene was voted Canada's Female Athlete for the 21st century, for her ability on the ski slopes.	**Donovan Bailey** As well as being a top sprinter, Donovan Bailey has also been a successful stockbroker! 
 **Catriona LeMay Doan** Catriona LeMay Doan is known as "the fastest woman on ice."	**Mark Tewksbury** Mark Tewksbury is famous both in the pool and as a spokesperson for human rights. 
 **Jamie Salé** Jamie Salé loved working with her partner, David Pelletier, so much that she married him.	**Alexandre Despatie** Alexandre Despatie isn't just a star on the diving board. He also stars in television commercials. 
 **Chandra Crawford** Growing up in the mountains, Chandra Crawford skied the hills in the winter and hiked them in the summer.	**Elvis Stojko** Elvis Stojko won the Canadian Figure Skating Championships seven times and the World Figure Skating Championships three times. 

Facts

Right to Play

Benoît Huot, a six-time Paralympic gold medal winner in swimming from Longueuil, Québec, is an ambassador for an organization called Right to Play. Right to Play uses sports and play programs to improve health, build life skills and promote peace in areas of the world affected by war, poverty and disease. Huot worked to raise 100 000 dollars to support programs in Francophone and West Africa, in Mali, Benin, Chad, Ghana, Liberia, Rwanda and Sierra Leone. He also visited Mali to observe these programs in action. Right to Play designs their programs to reach the specific needs of the community they are working with through sports. Benoît is just one of the many Canadian professional and Olympic athletes who believe that sports have the power to change lives and who has seen this first-hand.

2 Learn about Tara's experience as a wrestler.

The Olympic event with the longest history is wrestling. In Ancient Greece, men tested their strength by wrestling one another. Today, women compete in wrestling, but they aren't allowed to compete against boys after puberty. You will watch a video about a girl who tried to fight the system.

Sumo Wrestler, 1869, Hirasawa Kuniaki (1835–1888)

> Before watching the video, as a class, make a list of reasons why girls exercise and a list of reasons why boys exercise. When you have finished, answer the following questions individually.

1. Do boys and girls exercise for the same reasons?
2. Do they have equal opportunities to play and practise sports?
3. What kind of problems do girls face in accessing and playing sports?
4. Do boys face any of these problems?
5. Can you name one reason why girls shouldn't be allowed to wrestle against boys?
6. Can you name a reason why they should be allowed?

> Before watching the video, read the quiz questions below.
> After watching the video, in a small group, find the answers to the questions.
> Try to be the first team to finish the quiz!

"Girl Wrestler" Quiz

1. In the introduction, what do the girls say wrestling teaches you?
2. How many girls are on Tara's team?
3. Is Tara a successful wrestler? How do you know?
4. At what age must Tara stop wrestling boys?
5. Can she still keep wrestling after this age?
6. What will happen if Tara can't find another girl her weight to wrestle against when she is older?
7. What positive things do people at the tournament say about girls wrestling?
8. What reason do people at the tournament give against girls wrestling?

Pay attention while listening and watching.

Self-Evaluate

Did I cooperate with my group to complete the quiz?

Did I answer the questions accurately?

Sound and Transition Techniques in Video

Video is a very effective way to get a message across, because it combines images with movement and sound. In "Girl Wrestler," the director uses many different kinds of sounds. Can you find an example from the video for each of the following types of sound?

Sound	Used for
Direct sound Sound that is recorded at the same time as the film	• Creating a realistic effect
Voice-over narration A voice that comments on, explains or gives facts during a film	• Giving specific information directly to the viewers
Sound effects Recorded sounds of specific action added to the film after filming	• Emphasizing certain sounds, such as footsteps • Creating ambience or a context
Music Songs with or without words that are played over the action (so that you don't hear the other sounds) or in the background (so that you can hear other sounds)	• Creating the mood or emotion of a scene

In film, a scene is made up of a sequence of shots. Each shot is joined together using a transition technique. Here are the four most common types of transitions used in films:

Transition Technique	Used for
Pan left / right Moving from one part of the set to another	• Giving the viewers the impression that they are in the room and seeing the story through their own eyes
Cut Ending one shot and immediately starting another	• Ending one storyline and starting another • Changing the focus to another character • Changing the location of the storyline
Fade in / out Gradually showing / ending a shot	• Indicating the end of a sequence or the end of the movie • Indicating death or the afterlife
Dissolve Turning one shot into another	• Signalling the passing of time • Signalling a change in the location of the storyline

3 Share your opinion about sports on a poster.

The issue of women and men competing together in sports isn't a simple one. There are many arguments for and against it. You will choose a side of the debate, and then publicize the reasons behind your choice on a poster to be displayed in your classroom.

Step 1 **Prepare**

> With a partner, decide which side of the debate you will represent. Are you for or against women and men competing together in sports?

> Brainstorm and write a list of reasons to support your position.

> Choose a title or slogan.

> Think about the format of the poster:
  - Who is its target audience?
  - What is its purpose?
  - What kind of pictures will best support your argument?
  - What colours would be effective?
  - What materials do you need?

Step 2 **Produce**

> Create a rough sketch of the poster. Decide where to put the title, images and text. Use comparative and superlative adverbs (see the Smart Structure on the next page).

> Revise the poster. Is the poster effective at sending its message? Will people be convinced by the poster's arguments?

> Ask a classmate to give you feedback and suggestions for improving the poster. Edit the poster and correct your mistakes.

> Make a final copy.

Step 3 **Present**

> Display the poster in the classroom.

> Look at your classmates' posters and give them feedback and suggestions for improving their work.

> Vote for the best poster.

Plan. Read the instructions twice.

What resources do you need to create your poster?

Options

Use a digital camera to take pictures to include in the poster.

Use software to design a professional-looking poster with typed text and digitally modified images.

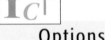

Self-**E**valuate

Did I cooperate with my partner and remain open to her/his ideas and suggestions?

Did I use comparative and superlative adverbs correctly?

Structure

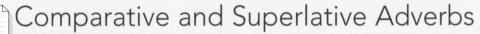

Comparative and Superlative Adverbs

When you talk about women and men competing together in sports, you use comparative and superlative adverbs.

Adverbs
An adverb is an adjective that used to describe a verb.   *She writes* **quickly**. (The adverb *quickly* describes the verb *writes*.)   An adverb is formed by adding *-ly* to the end of an adjective.   *quiet* → **quietly**   If the adjective ends in *-y* (for example, *happy*), you change the *y* to an *i* and then add *-ly*.   *happy* → **happily**   **Exceptions:**   Some adjectives stay the same when they become adverbs, for example: **fast**, **hard**, **early** and **far**.

Forming Comparative and Superlative Adverbs			
For adverbs ending in *-ly*, add the word *more* to form the comparative and the words *the most* to form the superlative.			
Adjective	**Adverb**	**Comparative Adverb**	**Superlative Adverb**
quiet careful happy	quietly carefully happily	more quietly more carefully more happily	the most quietly the most carefully the most happily
Adjective → *Jeff is* **quiet**. Adverb → *Jeff works* **quietly**. Comparative adverb → *Jeff works* **more quietly** *than Steve*. Superlative adverb → *Jeff works* **the most quietly** *of all the students*. **Pay attention:** Usually the comparative adverb is followed by *than*.			

Exceptions			
For most exceptions, add *-er* to form the comparative and *-est* to form the superlative.			
Adjective	**Adverb**	**Comparative Adverb**	**Superlative Adverb**
hard fast early good bad far	hard fast early well badly far	harder faster earlier better worse farther	the hardest the fastest the earliest the best the worst the farthest
Adjective → *Karen is a* **fast** *runner*. Adverb → *Patricia runs* **fast**. Comparative adverb → *Mary runs* **faster** *than John*. Superlative adverb → *Mary runs* **the fastest** *of all the runners on the team*.			

Raising Interest in Sports

Sports associations raise interest in women's sports by emphasizing the beauty and attractiveness of female athletes. They believe that if people buy magazines and watch television shows to see beautiful women, the same tactic will work for sports. What do you think? Is this a good way to raise interest in women's sports, or does it prevent people from taking female athletes seriously?

C1 1 Play a word association game.

What do you think of when you hear the word *athlete*? How about the word *sport*? We often associate words with specific ideas. Try the experiment below to find out which ideas you associate with words relating to certain sports.

| athlete | ...... | strong | ...... | muscles |
| sport | ...... | fun | ...... | hobby |

Smart Talk

What words did you write down for *Olympics*?

Why did you think of these words?

… is an interesting choice!

Do you agree?

> Write the following words on a piece of paper: *Olympics*, *beach volleyball* and *uniform*.

> Now write down the words that come to your mind when you read each of the above words. Take only fifteen seconds for each word.

> When you have finished, sit with a partner and compare your lists. Do you have any of the same words? Which words are different?

> Are you surprised by any of the words that you or your partner chose? Why?

> Try the game again using three new words related to sports.

Self-Evaluate

Was my message on topic?

Did my partner understand what I was saying?

2 Read about a sports magazine.

What do the words *bikini* and *volleyball* have in common? In most professional beach volleyball competitions, female players must wear bikini-style uniforms in order to play. Why do you think they have to show off their bodies? Do you think it makes the sport easier to play or more fun to watch?

⟩ Before reading the article below, look at the headline. Can you guess what the text will be about?

Don't panic even if the text seems difficult at first.

Plan. Look at all the Smart Words before you read.

Sports Illustrated Swimsuit Issue

In his 1928 book, *The Future of Sport*, British author G.S. Sandilands wrote, "Only a very few years ago, no man would have dreamed of mentioning in society the subject of ladies' **knickers**. Now girls in sports appear in running shorts and reveal great lengths of **unclad**
5 legs. Even naked **thighs** are displayed as if they don't matter."

Seven decades later, G.S. Sandilands would open any American sports magazine and discover plenty of naked thighs, and many other **unencumbered** body parts. The Canadian Association for the Advancement of Women and Sport and Physical Activity reacts more
10 with sadness than anger.

"It's kind of disappointing when you consider what they could do if they wanted," says Marg McGregor, executive director of the Ottawa-based group that for nearly twenty years has encouraged and promoted the role of girls and women at all levels of sport.

15 "They could profile strong, athletic, powerful, muscular women in a respectful and artful way. You'd expect a sports magazine to do that, but instead they go with a sexy approach."

But there are more **compelling** issues that concern us, such as volleyball's governing body, which in a **bid** to attract more male spectators has dictated
20 that women playing indoors must wear second-skin, Speedo-like uniforms to give the sport the sex-appeal of the game served up on the beach.

"Why aren't male athletes stuffed into tight-fitting uniforms as a way to get more women to watch?" Donna Lopiano, director of the U.S.-based Women's Sports Foundation, asks rhetorically.

25 McGregor would laugh at such ignorance if it weren't subscribed to by so many. Her group's mission is to achieve gender equity and respect for sportswomen. McGregor is encouraged by progress in the coverage and treatment of women's sports, "There is a recognition that it's passé to be sexist and objectify women," she says.

30 We're far removed from the 1920s, thankfully, and seven decades later, women continue to make long, overdue **strides** in sports. Yet we wonder how much higher they might fly if they needn't satisfy the cavemen who either run the games or **drool** as they report them.

On the Beach, (20th century), Janus Januszewski

Words
knickers = underwear
unclad = without clothes
thigh = part of the leg between the hip and the knee
unencumbered = unrestricted
compelling = important
bid = attempt
stride = progress
drool = let saliva run from the mouth

Dave Stubbs, "Sports Illustrated Swimsuit Issue," *The Gazette*, June 14, 1999

Self Portrait, circa 1930, Helen Newington Wills
(1905–1998)

> Decide whether the following statements are true or false.

1. In 1928, women in sports did not wear shorts or show their bare legs.

2. Some sports magazines do not choose to feature women athletes in a respectful and artistic way.

3. The indoor volleyball governing body asks women athletes to wear tighter uniforms to attract more viewers.

4. It also requires male athletes to wear skin-tight swimsuits to attract more female spectators.

5. Marg McGregor says people recognize that it's acceptable to objectify women.

> Finish these sentences individually.

6. I think the main idea of the text is that …

7. I was surprised to learn that …

8. I think that athletes should / shouldn't use their looks to attract spectators because …

Go Further

> Find a sports magazine or the sports section of a newspaper. Then write ten sentences describing the images that you see on the pages.

> Imagine that you are accompanying Mr. Sandilands to the beach volleyball finals at the next Olympic Games. Write a short story (with dialogue) about what happens at the event and how the women's and men's events are similar or different.

Self-Evaluate

Did I find the main idea of the text?

Did I clearly link my answers to the text?

Professional Sports

The differences between women's and men's sports can be clearly observed in professional sports, where athletes are paid to play. The public is more interested in watching professional sports played by men than by women, and most TV sports shows are hosted by men and cover male professional sports.

 1 Discuss the controversy.

Why are there very few women hosting sports shows on TV? Is this because women don't watch them? How about professional sports? Why aren't women being paid high salaries to play professionally?

> With a partner, make a list of as many professional sports as possible.

> Put check marks next to the sports in which women or men take part.

Professional Sport	Women	Men
Race-car driving	✓	✓
Football		✓

> Decide how much you agree with each of the following statements. Write your answer using the following scale:
> 1 = strongly agree   3 = disagree
> 2 = agree   4 = strongly disagree

> Share your answers with a partner or a small group.

Rachel Thompson and Emily Tidwell challenge one another in a "fantasy" soccer game, 1999, Bill Hall (1948–)

Statements

1 There are professional sports in which women should not participate.

2 Men are better at some sports than women, and that is why they are professionals.

3 Women and men should both be allowed to compete in all the professional sports.

4 Women playing professional sports would be as popular as men.

5 Women and men should earn an equal salary for playing the same sports.

6 Watching women's professional sports is as interesting as watching men's professional sports.

Use Smart Words from this unit to help you while you are speaking.

 Talk

I think that …

I agree / disagree, because …

I put number … because …

What do you think?

Which number did you put?

Self-**E**valuate

Did I speak without hesitating?

Did I use Smart Talk?

2 Read about girls who skateboard.

One sport in which more men participate than women is skateboarding—at both the amateur and the professional level—but there are women who are changing this.

> Take turns reading a paragraph of the text below out loud with a partner.
> While you are reading, write down the words that are new to you.

Skateboarding Girls

1 It is late afternoon in the park. Many people are enjoying the sun. There are business people, students, musicians and some skateboarders practising tricks. It is obvious that summer will soon be here. What is **unusual** about the park isn't the number of people in it, but how many female skateboarders are skating, talking and practising together.

2 Usually, if you see skateboarders in a park, they are all guys, but this group is special. They are a gang of skater girls who love everything about skateboarding. The group of women are between the ages of five and thirty-five. They often meet in the park to skate together, give each other advice, plan skateboarding trips and discuss upcoming competitions.

3 Of course, there weren't always female skateboarders. Like most sports, it is mostly men who practise skateboarding, but that is slowly changing. A few years ago, some young women grew tired of watching their brothers and guy friends skateboarding and decided to give it a try. It wasn't easy at first. Many of the women say that it was hard to ignore the voices that told them: "I'm not as good. It's normal. I'm just a girl." They knew it was stupid, but it was difficult to stay motivated. Besides, there weren't many female role models to look up to for an example.

4 Then, several years ago, these women started **running into** other women like them in skate parks in Montréal. They were in the minority, but it felt good to meet other women who also loved skateboarding.

5 "The guys were really nice to us, but it just wasn't the same," one skateboarder explains. "In all the skateboarding magazines, Internet sites and videos I saw, there were never any women. It was always pictures and videos of guys." "It was so great to finally meet other women who loved skateboarding like me," her friend adds.

6 Finally, enough of the women decided to get together and make their own skateboarding videos—of themselves—to post on the Internet. They started a website entirely for women skaters, and one of the women now writes a regular article about women skaters in a skateboarding magazine.

Words

unusual = different, strange

run into = meet by chance

7 There aren't just women skateboarders in Montréal; they exist all over Canada and the rest of the world. Some of them even have sponsorship deals. Many enter international competitions.

8 So why the sudden interest in women skaters? Why are they starting to get some of the same money and publicity that only men skaters got for so long? Many people believe that advertisers realize that there is money to be made selling products to women skaters, and that is why so many more women are getting sponsors.

Words

complain = protest, criticize

9 "Lots of people are **complaining** that the girls no longer skate because they love skateboarding—they do it for the money—but I don't think that's fair," one skateboarder says. "Why shouldn't women accept sponsorships just like the guys do if it helps them to spend more time in competitions? Women should be able to earn a living from sports just like the guys do."

10 "Having a place to go and skate with other women is great—It is truly motivating," one young skater remarks. It seems like the women's enthusiasm is also a good influence on the guys. "Wherever there are women skating, I notice that there's less competition between the guys, less talk centred around sponsors and much more fun," she says.

11 Are there places where women skaters are still unusual? "Absolutely!" one skater responds. "Sometimes we go to competitions in places where they have never seen a girl skateboarder before, but it is changing fast. Now there are more and more girls who are trying it out—and they are really good!"

12 "The younger girls are so athletic and smart—they improve really quickly," another woman adds. "I guess it helps that they have some women to look up to."

> **Answer the questions below individually.**

1 What are the main ideas of paragraphs 2, 3, 8, 9 and 10? Refer to the Smart Stop in Unit 3 (page 54) for help. For example, the main idea of paragraph 1 is that there are women skateboarders in the park.

2 Why were women skaters discouraged at first?

3 What made it easier for women skaters to start skateboarding?

4 Is skateboarding popular with girls in your area? Why or why not? Are there girls you know who would like to try skating? Why aren't more girls participating in skateboarding?

5 Do you think that women who accept money from sponsors are skating because they want the money or because they love the sport? Explain your answer.

6 How do you think male skateboarders felt when they first saw girls skateboarding? Explain your answer.

Go Further

> Compare your answers to question 1 on page 133 with a partner's answers. How many of your answers are the same? How many are different? Can you find spelling and grammar mistakes in your partner's answers?

> Write a paragraph answering these questions: How could you get women or men interested in skateboarding? Do you think that creating a website or starting a club would help? Why or why not?

Self-Evaluate

Did I make a meaningful connection between the text and my life?

Did I give my personal opinion?

C3 3 Create a scrapbook page for a professional or amateur athlete.

Do you admire any athletes? Can you imagine yourself being a professional athlete one day? In this activity, you will collect photographs of an athlete you admire. The athlete can be a professional or an amateur.

Maryse Turcotte, Olympic medallist in weightlifting

> Find at least five photographs of the athlete participating in a sport.

> Write a description for each image.

> Include comparative and superlative adverbs in the descriptions of the images.

> Write at least three sentences for each photograph.

> Write a short introduction to your scrapbook page. Include the following details:

- The athlete's name;
- The athlete's sport;
- Whether she/he is a professional athlete or an amateur;
- Whether more women or men participate in the sport and why.

Self-Evaluate

Did I use comparative and superlative adverbs?

Did I use a dictionary or other resources to help me?

Help Change Sports

It is time to put all the information you learned about sexism and sports into practice and send your own message.

Write about a sporting event.

Option A

Write an article on sports and sexism.

Option B

Publicize a sporting event in your community.

Option A

Write an article on sports and sexism.

I c^T

Options

Use software to create a newspaper article with photos.

Submit your article to a popular sports blog.

Step 1 **Prepare**

> Define your purpose. Why are you writing the article: to encourage more people to support women's athletics, to discuss sexism in a particular sport, to address a specific problem in your community?

> Define your target audience. Who you are writing the article: other students, adults, young children?

> Brainstorm for ideas. What arguments will you include in your article?

> Organize your ideas into a plan. Include an introduction, main body of text and a conclusion.

Step 2 **Write**

> Create a draft of the article based on your plan.
> Research facts, statistics and people with the help of the Internet.
> Include photos to support your text.
> Use comparative and superlative adverbs.

Step 3 **Revise**

> Reread the article. Does it make sense?
> Ask someone to read your article and give you feedback.
> Make the necessary changes.

Step 4 **Edit**

> Check your spelling in a dictionary and verify your grammar using the Smart Reference section (pages 268–280).
> Correct your mistakes and write a final copy.

Step 5 **Publish**

> Give your article to your teacher, school newspaper or community paper, or post it on the Internet.

Publicize a sporting event in your community.

Step 1 Prepare

> Use the Internet to research sporting clubs and upcoming sporting events in your area.
> Decide which sports event you wish to promote.
> Your advertisement should focus on an athlete or a team's achievements.
> Choose the format you will use for the advertisement. Will it be a poster, a video, a radio ad, a printed ad in a local newspaper?
> Where will you put the ad so that people will notice it?
> What important information will you include in the ad: the date of the event, the time, the place, the cost of admission, reasons why people should attend the event?

Step 2 Produce

> Create a rough copy of the ad. Make sure that you use all the important features of the medium you chose: images, sound, …
> Revise your text. Are your ideas clear? What could you add or remove to improve the ad?
> Edit: Check your spelling and grammar using a dictionary, the Smart Reference section and other resources. Did you use comparative and superlative adverbs correctly?

Step 3 Present

> Present the ad to your classmates.
> Place the ad in your community. Post it on bulletin boards, publish it in a newspaper, upload it onto the web, …

S elf-Evaluate

Did I use the ideas that I learned in this unit?
Did I express my ideas effectively in the text?
Did I use comparative and superlative adverbs correctly?
Did I use a dictionary and other resources to help me?

Reflection

1. Which activity did you like the most? Why?
2. Which activity was the most challenging for you?
3. Name two strategies that you learned to use in this unit.
4. If you had to do this unit over again, what would you do differently?
5. What are your goals for the next unit? What would you like to improve?

I_CT

Options

Use a digital camera or voice recorder to record the ad as a podcast.

Sm$a$rt Words
R E V I E W

1. bid
2. compelling
3. complain
4. counterpart
5. coverage
6. deserve
7. drool
8. drop out
9. gimmick
10. knickers
11. lack
12. opponent
13. run into
14. slanted
15. springboard
16. stride
17. thigh
18. unclad
19. unencumbered
20. unusual

Changing How We Play

The media covers men's sports much more than it covers women's sporting events. What will it take to change this? Is it just a matter of time before we see changes in newspaper articles and televised news? With more and more women succeeding in major sporting events like the World Cup and the Olympics, change is inevitable. Is there anything you can do to encourage it?

Before the Nagano Winter Olympic Games in 1998, not many women were playing hockey. Since then, the number of girls playing hockey here in Canada alone has more than doubled. Now teams of girls as young as nine and ten years old are playing girls-only hockey. For them to continue playing their sports at a higher level, girls need to be told that they are as important as boys. But whose responsibility is it to do so? The professional athletes'? The coaches'? The parents'?

We cannot expect female professional athletes to be the only ones promoting women in sports. It must come from the whole sporting community. Still today, not many women want to be head coaches or presidents of sports federations. As women continue to build the confidence they require to step into these high level positions, the younger generations will follow. The role models are already out there. In the last World Cup, Germany was the only country led entirely by women coaches. There's no reason we can't have more women leading teams in major sporting events!

FIFA and Unicef are doing their part as well with *Goals for Girls!*, an organization focused on gender equality and women's empowerment. *Goals for Girls!* uses competition as a **platform** to explain how educating girls helps eliminate gender discrimination and contribute to addressing serious problems in their communities.

What can you do? If you are a coach, a friend, a **sibling** or an athlete who attends local sporting events in your community, send the results to your local radio station or newspaper right after the game. The media doesn't always have reporters covering local sports events. If these events are brought to the attention of local media, media will take notice and begin reporting them.

You can also make a difference by writing letters expressing your **concerns** to local newspapers or radio and television stations. Take the time to examine which events their sports editor gives the most time to. Let them know that you are a concerned reader or listener who is interested and paying attention. Once you have sent your note, write an e-mail to all your friends asking them to do the same.

As more and more women become involved in sports at the various levels and gain the respect and support of men, as they progress from being spectators to playing or even coaching, change will happen. Will it be easy? No, it won't be easy. But we will keep trying all the same!

Sm**a**r**t**
Words
platform = opportunity to express ideas; forum

sibling = brother or sister

concern = worry

Olympian Too Sexy for Own Good?

ATHENS, Greece—She graces the cover of the men's magazine, pressed close to four other women. Barely concealed in their white bikinis, they look like models.

5 But look more closely at this magazine and you'll see that it's Olympic high jumper Amy Acuff, along with volleyball player Logan Tom, long jumper Jenny Adams and swimmers Amanda Beard 10 and Haley Cope.

"We work hard for our bodies," said Ms. Acuff, twenty-nine, of Austin.

All are competing at the Athens Games, except Ms. Adams, who failed to qualify.

15 "Ten or twenty years ago, it wasn't **in vogue** to be competitive, aggressive or **sweaty**," Ms. Acuff said. "Now you see the athletic body has become the standard."

The athletic body, in various states of 20 undress, is getting a lot of exposure these days, as several female Olympic athletes have decidedly gone sexy. And while it's true that athletes in the ancient Games competed in the nude, 25 the modern-day athletes have the benefit of magazines and the Internet.

Advocates for women's sports don't blame the athletes for taking advantage of the Olympic spotlight—and potentially 30 earning more money and corporate sponsorships. But they argue that this "sexualization" of female Olympic athletes diminishes their accomplishments—and ends up hurting 35 other women.

The Olympic athletes "get so little exposure and have such a short period when they're in the news," said Dr. Kane, professor of kinesiology. "It costs a lot of 40 money to be an elite athlete.

I understand why they do what they do. But it's not about advancing the cause of women's sports."

Even as the popularity of certain 45 women's sports **soars**, some assert that there's a backlash against women participating in more aggressive sports, like basketball, softball and track and field.

50 "It's a predominantly male culture. They're deciding what sells, and they're not willing to sell legitimate female athletic achievement. ... It's a way that culture has tried to diminish a woman by 55 **relegating** her to sex object or decorative object."

"This is an entertainment medium," she said, "the media is going to cover it as it's used to covering it—as an entertainment 60 and celebrity deal. For every image of a male athlete that supposedly sexualizes him, there are thousands and thousands of pictures of male athletes who are simply great athletes."

65 Others argue that such calendars and magazine photo spreads don't belittle the accomplishments of women athletes—they help them.

Ms. Beard, who won the gold in the 200- 70 meter breaststroke Thursday, said she has fun posing for magazines. "It's a thing to do outside of swimming, and I enjoy it. And as long as I enjoy it, I'll keep doing it. I don't see it as **shameful**," she 75 said. "We're promoting pride in our bodies."

Dr. Kane said, "Let's at least be honest about what the purpose is: to have men buy those images of her."

Thomas Huang, "Olympian Too Sexy for Own Good?", Women's Sports Foundation website, August 22, 2004

Etiquette
Essentials

Unit

In this unit, you will explore etiquette rules in our society for all kinds of social situations. You will take an etiquette quiz and reflect on the importance of politeness when writing e-mails, talking on cellphones, taking public transportation and eating at a restaurant or at home. Finally, you will discover etiquette essentials in different countries and learn how to write thank-you notes.

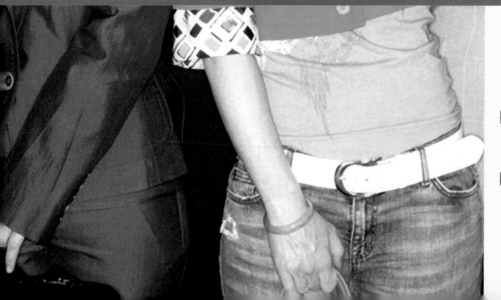

WHAT IS ETIQUETTE IN THE 21ST CENTURY?

Final
TAsk

List etiquette rules in modern society.

Option A

Write a children's book on etiquette rules.

Option B

Write a letter to your principal about etiquette rules in your school.

Smart Start

What is etiquette? Etiquette gives recommendations and restrictions for interacting with and showing respect towards others. Etiquette differs from culture to culture. It is meant to prevent you from making a faux pas in front of other people. Knowing how to use your knife and fork properly at a restaurant, how to dress appropriately for certain occasions and how to write suitable e-mails are all part of etiquette. How many etiquette rules do you know?

1 Take an etiquette quiz.

Take this etiquette quiz to find out what you already know about etiquette.

> Read the following situations out loud with your classmates and decide together on the best answers.

> Check the answers with your teacher. Are you surprised by any of them?

Read the question twice to make sure you understood.

Think of what you have done in similar situations in the past.

Words

apologize = express regret

shout = talk very loudly

1 **You are invited to a party and the invitation indicates that it starts at 7 p.m. You should arrive:**

a) One hour early.
b) On time.
c) One hour late.

2 **Your mom forgets about a lunch with a business associate. She feels badly about it and knows that the associate is upset. She should:**

a) Send flowers.
b) Not talk about it.
c) Call to **apologize** and set up another appointment.

3 **You answer the phone at your part-time job. How should you answer?**

a) XYZ Company. Hello, this is John speaking.
b) Hey dude, what's up?
c) Hello?

4 **If you have headphones on and someone talks to you, you should:**

a) Remove them.
b) Lower the volume but keep them on.
c) Ignore the person.

5 **Should you write an e-mail using all capital letters?**

a) No, because it means that you don't know how to use a keyboard.
b) Yes, because it means that you are happy.
c) No, because it means that you are **shouting** at someone.

The Garden Party,
early 20th century,
Ludwik Strimpl
(1880–1937)

6 **If you are talking on the phone and you receive a call on another line, you should:**

a) Not take it.

b) Excuse yourself, answer the other line and return to the initial call.

c) Always pick up the other line.

7 **At a wedding, you should wear:**

a) Anything you want.

b) Formal wear.

c) Something flashy.

8 **At a restaurant, the fork goes on the _____ and the knife and spoon go on the _____.**

a) Left / right

b) Right / left

c) Left / top of the plate

9 **On your business card, you should put your name and:**

a) Zodiac sign.

b) Address.

c) Phone number.

10 **When you are listening to your MP3 player on the bus, you should:**

a) Make sure that other people can hear your music.

b) Sing along to the music.

c) Keep the volume low enough so that others don't hear your music.

Words

wedding = marriage

Results
10/10
Good start! You're ready for more etiquette!
6–9/10
You could get into trouble!
0–5/10
You need an etiquette class!

2 Name all the etiquette rules you know.

Every day, you follow many etiquette rules. For example, you raise your hand when you want to speak to your teacher, you put your hand in front of your mouth when you cough or yawn, you bring a present to a birthday party, …

> Write as many etiquette rules as possible in five minutes.

> When trying to find etiquette rules, think about the following situations: dining at a restaurant, using public transportation, dressing for different occasions and places, talking on a cellphone, sending invitations, …

> Use the graphic organizer below to keep track of your ideas.

Put your garbage in the garbage can, not on the bus floor!

Think of all the rules you follow at school and at home.

Use a dictionary to help you.

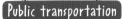

Public transportation

> Share your answers with a partner.

> Complete your list with the class's answers.

Talk

I wrote …
What about …?
What do you think?
I'm not sure that is a rule …
First of all … Then …
Finally …
Are we finished?
Good job!

S e l f - **E** v a l u a t e

Did I share all my answers with my partner?
Did I pronounce the words clearly?

Facts

Do You Know Emily Post?

Emily Post was an American author who promoted what she considered to be "proper etiquette." Her name has become synonymous with manners. In 1922, her book *Etiquette* was a bestseller, and updated versions continue to be popular today. In 1946, she founded the Emily Post Institute.

Peggy Post, Emily's great-granddaughter-in-law, is the current spokesperson for the Emily Post Institute and writes etiquette advice. Peter Post, Emily's great-grandson, and Lizzie Post, Emily's great-great-granddaughter, also write books about etiquette.

Teaching High School Students Table Manners, 1940, New York, U.S.A.

Modern Etiquette

The digital age has brought new rules to etiquette books. Since e-mails, MP3 players and cellphones are still relatively new, people don't always know how to use them properly, and therefore can accidentally be very rude! Do you know that you should turn off your cellphone in museums, restaurants and theatres? Do you know that you should lower the volume on your MP3 player when taking public transportation?

 1 Read about e-mail etiquette.

People write e-mails instead of writing letters or even using the telephone. Find out the rules you need to know regarding e-mail etiquette.

> Before reading the text, look at the list that you wrote in the Smart Start activity. Underline all the rules that relate to e-mails, cellphones and MP3 players. If you didn't write any rules related to technology, try to think of three rules now.

> Read the text below and answer the questions that follow.

E-mail Rules

You probably think that writing e-mails is much easier than writing letters. You are right. E-mails are shorter and take less time to write. However, it is important to remember that writing and grammar rules still apply. If e-mails are too **casual**, they can lead to problems such as spelling mistakes. Many people treat e-mails as everyday conversation and don't take the time to reread what they have written.

Communicating a clear message with an e-mail may be difficult because you can't rely on facial expression, tone of voice and other cues. Humour may also be difficult in an e-mail.

Here is a list of tips to help you write a proper e-mail.

❶ Don't forget to put in a subject line. This will help the **recipient** decide whether she/he should open your e-mail right away. It will also help her/him to find your e-mail in order to read it again.

❷ Only use cute symbols :) if you know someone well.

❸ Use the "To" line for the people who need to take action or are in the subject of the e-mail, and the "Cc" (or "carbon copy") line for people who are meant to use the e-mail as information only.

❹ Don't use e-mail if you know that calling the person will be more efficient. Remember: Phones still exist!

❺ Keep e-mails concise. Reading text on a computer screen isn't as easy as reading text on a sheet of paper. Get your message across as quickly as possible.

Smart Words

casual = not formal

recipient = person who receives something

6 Mention the e-mail's importance. This is very useful for recipients who receive hundreds of e-mails per day. It helps them choose which e-mails to open right away.

7 Use a signature at the bottom of the e-mail with your contact information (your address and phone number). This will help the recipient save time if she/he needs to contact you. If you can, try to choose an e-mail address that is easy to remember.

8 Don't send an e-mail when you are angry. Remember: Written words don't go away!

9 Don't waste time forwarding a joke to everyone in your address book. Choose a few people who will appreciate it or don't send it at all.

10 Use complete sentences. You aren't chatting—You are writing a note to someone. Reading shorthand or abbreviations can be confusing (and annoying) in an e-mail.

The next time you write an e-mail, try to follow these rules.

❯ **Answer the questions below individually.**

1 Which rules are new to you?

2 Which rules do you think are the most important? Why?

3 Why is it harder to communicate with e-mails?

4 When should you use the phone instead of writing an e-mail?

5 Why shouldn't you send an e-mail when you are angry?

6 Is this statement true or false? Explain why in your own words.
Everybody loves to see funny faces and symbols in an e-mail.

7 Is this statement true or false? Explain why in your own words.
Long e-mails are better because they explain the situation well.

Go Further

❯ Research English abbreviations used in e-mails and share their meaning with the class. For example, *BTW* means "by the way."

❯ Write an e-mail using English abbreviations. Then write the e-mail again using complete sentences. Which e-mail do your classmates prefer?

S e l f - **E** v a l u a t e

Did I answer the questions as completely as possible?
Did I answer the questions correctly?

2 Identify rules for public transportation.

Taking public transportation can be stressful since hundreds of people use it at the same time. Respecting a few simple rules of behaviour can help make the ride more pleasant for everyone.

> Play a memory game with the following words, which were taken from the audio segment.

> Take a minute to look at the words.

> Close your book and write down as many words as you can remember.

> Guess: What do the words mean?

> Ask your teacher for definitions or look up the words in a dictionary before listening.

bang	cough	courtesy	in a hurry
shoulder	sneeze	spreading	straightforward

> Before listening to the audio segment on subway etiquette, guess two rules that you should follow when taking public transportation.

> Listen to the audio segment and identify the five tips that are given.

> Summarize the tips in your own words.

> Share your summaries with a partner. Did you identify the same rules?

> These rules also apply when you take the school bus. Do you usually respect these rules? Which ones? Which ones don't you respect? Why not?

Predict the information that you need to find.

Take notes while listening to the audio segment.

Use gestures when you are speaking.

Self-Evaluate

Did I share the five tips?

Did I pronounce clearly?

Talk

I missed something.
What did you write?
I'm not sure, but …
Good! We have all the tips!

3 Learn about cellphone dos and don'ts.

Are you disturbed by people talking too loudly on cellphones? Do you find some ring tones annoying? A special code of behaviour also applies to cellphones. In the text on page 146, you will learn what you should and shouldn't do in order to follow cellphone etiquette.

> Read the rules for cellphone etiquette.

> While reading, think of five questions to ask about the text.

> After reading, write the five questions on a sheet of paper and quiz your partner.

Cellphone Dos and Don'ts

1 When you are with someone, excuse yourself before taking the call. The call may be important to you, but you must realize that you are also important to the person you are with.

2 Don't speak too loudly. Have you ever noticed how some people feel the need to scream at the top of their **lungs** while speaking on a cellphone? For some reason, most of us speak more loudly when we talk on the phone. Try not to do this.

3 Maintain at least a three-metre zone from anyone while talking on a cellphone.

4 Never talk on a cellphone in elevators, libraries, museums, restaurants, cemeteries, theatres, dentists' and doctors' offices, waiting rooms, auditoriums or other enclosed public spaces, such as hospital emergency rooms, buses and trains. People around you should have the option of not listening to your telephone conversation.

Smart Words

lung = organ used to breathe

refrain = stop

5 When in doubt, set your cellphone to silent. Many establishments ask customers to **refrain** from using cellphones, but almost all cellphones offer a vibrate feature, so you don't have to miss a call. Make sure to place the cellphone in an easily accessible spot.

6 Choose ring tones you won't regret. You might love your funny ring tone, but it might annoy people around you who have to hear it ten times a day.

7 Don't dial and drive. Driving a car and talking on a cellphone is very dangerous!

8 Before you take a picture with a cellphone, ask the person for permission.

9 When you are with a group of people, leave the room or move away to answer an incoming call so that you don't disrupt the group's conversation.

10 To make a good impression, ask the people with you: "Do you mind if I make a call?"

Self-Evaluate

Did I formulate the questions correctly?

Are the questions directly related to the text?

Structure

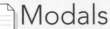

Modals

When you learn about etiquette, you often use modals, for example:

*You **should not** make noise when you eat.*

Modals are auxiliary verbs that allow you to express a mood of possibility, capability, permission, …

Function	Modal	Example
Possibility	**may, might**	I **might** take your advice.
Capability	**can, could**	I **could** lower my tone of voice.
Permission	**may, can**	**Can** I forward this e-mail?
Suggestion or advice	**should**	You **shouldn't** eat with your fingers.
Obligation	**must, have to**	You **have to** follow these rules.
Intention or promise	**will**	I **will** try to change my behaviour.
Politeness	**would, could**	**Would** you help me, please?

Future Tense

After learning new etiquette rules, you will probably want to change some of your behaviours. You will be able to say: *I'm **not going to** talk on my cellphone in a restaurant.*

Will and **Be Going To**		
Use **will** or **be going to** to express the future tense.		

	Will	**Be Going To**
Affirmative	*Claudia **will** use the right fork.*	*He **is going to** eat with his fingers.*
Negative	*Claudia **will not** use the right fork.*	*He **is not going to** eat with his fingers.*
Question	***Will** Claudia use the right fork?*	***Is** he **going to** eat with his fingers?*

Use **will** or **be going to** to express a prediction.
*We **will** invent new etiquette rules.*   *We **are going to** invent new etiquette rules.*

Use **be going to** to express a plan.
*I **am going to** learn etiquette rules.*

Use **will** to express an intention.
*I **will** answer the phone.*

You will often hear people using the informal pronunciation of **going to**: "gonna." Even though it is technically incorrect, you can use **gonna** when speaking. However, you shouldn't use it when writing:

incorrect   *I'm **gonna** help with these new rules.*   correct   *I'm **going to** help with these new rules.*

Key Words:
tomorrow, later, next week, today

Task 2 Food Etiquette

Going to a fancy restaurant or eating food at a dinner party can raise different etiquette questions. Which fork should you use for salad? Can you eat shrimp with your fingers?

C1 1 Discuss the utensils in a table setting.

At home, we usually use a knife, a fork, a tablespoon and a teaspoon. Most of us are surprised by the number of utensils, plates and glassware in a table setting at a fancy restaurant. Do you know how to use all these utensils?

> Look at the illustration and identify the objects in the table setting.

> Don't look at the vocabulary list.

> Match the words in the list below with the numbers on the illustration.

> Compare your answers with your partner's and discuss where each item goes in the table setting, for example:

The coffee cup and saucer go to the right of the table setting.

- **A** Bread plate and butter knife
- **B** Dessert / coffee
- **C** Meat course knife and fork
- **D** Red wine glass
- **E** Seafood fork
- **F** Water glass
- **G** Coffee cup and saucer
- **H** Fish course knife and fork
- **I** Plate and napkin
- **J** Salad course knife and fork
- **K** Soup spoon
- **L** White wine glass

Self-Evaluate

Did I show a positive attitude in this activity?

Did I cooperate with my partner?

2 Read about finger foods.

In some countries, people don't use utensils—They use their fingers. In Canada, people eat finger foods at parties. Finger foods are fun to eat because you don't need a plate and you can walk around the room talking to people while you eat. However, there are rules associated with eating finger foods. Read the text below to learn how to eat finger foods properly.

> Before reading the text, name five finger foods. What are you allowed to eat with your fingers?

> Read the text twice. Your partner will then ask you the questions found on page 150.

Finger Foods

Hors d'oeuvres are one of the few foods that adults are encouraged to eat with their fingers. That said, there are **pitfalls** to avoid. In addition to certain hors d'oeuvres, there are more common foods that require a bit of **dexterous** handling, such as the proverbial "hot dog with everything" at the ball game.

5 Cherry tomatoes—This is a one-bite food, so choose your tomato wisely.

Buffalo chicken wings and spareribs—It's assumed that spicy wings and ribs are finger food, so enjoy yourself. But be sure to have a "bone **bucket**" before digging in.

Pizza—Even the common "slice" can be eaten with grace. Hold the pizza
10 with your fingers and curl the sides so that the topping doesn't slide.

Radishes and celery—If garnishes are passed at dinner, spoon them onto your butter or cocktail plate. If the radishes aren't neatly trimmed and the celery still has its "feathers," make as discreet and **tidy** a pile as possible on the side of your plate.

15 Shrimp—One dip and two bites are recommended. The tail should be disposed of as quickly as is convenient.

Corn on the cob—Whether you eat yours typewriter style (across) or around, the cleanest way to eat fresh corn is to salt and butter it as you go. On the other hand, if you're among close friends or family, you may not need to be
20 as tidy—as long as you don't let familiarity breed poor manners.

Devilled eggs—This always delicious food is also always **messy**. No one expects you to eat this in one bite (unless you want "beaver cheeks"), so use a napkin and be as tidy as possible.

Caviar—Use the serving spoon to put some caviar on your plate, and your
25 own knife or spoon to gently prepare your portion. Take care not to overload your cracker or toast point with the sieved chopped egg and caviar. Nothing is worse (and more wasteful) than little grains of expensive caviar falling onto the carpet.

Words

pitfall = danger or difficulty

dexterous = skilled with the hands

bucket = container

tidy = neat

messy = dirty

The first time you read the text, read it quickly to get a general idea.

The second time you read the text, look for specific information.

Asparagus—Although not traditionally considered a finger food, there
30 are times when you can pick up the asparagus and eat it in a single stalk.
It's easier to plate this vegetable and use a knife and fork.

French fries—No fork ever made french fries taste better. Use your fingers
and enjoy yourself.

Trouble Foods

Some foods are described as "trouble food" because they pose a problem:
35 What do you do with the leftover shells and bones? What's a discreet way
to bite into a triple-decker club sandwich? And what about fruit pits and
banana peels? Nothing is more **awkward** than trying to take a spoonful of
French onion au gratin and winding up with a **skein** of cheese a foot long.
(If it happens, twirl the cheese around your soup spoon.)

40 Fruit and olive pits—These do not go into your napkin, but are best placed
in the cup of your hand and set to the side of your plate. This applies to
watermelon seeds too.

Oversized sandwiches—This is not a contest between you and the
sandwich. Triple-deckers or mega-size roast beef sandwiches are best cut
45 into smaller, more manageable pieces. Always use a knife and fork to eat
an open-ended sandwich.

**Smart
Words**

awkward =
embarrassing

skein = tangled piece

Kate Spade, *Manners*, Markham, Ontario, Simon & Schuster Canada, 2004, pp. 22–23

The Wedding Banquet [detail], circa 1567, Pieter Brueghel, Sr.
(1525–1569)

> Ask your partner questions 1 to 5. Your
> partner should close the Student Book.

> Switch roles and answer questions 6 to 10.

> Try to answer the questions without referring
> to the Student Book.

1 What should you do with pits?

2 When a sandwich is too big, what
should you do?

3 Is it more polite to eat french fries
with a fork?

4 How should you eat shrimp?

5 Why is it better to put butter and salt
on corn on the cob as you go?

6 Why should you curl the sides of
a piece of pizza when eating it?

7. Where should you put the ribs and bones once you finish eating the meat?

8. Do you remember making a faux pas with food? Explain what happened.

9. Do you think your parents know about these rules? Which ones do you want to share with them?

10. How will this information help you at the next party you attend? What will you do differently?

> Write the answers to the above questions.

Go Further

> Design a menu including finger foods to serve at your next party. Say why you would or would not serve certain food items. Then compare your party menu with a classmate's.

> Do research on another country where etiquette rules for eating with your hands differ from those in North America. Present your findings to the class.

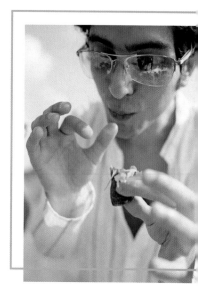

S e l f - E v a l u a t e

Did I answer the questions as completely as possible?

Did I answer the questions correctly?

Facts

More about Table Manners

1. Use silverware from the outside in.
2. Never cut more than three bites at a time.
3. When passing main dishes, always pass to the right.
4. To indicate that you have finished eating, place your silverware together on your plate in a clock position of ten to four, with the handles pointing at four.
5. Don't put your elbows on the table.
6. Don't put lipstick on at the table.
7. If you are serving food, serve all the guests before serving yourself.
8. If you are asked to pass the salt, pass the pepper as well.
9. If you can't use chopsticks, use a fork.
10. Put your napkin on your lap as soon as you sit down at the table.
11. If you leave the table during the meal, put your napkin to the left of the plate.
12. To butter bread, break off a small piece and butter it over your bread plate.

T^Ask 3 Etiquette in Different Countries

Knowing international etiquette rules is an important element of successful relationships if you visit other countries for pleasure or business. What is considered polite in one country may be considered offensive in another.

 1 Guess the etiquette rules in different countries.

How much do you know about etiquette in other countries?

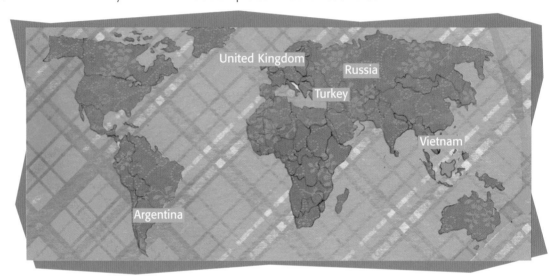

> Read the statements below out loud with a partner and decide whether each statement is true or false.

> Check the answers at the end of the quiz.

> Answer the following questions with your partner:

• Which country's etiquette did you find the most surprising? Why?

• In which country might you make a faux pas?

• Based on the etiquette rules, is there any place you would be reluctant to visit? Why?

• What kinds of faux pas do you think people visiting Canada from these countries might make?

Argentina

1 Argentines like to touch people and stand close to one another when they are speaking.

2 The "O.K." and "thumbs-up" gestures are considered vulgar.

3 Arriving on time for Argentines is very important.

United Kingdom

4 It is important to give a firm handshake when meeting or greeting someone in the United Kingdom.

5 You should leave a very small amount of food on your plate when you have finished eating.

6 It is impolite to ask for a tour of your host's home.

Turkey

7 When speaking to a Turk, always look her/him in the eyes.

8 Hosts expect you to eat little. Eating too much is considered impolite.

9 Avoid wearing short skirts and **low-cut** blouses in Turkey.

Vietnam

10 Bow your head slightly to show respect.

11 Men and women often show affection in public. Don't be surprised if people kiss in front of you in Vietnam.

12 The Vietnamese don't dress up often, so try to dress down to make them feel more comfortable.

Russia

13 Don't clink your glass to toast if you are drinking a non-alcoholic beverage.

14 If you want people to see you as a professional, you should wear bright colours.

15 Smoking in a public place is considered very impolite in Russia.

Smart Words

low-cut = showing a lot of skin

Go Further

> Quiz a friend from another class to practise your English.

> Research more international etiquette rules on the Internet and prepare a short quiz for your classmates.

Self-Evaluate

Did I keep talking even if I made a mistake?

Did I ask my partner about her/his opinion?

Answers: 1T, 2T, 3F, 4F, 5T, 6T, 7F, 8E, 9T, 10T, 11F, 12F, 13T, 14F, 15F

Pay attention to the different English accents.

Take note of new words.

Use a dictionary to help you.

2 Learn about a Japanese etiquette school.

Surveys say that people are becoming ruder and ruder. Maybe it is because people have simply forgotten the etiquette rules. The video you will watch is about Mrs. Tamami Kondo, a professor of politeness who has been teaching classes on good manners for almost thirty years in Japan.

Japanese Teahouse Maid Okita of Anaiwaya, 18th century, Kitagawa Utamaro (1753–1806)

〉 Before watching the video, answer these questions:
  • Which teens are more polite: North American or Japanese?
  • In Japan, is it bad behaviour to smoke, eat or talk on a cellphone on the street?

〉 Watch the video.

〉 While watching the video, write down five new vocabulary words.

〉 After watching the video, answer the questions below individually.

❶ What surprised you in the video?

❷ What amused you?

❸ In two sentences, summarize the subway incident. What did the young woman do? What did the older woman do?

❹ Do you think that smoking rooms are a good idea? Should we have them here in Canada? Explain your answer.

❺ Find definitions for the five new words that you found in the video.

Self-Evaluate

Did I find five new words and definitions?

Did I give my personal opinion?

How to Write Formal Letters

Many students write e-mails but have little experience writing formal letters. Look at the following letter and its features.

Kyara Desgagné
123 English Street
Anytown, QC

August 29, 2012

Dear Kyara,

Have you ever received a letter in the mail? If so, you must know how exciting it is to open the envelope and read the message inside.

When you write a letter to a friend or relative, it is called a friendly letter. You can write about a new pet, a vacation that you took or a big event in your life. When you write to someone you don't know, it is called a business letter, and it is more formal.

You will write to someone famous, such as an author or an athlete, or to the owner of a business to express your ideas.

Follow the steps on this page to write your letter.

Yours truly,

Daisy Nahas

Daisy Nahas
Your English Teacher

Inside address

The name of the person you are writing to, her/his title (when applicable), the name of the company and the complete address where you are sending the letter

Date

Month, day and year

Salutation

The name of the person you are writing to, preceded by "Mr." for a man, "Ms." for a woman, or by another title such as "Dr."

Body

Explain why you are writing the letter and include a space between each paragraph.

Closing

There are several words and phrases you can use to close a letter: *Sincerely, Yours truly, Cordially,* … Don't forget to add a comma at the end of the word or phrase.

Signature

Sign your first and last name under the closing. Then type your first and last name (and title) under your signature.

How to Write a Thank-You Note

Paper and Timing

Don't use regular school lined paper. If you are thanking a close friend and have a lot to say, use a letter-sized sheet or buy nice stationery. When you only want to share a few words, choose a decorated card. Remember: The smaller the paper, the easier it will be for you to fill. Write your thank-you note by hand unless your handwriting is hard to read.

Write the thank-you note within a few days. Sooner is better, but later is better than never!

E-mail versus Handwriting

Feelings are best expressed with a handwritten note. E-mail might be acceptable for school friends, but for family and formal occasions, pick up a pen.

3 Write thank-you notes.

In some cultures, writing a thank-you note is obligatory after receiving a gift or being invited for dinner. Have you ever received a thank-you note? Not only are they fun to receive, they are also a polite way to thank someone. Thank-you notes give you a chance to say on paper what you might otherwise be too shy to say in person.

> Write three thank-you notes to people you would like to thank, such as a teacher for spending extra time with you, a neighbour for helping you with your homework, a friend for giving you a gift, ...

Ic**T**

Options

Use your computer to create interesting-looking thank-you notes.

Use an online dictionary to help you revise and edit your thank-you notes.

Step 1 **Prepare**

> Brainstorm: Choose three people you would like to thank. For what do you want to thank them? Which situations do you think merit a thank-you note: receiving a gift, being invited for dinner, being helped out by someone? How has the person's generosity impacted you?

> What kind of paper or cardboard will you use for the thank-you notes? What size will they be? What colour? Do you want to add illustrations?

Step 2 **Write**

> Write initial drafts of the three thank-you notes.

Step 3 **Revise**

> Reread the drafts. Are your messages clear? Did you explain why you are thanking the person?

> Ask someone to look at the thank-you notes and comment on your work.

> Make changes if necessary.

Step 4 **Edit**

> Check your spelling in a dictionary and verify your verb tenses using the Smart Reference section (pages 268–280).

> Write final copies.

> Add illustrations and colours.

Step 5 **Publish**

> Show the thank-you notes to your teacher.

> Give the thank-you notes to the people you wrote them for.

Reception of the Grand Condé at Versailles by Louis XIV, 19th century, Jean Léon Gérôme (1824–1904)

Self-**E**valuate

Did I use the correct verb tenses?

Did I use a dictionary to check my spelling?

Become an Etiquette Specialist

People's actions are influenced by their personal etiquette. Use your own etiquette rules and those you have learned in this unit to become an etiquette specialist for the twenty-first century.

List etiquette rules in modern society.

Option A

Write a children's book on etiquette rules.

Option B

Write a letter to your principal about etiquette rules in your school.

Option A

Write a children's book on etiquette rules.

Step 1 Prepare

> Reread this unit to review all the etiquette rules you have learned.

> Research more etiquette topics on the Internet and in magazines if necessary. Remember to write down your sources.

> Here are a few ideas to get you started:

 • Write an outline of the story, with a beginning, middle and end. Remember: A good story often includes problems to be solved.

 • What kind of etiquette rules do you think are important for children to learn: school rules, house rules, cafeteria rules?

 • What will the title of the book be?

 • Who will tell the story: an animal, a flower, an adult, a teenager, a grandparent? Include details about the character's physical appearance and personality. Don't forget to give the character an amusing name.

 • Think about ideas for colourful drawings to illustrate the book.

Options

Use your camera or cellphone to take pictures to include in the children's book.

Use software to create the children's book.

Step 2 Produce

> Write a draft of the children's book.

> Try to add humour.

> Ask a friend or a parent to read the story.

> Did you use modal auxiliaries and the future tense correctly?

> Check your spelling in a dictionary.

> Make changes and write a final copy.

Step 3 Present

> Give your story to your teacher.

> Read the story to a child you know.

Write a letter to your principal about etiquette rules in your school.

Step 1 **Prepare**

> Reread this unit to review all the etiquette rules you have learned.
> Think of the effective etiquette rules that apply in your school.
> Think of the rules that need to be changed and why they are outdated.
> Find pictures or illustrations to include in the letter.

Step 2 **Write**

> Include all the features of a formal letter found in Smart Stop (page 155).
> Provide examples to support your choice of rules that are effective and rules that need to be changed in your school, for example:

> *In our school, we are not allowed to wear hats and I think this rule should be changed. Baseball hats and different kinds of hats are part of fashion and do not make students who wear them impolite.*

Step 3 **Revise**

> Show the letter to a partner for feedback. Is your message clear?
> Reread the letter out loud and make changes.

Step 4 **Edit**

> Check your spelling in a dictionary.
> Did you use modal auxiliaries and the future tense correctly?
> Make corrections and write a final copy.

Step 5 **Publish**

> Give the letter to your teacher.
> Publish the letter in your school newspaper.

Smart Words
REVIEW

1. apologize
2. awkward
3. bucket
4. casual
5. dexterous
6. low-cut
7. lung
8. messy
9. pitfall
10. recipient
11. refrain
12. shout
13. skein
14. tidy
15. wedding

Self-Evaluate

Did I follow all the steps or adapt them for my text?
Did I use the ideas I had learned in an original way?
Did I check my grammar and spelling?
Did I use different resources?

Reflection

1. Which activity did you like the most? Why?
2. Which activity was the most challenging for you?
3. Name two strategies that you learned to use in this unit.
4. If you had to do this unit over again, what would you do differently?
5. What are your goals for the next unit? What would you like to improve?

First Date Etiquette

That boy or girl that you have been drooling over has finally asked you out! Yes, guys: girls do ask boys out on dates in this day and age! Planning and preparing for your date will help to make it a success. Here are a few etiquette tips to think about.

5 Have a conversation over the phone before meeting. Taking a few minutes to chat with your date can save you from a disastrous and uncomfortable evening. Find out what your date likes to do to help you plan your meeting.

Make the first date a short one. Two to three hours is enough time to go for a movie, for a quick lunch or to the mall. You can always leave time open in your schedule to keep the date going if you are enjoying yourself.

10 Be respectful and polite by arriving on time. Don't **stand up** your date. If you are picking up your date at home, be prepared to meet the parents. Go to the door and ring the bell. Don't sit in the car and **honk** the horn or call from your cellphone from the other end of the street. Show your face and introduce yourself. Make **small talk** with your date's parents. The conversation should be light, casual and positive. If you are
15 asked a question you are not comfortable answering, say so.

Don't bring your pet fish, best friend, grandma or anyone else along on your date! Don't plan to meet anyone "unexpectedly" either. Choose an interesting place for the date to begin to help you both relax. A nice coffee shop is a good place to start. Dating should be fun! Do everything you can to make the date enjoyable for you both.

20 When you are talking with your date, choose your topics carefully. Too much information might scare your date away. Always ask questions to show that you're interested in your date. Making eye contact and listening when your date is talking will help them to relax as well.

If you are driving your date home, make sure you meet curfew. Helping your date
25 respect the guidelines set by parents shows that you respect them. You'll get **brownie points** with the parents, too! If something comes up and you're late back, make sure your date calls home so that mom and dad don't stay up worrying and waiting for you.

Finally, NEVER **dump** your date on the side of the road. Walk them to the door and make sure they get in safely. A kiss usually doesn't happen on a first date, but if the
30 date goes well, you may want to give your date a kiss on the cheek. The way you treat your date will show them how you like to be treated. Happy dating!

Smart Words

stand up = not show up at a set time and place

honk = make a loud noise with the horn of a car

small talk = polite, friendly conversation about nothing important

brownie points = praise for something

dump = drop off in a hurry

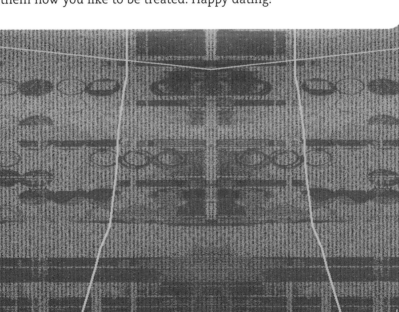

Josh Freed on Manners in the Digital Age
My post-Emily Post guide to etiquette for the 21st century

CELLPHONE ETIQUETTE: Cellphones should not be confused with **megaphones**. Do not speak into them as if addressing a stadium of anti-war protesters. It's difficult to grasp,
5 but your conversation about your daughter's horse show is not compelling to everyone—Some of us are self-centered **egomaniacs** who just don't care that she won the silver medal for dressage.

10 When using your cell, it's best to assume the people nearby don't want to hear your conversation. Speak as if you're having a personal talk between two people—not like you're onstage in Hamlet. Think cellphone,
15 not yellphone.

Fortunately, cellphones ringing in movies have now become quite rare as everyone knows this is the worst social mistake on the planet. Audience reactions can become
20 so violent, I feel bad for the person whose phone is ringing.

If you get stuck in this situation, it's advisable not to answer your phone at all—just look around **indignantly** like everyone
25 else until the ringing stops.

EMAIL ETIQUETTE is also just evolving. A new book called *Send* offers many tips that are among my own rules. For instance, some spelling mistakes are fine ocasionly,
30 bt nt in evy wrd becse is annoying nd hd to red.

CAPITAL LETTERS ARE NOT TO BE OVERUSED. IT'S LIKE SHOUTING, UNLESS YOU ARE SENDING NIGERIAN EMAIL,
35 WHERE THIS IS THE PROPER STYLE.

It's okay to check your mail while walking or jogging—but not while conversing with someone or driving or at symphonies, funerals, operas or temples of worship. It's
40 okay to hire someone by email, but don't use it to fire them.

You do not have to sign your name at the bottom of your email—We already know who it's from. But it's charming anyway.

45 AIRPLANE ETIQUETTE is awkward, too, nowadays, because you and your seatmate are sharing a seat that's only big enough for one. Incredibly, just because you weigh three times as much as your neighbour
50 doesn't mean you get three times the room.

The border between seats starts officially at the armrest, which is exactly big enough for half an arm each. The line extends right up to the ceiling, which means you
55 shouldn't fall asleep with your head resting on your seatmate's shoulder or on their lap.

It's fine to use your computer or DVD, but your screen width should not exceed your
60 seat width. When placing your seat in the **recline** position, remember to do so gently, because you may be crushing the person behind you to death.

The one nice thing about modern flights is
65 you don't have to worry about spilling food on your neighbour anymore—because there isn't any food.

BUS SEATS: Giving your seat up to an elderly person is tricky today because
70 many of them don't consider themselves old. They may even feel you are announcing to the whole bus that THIS PERSON IS AN OLD PERSON! In fact, in some U.S. states, they might bring a suit
75 against you **alleging** discrimination and psychological abuse.

Study the aging person carefully and ask yourself how they see themselves. If they're wearing jogging shorts or a Boston
80 marathon nose ring, do not offer your seat. If they're carrying a cane and five shopping bags, give it a try.

If they're bald with a grey beard, that's me—and I like standing, punk.

85 CONVERSATIONAL ETIQUETTE: Last millennium, when someone said, "Thank you" it was **customary** to reply, "You're welcome"—but this is becoming an extinct phrase replaced by more modern
90 expressions.

Today, when you say "Thanks" to a movie usher, he's likely to say something like "Sure, man" or "Yep" or "No problem(o)" or "Cool" or "Enjoy." He might also say
95 "Uhhuh" or just "Huh" or "Uh?" or the all-purpose "Whatever."

We live in informal times. In fact, now that I've taught you modern etiquette, you don't even have to say thank you. Just
100 whatever.

Josh Freed, "My post-Emily Post guide, to etiquette for the 21st century," *The Gazette*, Montréal, May 19, 2007

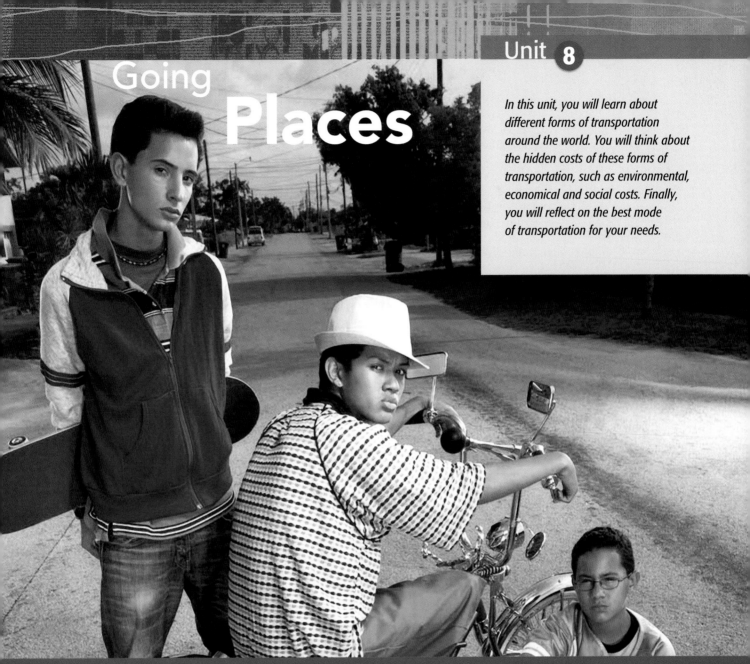

Going **Places**

In this unit, you will learn about different forms of transportation around the world. You will think about the hidden costs of these forms of transportation, such as environmental, economical and social costs. Finally, you will reflect on the best mode of transportation for your needs.

WHAT IS THE REAL COST OF YOUR RIDE?

Final
T A S k

Encourage better transportation choices.

Option A

Write an e-mail to a car company asking it to create or promote better transportation.

Option B

Publicize the benefits of one kind of transportation in an advertisement.

Smart Start

There are many ways to reach a destination. In Canada, we can walk, bike, drive, take a bus, a train or an airplane, among other transportation choices. What do people in other countries use as transportation? There are as many ways to get around as there are types of people in the world.

1 Learn about different types of transportation.

Have you ever taken a "publico"? Have you ever ridden an elephant? Even if you haven't, you might like to try it someday! In this game, you will match pictures with descriptions of types of transportation.

> Look carefully at each picture.
> Match each picture with a description.
> Compare your answers with those of your classmates.

Gondola

Chinese junk (boat)

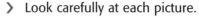
Rickshaw

Horse and buggy

Personal transporter ("Segway")

Seaplane

Skytrain (monorail)

Unicycle

Descriptions

a) Like a bicycle, this kind of transportation uses a wheel and pedals to propel it, but it takes a lot of practice to learn how to balance it!

b) Many people like to use this mode of transportation between the city and the forests up north. It is an easy way to travel quickly through the air and on water.

c) Venice is known as the "City of Love." However, the city is slowly sinking under water, which is why these boats replaced horses many hundreds of years ago.

d) This new form of transportation was invented in 2001. A computer and a motor keep the driver balanced upright on its platform and two wheels.

e) Although most people prefer to use cars, communities such as the Amish and the Mennonites still use this method of transportation.

f) This two-wheeled form of transportation has existed in Asia for hundreds of years. One person pulls another person seated in a carriage.

g) This type of transportation, designed for public transport in cities, runs on only one track. It is quiet and uses electricity, not gas. However, it is expensive to build and maintain.

h) This method of transportation is big enough to carry many supplies and efficient enough to adapt to different types of wind. It first appeared in Asia around 200 BCE.

2 Decide on the type of transportation.

Now you will use what you learned in the first activity to decide which types of transportation best suit different environments and needs.

> Look at the chart below.
> Write down modes of transportation to suit each situation.
> Then sit with a small group and compare your answers.
> Try to think of as many forms of transportation as possible for each environment.
> Decide together on the best overall method of transportation for each situation.

	Environment / Situation	Possible Modes of Transportation	Best Mode of Transportation	Reasons Why It Is the Best Mode
1	In the desert	• Camel • Jeep	Camel	Doesn't need gas
2	In the Arctic	▬▬▬	▬▬▬	▬▬▬
3	In a large city where most people can't afford cars and the air is polluted	▬▬▬	▬▬▬	▬▬▬
4	On an island in the middle of a large lake	▬▬▬	▬▬▬	▬▬▬
5	On a mountain	▬▬▬	▬▬▬	▬▬▬
6	Across a large ocean	▬▬▬	▬▬▬	▬▬▬
7	Across a large country (like Canada, China or Russia)	▬▬▬	▬▬▬	▬▬▬
8	In a city surrounded by water (like Sydney or Venice)	▬▬▬	▬▬▬	▬▬▬

Repeat what your classmate said to show that you understood the message.

Cooperate. Share your ideas with your classmates and listen to theirs.

Talk

I think that a good form of transportation here would be … because …

I agree / disagree with you, because …

What do you think?

What about using …?

Do we all agree that … is the best form of transportation?

Self-Evaluate

Did I cooperate and share my ideas with my classmates?

Did I use Smart Talk and strategies to help me?

Task 1 Different Places, Different Ways to Get Around

Most people's choice of transportation is a combined result of what they can afford and what is available to them. Some decide to use a form of transportation because it is environmentally friendly. In general, people like to ride in as much comfort and style as they can!

1 Learn about publicos and mopeds.

Many people in Puerto Rico can't afford to own a car. They created a unique method of public transportation called *publicos*, or public buses. The Italians invented the moped, a cross between a motorcycle and a scooter. In this activity, you will listen to Cristina Lopez and Carlo DiNicola talk about their preferred modes of transportation.

> Before listening, answer the questions below individually.

1 What is more important when considering the kind of transportation to use: the money it costs, the environmental impact, the comfort and style of your ride or the safety standards? Why is this important to you?

2 Do you think that everyone in your class has the same opinion as you? What about people in other countries?

3 What methods of transportation do you think people use in Puerto Rico, a Caribbean island? What types of transportation do you think people use in Italy, a European country? How do you think they are different? How do you think they are similar?

> When you have finished listening to the audio segment, answer the following questions.

4 Think of at least one question to ask Cristina and one to ask Carlo. Write down your questions and exchange them with a partner. Answer your partner's questions as if you were Cristina or Carlo.

5 What form of transportation do you think would be more useful in your community: a publico or a moped?

Self-Evaluate

Did I use Smart Words to help me?

Did I persevere and try to answer the questions even when they were difficult?

2 Read about transportation in China.

Not long ago, China was known as "the kingdom of bicycles," because bicycles were the most popular style of transportation. Today, more and more people in China are buying cars. The decision to exchange bicycles for cars has important consequences, not just in China, but around the world.

> Before reading the text, think about what you already know about bicycles and cars.

Bicycles Crowd a Street and Sidewalk in Canton, 20th century, Franklin McMahon

> Create a Venn diagram comparing the characteristics of both types of transportation. Give as many examples as you can. Think about their cost, speed, environmental impact, …

Use your Venn diagram to compare information.

Use the information in your Venn diagram to help you predict the problem.

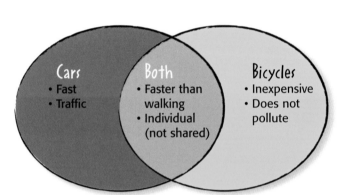

Cars
- Fast
- Traffic

Both
- Faster than walking
- Individual (not shared)

Bicycles
- Inexpensive
- Does not pollute

China: Kingdom of Bicycles No More

The most populous country in the world is moving to a car-based economy, which is more bad news for global warming

Be worried. If you have given even a moment's thought to **climate warming** and its potential impact on our planet, be very worried. China, a nation of 1,3 billion people, has abandoned the bicycle as a principal mode of transportation and is now moving at a frightening **pace** to a car-based
5 economy.

A friend who works for the World Health Organization recently pointed out that when Chinese officials are **drawn into** discussions about bicycles as a means of transportation, they respond by asking how many people use bicycles in Los Angeles, New York or Toronto. Automobiles are rapidly
10 replacing the bikes that are disappearing from the streets of Chinese cities at a phenomenal **rate**.

According to the China Association of Automobile Manufacturers, car sales in China in the first half of 2006 climbed almost 50 percent, year-on-year, to 1,8 million.

Words

climate warming = increase of the earth's temperature due to pollution

pace = speed

drawn into = pulled or guided into

rate = speed

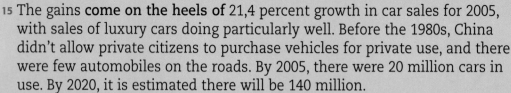

15 The gains **come on the heels of** 21,4 percent growth in car sales for 2005, with sales of luxury cars doing particularly well. Before the 1980s, China didn't allow private citizens to purchase vehicles for private use, and there were few automobiles on the roads. By 2005, there were 20 million cars in use. By 2020, it is estimated there will be 140 million.

20 Last November 22, the *China Daily* reported that in the first half of 2006, emissions of sulphur dioxide increased by 4,2 percent, and chemical oxygen demand, a major index of water pollution, grew by 3,7 percent compared to the same period in 2005.

Perhaps the only hope would be for western trendsetters—young actors, 25 business leaders, politicians—to adopt a non-car lifestyle, since western trends seem to influence the behaviour of much of the world.

Of course, that is not going to happen. Even if by some miracle it does, there is no guarantee that a world that has watched the West **stuff its collective face** with energy-consuming habits will join in its new-found environmental 30 sensitivity.

So be worried. It is really the only option. And if 1,3 billion car users don't scare you, remember that Indians, who number a mere 1,2 billion, are close behind. Our western ethos and lifestyle has triumphed, all right.

Sm**a**r**t**

W o r d s

come on the heels of = follow

stuff its collective face = use up its resources

Henry Gold, "China: Kingdom of bicycles no more," the *Toronto Star* online edition, January 15, 2007

> Decide whether these statements are true or false. If a statement is false, explain why it is incorrect.

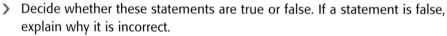

1 People in China use bicycles as their principal mode of transportation.

2 Car sales in China decreased by 50 percent in 2006.

3 People in China bought nearly 2 million cars in 2006.

4 Before the 1980s, the Chinese government didn't allow its citizens to buy cars.

5 By 2020, it is estimated that China will have 140 million more people.

6 In 2006, water and air pollution increased significantly in China.

7 According to the article, the use of cars by Indians in the future will cause problems as well.

> Answer the following questions:

8 What does the author identify as the main problem with people in China using cars? Did you predict the problem before reading the text?

9 Does the article present a positive or a negative view of the situation in China? What words or phrases give you this impression?

S e l f - E v a l u a t e

Did I use information from the text in my answers?

Did I choose an appropriate strategy to help me?

3 Participate in a transport conference.

Transportation is an important issue for people all over the world. Every year, governments and other organizations meet to discuss ways to make transportation safer, more efficient and environmentally friendly. In this activity, you will take part in an international conference on transportation and try to convince others to adopt a form of transportation.

In my country, we use bicycles. There are bike paths everywhere.

In Chile, there are so many mountains that biking takes a lot of energy. That's why we use public buses.

In my country, we prefer to use motorcycles. On the streets, you can often see a family of three all riding on one motorcycle!

Jan Verhoeven
Denmark

Juanita Flores
Chile

Kanya Narong
Thailand

Before the Conference

> Read your role-playing card carefully.
> Try to add advantages of your mode of transportation that are missing from your role-playing card.
> Take time to find solutions to the disadvantages of your form of transportation.

During the Conference

> Sit in a group of three.
> Introduce yourself to the other members of the conference.
> Take turns trying to convince the others to adopt your type of transportation.
> Find disadvantages of the other forms of transportation.
> Give solutions to the disadvantages of your type of transportation.

After the Conference

> Present the results to your teacher or your classmates.
> Who was the most convincing?
> What method of transportation did you decide was the best? Why?

Self-Evaluate

Did I listen to and encourage other group members?
Did I support my ideas?

Be Smart

Take your time. Think about what you will say before you speak.

Encourage other group members to speak. Ask them questions and give them positive feedback.

Smart Talk

My name is … and I'm from …

Just a moment, please. Let me think about that.

That's a good idea!

Doesn't … cause a lot of pollution?

Isn't … expensive / dangerous?

We think that … is best.

Dangers of Transportation

You have learned that cost and pollution are major concerns when using certain types of transportation. There are other factors to consider as well. For example, some forms of transportation are more dangerous than others, mostly because of dangerous driving behaviour.

Use words from the text to help you while you are speaking.

Listen to yourself talking. Try to correct any errors you make when you speak.

Cooperate. Share your ideas with your partner and listen to her/his ideas.

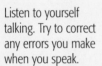

Talk

Most traffic offences are for …

More people … while driving than …

I was surprised that … because …

1 Compare impaired driving in Canada.

The most popular form of transportation in Canada is the car. There are over twelve million cars registered in Canada—That is one car for every two Canadians! Nearly 3000 people in Canada are killed in car accidents every year, and approximately 230 000 more are injured. What are we doing on our roads?

> Before looking at the pie chart on the next page, try to predict which age group is convicted most often of impaired driving: 16–18, 19–24, 25–34, 35–44, 45–54, 55–64, or over 65?

> Read the text and look at the pie chart.

> Use the information to discuss the following questionswith a partner.

1 Which age group is convicted of impaired driving most often?

2 What percentage of people aged nineteen to thirty-four received infractions for being impaired while driving?

3 Why do you think that so few sixteen- to eighteen-year-olds are charged with impaired driving?

4 Do you think that younger people are more likely than people over fifty-five to drive drunk, or are they just more likely to be caught?

5 Which age group did you predict would have the highest number of drinking and driving infractions? Did you guess correctly?

6 Were you surprised by these statistics? Why or why not?

Are Canadians Dangerous Drivers?

What do we do that makes the roads unsafe? One way of looking at our bad driving habits is to examine the statistics that Statistics Canada publishes each year. According to Statistics Canada, driver inexperience, drinking and driving, speeding and not using seatbelts are the cause of most traffic fatalities. New distractions such as cellphones are also causing people to be careless on the road. Statistics Canada keeps records on drinking and driving offences (impaired driving). Look at the following pie chart to see which age group is guilty of impaired driving most often.

Impaired Driving in Canada

Title → It is important to include a title to explain what the pie chart shows.

8%   2%   8%

14%   27%

20%   21%

Statistics
Pie charts represent statistics and percentages visually.

Colours
They use colours to differentiate between values.

Age:	16–18	25–34	45–54	Over 65
	19–24	35–44	55–64	

Legend
A pie chart can either include a legend or a key to explain what each colour represents, or arrows pointing to each section individually.

"Impaired Driving and Other Traffic Offences," 2002, Statistics Canada website

Smart Facts

Traffic Tickets

On average, 14 percent of Canadians get tickets for traffic offences every year, mostly for speeding. However, Canadians' driving habits differ from province to province. For example, 16 percent of the population in Alberta get tickets every year compared to only 8 percent in Prince Edward Island. In Quebec, drivers get fewer tickets for not wearing their seatbelts than any other province, but more tickets for not indicating a turn or change of lane. In Prince Edward Island and New Brunswick, drivers forget to bring their insurance or licence more often than anywhere else in the country!

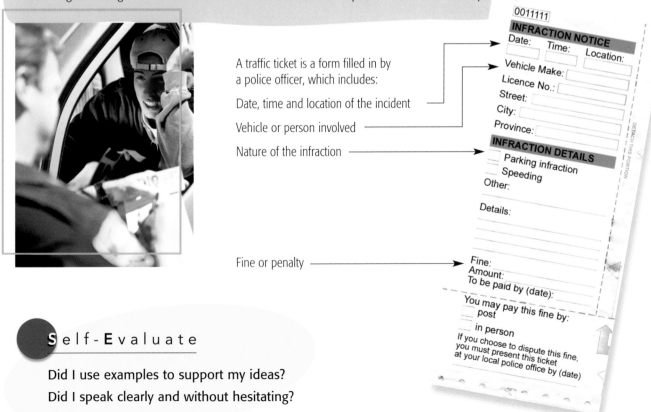

A traffic ticket is a form filled in by a police officer, which includes:

Date, time and location of the incident

Vehicle or person involved

Nature of the infraction

Fine or penalty

0011111

INFRACTION NOTICE
Date: Time: Location:

Vehicle Make:
Licence No.:
Street:
City:
Province:

INFRACTION DETAILS
___ Parking infraction
___ Speeding
Other:

Details:

Fine:
Amount:
To be paid by (date):

You may pay this fine by:
___ post
___ in person
If you choose to dispute this fine, you must present this ticket at your local police office by (date)

DETACH THIS PORTION

Self-Evaluate

Did I use examples to support my ideas?

Did I speak clearly and without hesitating?

Features of a Form

Most forms that you fill in ask for basic personal information, such as your name, address and age. Forms contain boxes to be filled in. Most forms require that you print the information so that the person receiving the form can read it easily.

Here is an example of a medical registration form:

Hospital logo

SNOWY HILL HOSPITAL

FAMILY MEDICAL CENTRE

Personal information

Name:		Age:	Sex: ❑ M ❑ F	Birth Date:
Street Address:		City:		Postal Code:
Mailing Address: ❑ Same as above ❑ Other		City:	Postal Code:	Religion:
Home Phone:		Work Phone:		Ext. / Dept:
Employer:		Address:		How Long?:
Medicare? ❑ Yes ❑ No	Medicare No.:	Social Insurance No.:		Referred by:

Personal information

Patient's parent or spouse

FATHER or HUSBAND				
Name:		Legal Guardian: ❑ Yes ❑ No		Birth Date:
Street Address:		City:		Postal Code:
Home Phone:	Work Phone:		Ext. / Dept:	Social Insurance No.:
Employer:	Address:			How Long?:

MOTHER or WIFE				
Name:		Legal Guardian: ❑ Yes ❑ No		Birth Date:
Street Address:		City:		Postal Code:
Home Phone:	Work Phone:		Ext. / Dept:	Social Insurance No.:
Employer:	Address:			How Long?:

Emergency information

Person to contact in case of emergency

In Case of Emergency (Friend or Relative Not Listed Above. ONE MUST BE LOCAL)			
Name (1):		Address:	
Home Phone:	Work Phone:		Relation:
Name (2):		Address:	
Home Phone:	Work Phone:		Relation:

List Any Immediate Family Member(s) Already Under the Dr.'s Care				
Name:	Relation:	Name:		Relation:

Insurance information

INSURANCE INFORMATION (A Copy of All Insurance Cards Is Required for Filing Purposes.)	
Primary Insurance:	Name of Insuree & Social Insurance No.:
Group No.:	Insuree's DOB:	Other Insurances (cont'd on back):

Authorization

I hereby assign to Snowy Hill Hospital all payments for medical services rendered to myself or my dependants. I understand that I am responsible for any amount not covered by insurance. The above registration information is correct to the best of my knowledge and I understand and accept the above payment policy.
I hereby authorize Snowy Hill Hospital to provide information to my insurance carriers concerning my medical care and that of my dependants.

Signature

_____   _____
Date   Signature of patient (or parent / legal guardian if patient is a minor)

2 Watch a video about dangerous driving.

One of the most dangerous driving habits is driving while under the influence of drugs or alcohol, or "DUI" for short. Thanks to massive publicity campaigns, fewer and fewer people are stopped for this traffic offence each year. In this video, you will see how someone who drove while under the influence was held responsible for his actions.

> Before watching the video, discuss this question as a class:

What is the worst thing that could happen to you if you drove while under the influence of alcohol or drugs?

> Read the following questions before you watch the video.

> After watching the video, answer the questions individually.

> Share your answers as a small group.

1. What was Kevin trying to do when he had the car accident that killed his friends?

2. Why did the judge change his mind about putting Kevin in jail? Who convinced him? Did this surprise you? Why or why not?

3. Did Kevin have a plan for an alternative way home? If so, why didn't he use it?

4. What did the police want to give Kevin as a punishment? Do you think that this would have been an appropriate punishment? Why or why not?

5. How did you feel when you saw Kevin talking in front of the high school students? Do you think that listening to someone like Kevin would convince you not to drive while under the influence?

6. What other driving behaviours can you think of that are as dangerous as driving under the influence? Do you think that publicity campaigns like the one in this video help change people's behaviour? Why or why not?

Think about your goal when you watch the video: Do you want to get a general idea? Do you need specific information?

Read the questions before watching to find out which information to look for.

Go Further

> Make a list of five things you can do (instead of driving home) if you are with someone who has been drinking or doing drugs. Write one sentence for each option.

> Imagine that you are the parent of one of the two boys who were killed in the accident. Write a letter to the judge convincing him either to let Kevin make public speeches or to give Kevin a jail sentence.

Self-Evaluate

Did I give my personal opinion?

Did I answer all the questions?

Structure

Passive Voice

When you read information articles in English, you will notice that many sentences are formed in the passive voice. The passive voice is formed using the verb *to be* and the past participle. For example:

*Our car **was manufactured** in Ontario.*

Passive Voice	
Use the passive voice	**Compare:**
• To be more polite.	*People **cause** traffic accidents.* (active voice)
• To appear more objective (fact-based rather than expressing an opinion).	
• When you don't know who is doing the action.	*Traffic accidents **are caused by** people.* (passive voice)

To make an active sentence passive, follow these steps:

1 Move the object of the sentence into the subject position (at the beginning of the sentence).
People cause **traffic accidents**. → **Traffic accidents** are caused by **people**.
Subject   Object

2 Change the main verb to the past participle. (See irregular verb list, page 270.)
*People **cause** traffic accidents.* → *Traffic accidents are **caused** by people.*

3 Add the verb *to be* to the original verb and conjugate it correctly.
Make sure to use the same verb tense as in the original sentence.
People cause traffic accidents. → *Traffic accidents **are** caused by people.*

4 If necessary, add the preposition *by*.
People cause traffic accidents. → *Traffic accidents are caused **by** people.*

Examples

Simple present tense:
*Car accidents **kill** pedestrians every year.*
(active voice)
*Pedestrians **are killed by** car accidents every year.*
(passive voice)

Simple past tense:
*They **introduced** two new hybrid cars on the market.*
(active voice)
*Two new hybrid cars **were introduced** on the market.*
(passive voice)

> Change the following sentences from the active voice to the passive voice.

1 Steve bought a new motorcycle.

2 The students handed in their reports.

3 Someone gave Sue a job at the bicycle factory.

4 We cleaned the car last week.

5 The police officer helped the children to cross the busy street.

6 They will complete the new highway next month.

7 The police officer gave Joe a ticket for speeding.

8 Jasmin invited you to the car show.

9 Someone in India made that bicycle seat.

10 The newspaper reported an increase in air pollution.

How Much Does the Planet Pay?

Cost, pollution and safety are all considerations when choosing a method of transportation. In fact, pollution may be the most important factor to consider. In this next task, you will examine how transportation can make the world an unhealthy place in which to live.

1 Learn about "In town without my car!" day.

Across the world, people are finding ways to live without their cars. Every year in Montréal, there is a special event called "In town without my car!" day, when the city centre is blocked off from traffic. You will read an authentic report from the Canadian transport ministry examining the impact of "In town without my car!" day.

> Before reading the text, think of three positive effects of "In town without my car!" day.

> Discuss your ideas with your classmates.

Be **s**m**a**rt

Use the features of the text, such as the headings and statistics, to help you understand.

In Town Without My Car!

Overview

"In town without my car!" is an international event intended to educate citizens about the negative impact of cars on quality of life and on the environment. On 22 September 2004, a sector in the downtown **core**, as well
5 as part of a neighbourhood that surrounds a shopping centre, was closed to car traffic. People could participate in many activities and travel from one to another by alternative means of transportation. The event has positive results: **widespread** participation, less air and noise pollution and awareness of alternative methods of transportation.

10 ### Community Context

Inspired by a 1998 French initiative, "In town without my car!" day is now an international event focused on raising community awareness of the effects of excessive car use. It also provides the public with information on the various methods of alternative transportation, specifically **carpooling**,
15 subway, commuter rail, bus, taxis, bicycle, scooter and walking. This day focuses on changing behaviour: if each individual takes action, it is possible to improve the quality of life in the city and combat climate change.

Montréal, like the 1500 cities that organize events like these, is concerned about pollution and urban mobility. Between 1987 and 1998, the number of
20 cars in the metropolitan region increased by 44 percent. Between 1998 and 2003, there was another 10 percent increase in the number of cars. In 1998, there were more than 6,5 million trips into the downtown area each day; most (78 percent) were made by motorists without passengers.

sm**a**rt
Words

core = centre

widespread = happening in many places

carpooling = travelling in a car together and sharing the costs

Words

sustainable = used without destroying the environment

greenhouse gases = chemicals that cause the earth's temperature to rise

borough = area or section of a city

Rationale and Objectives

25 Public transportation represents a **sustainable** choice that benefits individuals and society both directly and indirectly. Here are some examples:

- An individual who uses public transportation rather than buying a compact car has an annual net gain of $5000.

30 - Use of public transportation makes a significant contribution to decreasing **greenhouse gases** and therefore to achieving the objectives of the Kyoto Protocol.

- Finally, a city that is less polluted and less noisy provides a better quality of life, which attracts new residents and is advantageous to those who 35 already live there.

Actions

The **borough** of Plateau Mont-Royal met with business owners in person in order to explain the value of "In town without my car!" day before the event took place.

40 On 22 September 2004, downtown Montréal and the Plateau Mont-Royal were closed to traffic between 9:30 a.m. and 3:30 p.m. Street parking was prohibited. Citizens could get downtown and to the Plateau using transportation alternatives. Buses travelled the perimeter and a significant number of taxis were present.

45 Many free activities (street performers, shows, exhibits of hybrid cars) were offered to citizens to enable them to rediscover the streets downtown and on the Plateau.

Results

At the height of the day, the event drew more than 25 000 people to 50 downtown—close to twice the participation of the previous year.

That day, in the areas closed to car traffic, Environment Québec measured less air and noise pollution:

- A 90 percent decrease in both nitrogen monoxide (NO) and carbon monoxide (CO) between 10 a.m. and 3 p.m.

55 - The noise measurement recorded was fifty decibels (dB) compared to 80,5 dB at the same location and time one week later.

- Thirteen percent of people who usually drove their cars used mass transit (subway, bus, commuter rail, carpooling, etc.) on 22 September. Carpooling was the most common alternative.

60 - Thirty-nine percent of people who usually drove their cars acknowledged that the event encouraged them to consider modes of transportation other than cars for their daily travel.

Doug Hickey, "In Town Without My Car!", Transport Canada, Crown Copyright File No. 2007–22440, July 24, 2007

> After reading, answer the following questions with complete sentences.

> Compare your answers with those of a classmate.

1. What is "In town without my car!" day? What is this event trying to promote?

2. What are two benefits of choosing public transportation?

3. Which two initiatives took place in the Plateau to bring people to the area while it was closed to cars?

4. What are two positive results that were reported after the event?

5. Do you think that an event like this is an effective way to encourage people to change their transportation habits? Why or why not?

6. Would the event work in your community? Why or why not?

 Further

> Using the ideas presented in the text, list five reasons why you shouldn't drive your car downtown.

> Role-play with a partner: One of you lives in the suburbs and drives into the city alone every day, and the other lives in the city and takes public transportation. Discuss your reasons for choosing your form of transportation and try to convince your partner to be more flexible in her/his choice.

Self-Evaluate

Did I answer all the questions with complete sentences?

Did I use strategies to understand the text?

Facts

Transportation Costs

On average, it costs $0.53 a kilometre to drive your car in the country and $0.83 a kilometre in the city. Therefore, a driver who drives approximately 20 000 kilometres a year (the national average) spends between $10 600 and $16 600 a year on car payments, gasoline, maintenance and insurance. One way to cut this cost is to carpool (to give other people a ride and share the gasoline cost).

If you take public transport, a monthly pass in Canada's major cities ranges in price from $60 to $90 (or $720 to $1080 a year).

Activity levels are increasing among Canadians who walk or bike as a means of daily transportation, rising from 19 percent in 1996 to 25 percent in 2005. Biking and walking are great forms of alternative transportation, because not only are they free and non-polluting, but they also help keep you active and fit!

2 Send a message to others.

One way environmental activists send a message to people who choose to drive cars and SUVs (sports utility vehicles) that use a lot of gas is by creating and distributing informative bumper stickers. These bumper stickers are meant to serve as a reminder and are never used to deface private property. In this activity, you will look at the features of this useful medium and create your own informative bumper sticker.

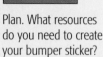
> Look at the bumper sticker below.
> Discuss the following questions with your classmates:

Who is this bumper sticker trying to reach? What makes it effective?

Picture

This bumper sticker includes a picture that matches the slogan.

Slogan

This bumper sticker uses a simple slogan to get its message across clearly.

Colours

This bumper sticker uses bright colours to attract your attention.

One Less Car = One More Tree!

> Create your own informative bumper sticker to distribute by following the steps below.

Step 1 **Prepare**

> Choose a target audience.
> Where will you distribute the bumper sticker?
> Decide what your message will be.
> Research real-life examples to help you make an effective bumper sticker.

Options

Use your computer to create a logo. Try using different fonts, colours and illustrations in order to create a great-looking sticker.

Step 2 **Produce**

> Create a draft bumper sticker.
> Include the features you learned about.
> Revise. What could you add or remove? Ask someone for suggestions.
> Edit. Check your spelling and grammar.
> Make any necessary changes.
> Produce a final copy.

Step 3 **Present**

> Present your bumper sticker to the class.
> Make copies and distribute the bumper sticker in your community.
> Reflect on your success.

Self-**E**valuate

Did I use the features of a bumper sticker effectively?

Did I use and adapt ideas and information from the Student Book?

How Much Does Your Ride Cost?

You may live in the city, in a village, on a farm or on an island. You may have a lot of money or you may need to consider your budget carefully. You may be concerned about the environment but find it difficult to walk, bike or take public transportation. All of these factors will determine what kind of transportation is best for you.

1 Consider your transportation options.

Think about your available options for transportation. When you consider all the factors, what is the best way for you to get around?

> Copy the chart below.

> Take a survey of your classmates by asking them the questions from the chart and writing down their answers.

> Try to ask as many classmates as possible.

	Question	Names and Answers
1	Where do you live (in a city, a suburb, a small town, the countryside, …)?	▬▬▬
2	What modes of transportation do you use to get to school, meet friends, go shopping, …?	▬▬▬
3	What conditions do you need to travel through (snow, heat, rain, …)?	▬▬▬
4	What challenges do you face getting where you want to go (traffic, long distances, finding parking, …)?	▬▬▬
5	How concerned are you about the environmental impact of your ride (a lot, somewhat, not at all, …)?	▬▬▬
6	What modes of transportation will you use after you leave high school? Where will you be going?	▬▬▬

> In a small group, discuss the results of the survey.

> Brainstorm to make a list of at least three forms of transportation that fit the needs of you and your classmates.

> Examine the options on the list and choose the best modes of transportation by ranking them from the most to the least effective.

Be Smart

Repeat what your classmates say to show that you understand them.

Take your time. Think about what you will say before you speak.

Smart Talk

Hi, could you answer a few questions for me?

How much …? Which …? Are you …?

What ideas can we think of for transportation?

I think … is a good method of transportation because …

Why don't we add … to the list?

Self-Evaluate

Did I present my message clearly?

Did I take my time when speaking?

2 Discover the truth about hybrid cars.

How can you drive more cheaply and with less damage to the environment? Car manufacturers are promoting hybrid cars, that is, cars that run on both electricity and gasoline. You will read about the facts and myths associated with buying, driving and maintaining a hybrid car.

> Before you read the text, think about hybrid cars. What do you know about them already? What are their advantages? What are their disadvantages? Would you consider buying one? Why or why not?

> As you read the text, fill out a T-chart summarizing the information about hybrid cars.

> Use "Fact" and "Myth" as your headings.

Fact	Myth
Hybrid cars run on a combination of electricity and gasoline.	Hybrid cars run only on electricity.

Going Green in a Time of Gas Guzzling: Busting Hybrid Car Myths

Words

ponder = think about

payoff = return on an investment

cruise = travel at a constant speed

With the rising price of oil and gas, many consumers are **pondering** the purchase of a hybrid car as a way of saving at the pump. But cost is not the only reason people are going hybrid. It is also good for the environment, reducing emissions and dependence on oil. Before you buy, here are some
5 hybrid myths and facts to consider.

Myth 1: I will save a lot of money by driving a hybrid car.

Hybrid vehicles cost anywhere from $5000 to $8000 more than their conventional counterparts. Ultimately, you will have to drive the vehicle for a very long time before seeing financial **payoff**. However, the cost of
10 technology will decrease overtime, which means hybrids may sell at lower prices in the future.

Myth 2: Hybrid cars have remarkable fuel economy.

The amount of gas you preserve depends on the speed at which you drive. There is excellent fuel economy when **cruising** in residential
15 neighbourhoods and slow city traffic, because the electric engine runs the vehicle at low speeds.

Hybrids are not necessarily fuel-efficient when it comes to highway driving. At faster clicks, the gas engine must kick in since more power is needed to run the vehicle at high speeds.

Myth 3: You need to plug your car in an outlet to recharge the batteries in your hybrid every night.

This is a common misperception. You never have to recharge the car by plugging the batteries into an outlet.

Myth 4: Hybrid cars don't perform as well as their conventional 25 **counterparts.**

The key concern with auto performance is the acceleration rate and some hybrids **measure up** while others are **left in the dust**. You don't have to sacrifice speed for fuel economy anymore.

Myth 5: Hybrids are unsafe.

30 The fact that a vehicle runs on a gas-electric motor has no bearing on its safety rating. Natural Resources Canada claims that "hybrid electric vehicles are as safe—or safer than—gasoline-powered vehicles." A hybrid must meet the exact same crash test and safety regulations as any 35 other light-duty vehicle sold in Canada.

Myth 6: Hybrids are the wave of the future.

Though there is an increasing demand for hybrids, they still only occupy a small portion of the auto market at one percent of the more than seventeen million vehicles 40 sold in North America today. Hydrogen fuel cell cars— zero-emission vehicles powered by fuel cell technology— are predicted to be the long-term solution to society's dependence on **fossil fuels**. But the shift to a hydrogen-based transport system is not expected for at least 45 another ten to twenty years.

Hydrogen record racecar

Words

measure up = be good enough

left in the dust = not good enough

fossil fuels = oil, gas or coal

Tiffany Quan, "Going green in a time of gas guzzling: Busting hybrid car myths," CTV News website, November 23, 2005

> After reading and filling out the T-chart, discuss the following questions in a small group.

1 Which myth surprised you the most? Why? Explain your answer.

2 Before you read the article, would you have considered buying a hybrid car?

3 Did your ideas change after reading the article? Why or why not? What made you confirm your ideas or change your mind?

Self-**E**valuate

Did I complete the T-chart?

Did I use a dictionary or other resources to help me understand the text?

Steamboat, 1923,
Fernand Léger
(1881–1955)

 3 Compare two forms of transportation.

In this activity, you will use a chart to compare the costs and advantages or disadvantages (financial, environmental, safety, …) of two forms of transportation.

> Choose two types of transportation that you would like to compare.

> Use the example in the chart below to help you.

> Research information on each type of transportation using the Student Book, newspapers, magazines, the Internet or other resources.

> Compare the costs and advantages or disadvantages of the two types of transportation using the chart below as a model.

> When you have completed the chart, write a short paragraph to answer the following questions:

• Which mode of transportation is best for you?

• Which is the best mode of transportation for people in your community?

• How can you and the people in your community modify your transportation choices in order for them to be more economically and environmentally friendly?

> Present your findings to your teacher, your class or a small group.

Take your time to find the right information.

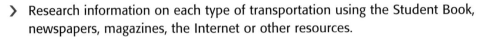

	Transport 1: Hybrid Car	Transport 2
Financial costs (per year)	Car payments = $4800 Insurance = $4000 Maintenance = $1000 Gasoline = $500 TOTAL = $11 300	
Environmental costs	A hybrid car cuts emissions by 25 to 35 percent compared to even the most fuel-efficient gas-powered vehicle.	
Advantages	• Better for the environment • Costs less in gas	
Disadvantages	Expensive to buy	
Possible modifications	Carpooling	

Self-**E**valuate

Did I find all the information necessary for the activity?

Is my opinion relevant and on topic?

Take a Stand

Now that you are familiar with many different kinds of transportation, you can encourage people to make better choices when they go places.

Encourage better transportation choices.

Option A

Write an e-mail to a car company asking it to create or promote better transportation.

Option B

Publicize the benefits of one kind of transportation in an advertisement.

Option A

Write an e-mail to a car company asking it to create or promote better transportation.

Step 1 Prepare

> Define your purpose. Why are you writing the e-mail: to ask a car company to create more environmentally friendly vehicles, to stop showing dangerous driving in its advertisements, …?

> Choose a specific car company. Find out to whom you need to write the e-mail and obtain the person's e-mail address.

> Brainstorm: What important ideas do you want to mention?

> Organize your ideas into a plan. Include an introduction, the main body of the e-mail (with your ideas in order) and a conclusion.

Step 2 Write

> Use your plan to write a draft e-mail.

> Include the passive voice to make the e-mail sound factual and polite.

> Use the features of a formal letter (see Unit 7, page 155).

Step 3 Revise

> Reread the e-mail. Does it make sense?

> Ask someone to read the e-mail and give you feedback.

> Make changes.

Step 4 Edit

> Check the spelling of words in a dictionary. Verify your grammar.

> Correct your mistakes and write a final copy.

Step 5 Publish

> Send your e-mail to the car company and copy your teacher.

> Reflect on your e-mail's effectiveness: Did you receive a response?

Options

Use the Internet to help you research car companies' practices or advertisements.

Start an e-mail campaign or create a website to inform people about the environmental impact of driving or about dangerous driving practices.

Solar energy plane

Option B

Publicize the benefits of one kind of transportation in an advertisement.

Step 1 Prepare

> What form of transportation do you want to promote or encurge people to use?
> Who is your target audience for the advertisement: men, women? Where are they living?
> What important information will you include in the advertisement: cost, advantages, disadvantages?
> What format will you use for the advertisement: a poster, an Internet ad, a radio ad?
> Research: Use the Smart Stop on page 40 to help you make an effective advertisement.

Step 2 Produce

> Create a draft of the ad.
> Make sure you use all the important features of the medium you chose.
> Include appropriate examples of the passive voice.
> Revise your advertisement. Are your ideas clear? What could you add or remove to improve the ad? Did you verify your grammar and use a dictionary?
> Make changes if necessary.
> Create a final copy.

Step 3 Present

> Present the ad to your class.
> Post it on the school walls.
> Reflect on the process. Do you think the ad will help change people's minds about using another form of transportation?

Smart Words
REVIEW

1. borough
2. carpooling
3. crowded
4. cruise
5. drawn into
6. fossil fuels
7. fuel-efficient
8. gleaming
9. greenhouse gases
10. measure up
11. neat
12. pace
13. payoff
14. ponder
15. rate
16. sleek
17. sustainable
18. wave
19. widespread
20. wrap things up

Self-Evaluate

Did I use and adapt the steps?

Does my text contain facts that support my ideas?

Did I use the passive voice correctly and appropriately?

Did I use a variety of resources?

Reflection

1. Which activity did you like the most? Why?
2. Which activity was the most challenging for you?
3. Name two strategies that you learned to use in this unit.
4. If you had to do this unit over again, what would you do differently?
5. What are your goals for the next unit? What would you like to improve?

Walkable Communities

For centuries, people used their feet as their primary mode of transportation. Can you imagine a world where your feet are your only way to get around town? It seems a bit extreme, but there are many groups across Canada who are doing just that. These groups are trying to get **urban** developers and city planners to put more effort into designing what they call "walkable communities" as a way of saving the planet.

What is a walkable community?

A walkable community is a well-designed, compact community where people can walk to school, work, the grocery store, parks or restaurants and go about their day-to-day activities without relying on a vehicle to get around. These communities can be small towns or **neighbourhoods** in big cities.

Why are walkable communities important?

There are many reasons why these communities are important. From a health perspective, walking helps reduce health problems such as obesity, diabetes and heart disease, all of which put great pressure on our heath care system. From an environmental perspective, cutting down on the amount of short car trips reduces air and water pollution. Walkable communities also help decrease the number of cars on the road, which reduces traffic congestion, improves road safety and diminishes the cost of repairing and maintaining the roads.

A walkable community promotes the community in general. This promotion helps people develop a higher sense of belonging and attachment to their community. People become aware of their **surroundings** and more involved in maintaining and improving their community. This, in turn, helps to lessen street crime in their area. These kinds of communities also help improve access to employment, education and social services.

Here are the four criteria used to determine a community's *walkability*:

Connectivity

Connectivity looks at how a community is connected literally. How big are the **sidewalks**? Could three or four people fit on them? Do all streets have sidewalks on both sides? What condition are the sidewalks in? Are they big enough for a wheelchair or a stroller?

Proximity

Proximity refers to how close businesses, stores, schools and homes are in relation to each other. Are there a variety of stores where people can buy groceries and which fill the basic day-to-day needs of the people in the neighbourhood? Are there clinics or other businesses like banks or pharmacies that are needed in the area? Are there a mix of homes, apartments and duplexes to accommodate a variety of income levels in the same community?

Aesthetics

Aesthetics refer to how the neighbourhood looks in general. Are walking routes attractive and pleasant? Are there **benches** for people to rest on? Are the businesses and shops well maintained and accessible to the public?

Safety

People will not be encouraged to walk in their neighbourhood if they do not feel safe. Are the sidewalks safe? Do the cars respect the crossing signals and signs? Are passages well-lit? Are people present on the street even in the evenings?

It may not be possible for you to walk everywhere, but if you can walk where you need to go, why not make the choice to do so? You will be improving your health and that of the planet. Encourage others in your community to do the same!

Fresh Air Will Kill You

Pulitzer Prize winner Art Buchwald's writing was filled with irony and made people think. This essay is comically set in a futuristic time when people have given up trying to solve environmental issues in our world and have accepted the consequences of living with pollution.

Smog, which was once the big attraction of Los Angeles, can now be found all over the country from Butte, Montana, to New York City, and people are getting so used
5 to polluted air that it's very difficult for them to breathe anything else.

I was lecturing recently, and one of my stops was Flagstaff, Arizona, which is about 7000 feet above sea level.

10 As soon as I got out of the plane, I smelled something **peculiar**.

"What's that smell?" I asked the man who met me at the plane.

"I don't smell anything," he replied.

15 "There's a definite odor that I'm not familiar with," I said.

"Oh, you must be talking about the fresh air. A lot of people come out here who have never smelled fresh air before."

20 "What's it supposed to do?" I asked suspiciously.

"Nothing. You just breathe it like any other kind of air. It's supposed to be good for your lungs."

25 "I've heard that story before," I said. "How come if it's air, my eyes aren't watering?"

"Your eyes don't water with fresh air. That's the advantage of it. Saves you a lot in paper tissues."

30 I looked around and everything appeared crystal clear. It was a strange sensation and made me feel very uncomfortable.

My host, sensing this, tried to be reassuring. "Please don't worry about it.
35 Tests have proved that you can breathe fresh air day and night without its doing any harm to the body."

"You're just saying that because you don't want me to leave," I said. "Nobody
45 who has lived in a major city can stand fresh air for a very long time. He has no tolerance for it."

"Well, if the fresh air bothers you, why don't you put a **handkerchief** over your
50 nose and breathe through your mouth?"

"Okay, I'll try it. If I'd known I was coming to a place that had nothing but fresh air, I would have brought a surgical mask."

We drove in silence. About fifteen
55 minutes later he asked, "How do you feel now?"

"Okay, I guess, but I sure miss sneezing."

"We don't sneeze too much here," the man admitted. "Do they sneeze a lot
60 where you come from?"

"All the time. There are some days when that's all you do."

"Do you enjoy it?"

"Not necessarily, but if you don't sneeze,
65 you'll die. Let me ask you something. How come there's no air pollution around here?"

"Flagstaff can't seem to attract industry. I guess we're really behind the times."

70 The fresh air was making me feel **dizzy**. "Isn't there a diesel bus around here that I could breathe into for a couple of hours?"

"Not at this time of day. I might be able
75 to find a truck for you."

We found a truck driver, and slipped him a five-dollar bill, and he let me put my head near his **exhaust pipe** for a half hour. I was immediately revived and able
80 to give my speech.

Nobody was as happy to leave Flagstaff as I was. My next stop was Los Angeles, and when I got off the plane, I took one big deep breath of the smog-filled air, my
85 eyes started to water, I began to sneeze, and I felt like a new man again.

Art Buchwald, "Fresh Air Will Kill You," *Have I Ever Lied to You?*, New York, G.P. Putnam's Sons, 1968

World **Action**

In this unit, you will learn about people around the world trying to improve the lives of others: a Canadian doctor helping children in war zones; a blind German woman who founded a school for blind children in Tibet; a British cook who improved the quality of cafeteria food in schools; and a Québécois woman volunteering in Kenya and Peru. Discover how you can use your passion to help others.

HOW CAN A PROJECT CHANGE THE WORLD?

Final **TASK**

Describe projects making an impact.

Option A

Produce a news report on a project that is helping to improve people's lives.

Option B

Make a class magazine about outstanding local initiatives.

Smart Start

We can be part of the solutions that already exist to build the future we want. The challenge is to start right now! In this task, you will discover how we all have a responsibility to become involved if we desire real change to happen.

1 Organize ideas for change.

In this activity, you will organize ideas for change into the following categories: businesses, cities, communities, homes, politics and products.

> Read the description of each category.
> Read the list of ideas and classify them into the appropriate categories. Note that some ideas will fit into more than one category.
> Compare your classifications with a partner.

Building of recycled shipping containers, London, England

Be Smart

Plan. Use a dictionary if you don't understand the sentences.

Guess. If you aren't sure where to put an idea, choose the best category according to what you understand.

Categories

Businesses	Cities	Communities
Business people, owners, economists, investors and consumers all have the power to change the business world's decisions, methods and practices.	Using transportation in a safe, cost efficient and environmentally friendly way, and incorporating nature into the places we live, can help improve the quality of life in our cities.	Communities can work together to educate people and reduce poverty, oppression, environmental and health problems.
Homes	**Politics**	**Products**
Homes are our shelters. Most homes around the world could be better designed.	We are responsible for making sure that governments are **transparent** and democratic, ruled by the people.	What we buy, use, keep, throw away and save determines the kind of life we can all live.

Smart Words

transparent = open to public observation

waste = material that goes in the garbage

List of Ideas

1. Buy cleaning products that are biodegradable.
2. Dry your clothes outside instead of in a dryer.
3. Learn another language.
4. Share a car.
5. Ban landmines.
6. Use less air-conditioning.
7. Reduce your **waste**.
8. Donate your old laptop to charity.
9. Grow plants inside to help clean the air.
10. Read books at the library.
11. Design your house to utilize natural light.
12. Educate people around the world.
13. Provide free medication.
14. Travel the world by volunteering.

2 Learn about extraordinary people.

In this activity, you will learn about women and men from different countries who have impacted the world in a special way.

> Read the list of names below and identify those you are familiar with.

> For each name you recognize, describe what the person has done to change the world, for example:

Bono (1960–) *This singer has organized and played in several benefit concerts for human-rights organizations.*

Martin Luther King, Jr. (1929–1968)

Mother Teresa (1910–1997)

David Suzuki (1936–)

Roméo Dallaire (1946–)

Shirin Ebadi (1947–)

Jane Goodall (1934–)

> Now match each name with one of the descriptions below.

> Check your answers with your teacher.

> Can you think of anyone else who has helped change the world?

Descriptions

a) This person is Canada's most well-known environmental activist. He has a TV program and criticizes governments for their lack of action related to global warming.

b) This person is a humanitarian, author and retired general. He is best known for his involvement in the United Nations peacekeeping force in Rwanda in 1993 and 1994. He tried to stop the Hutu from slaughtering the Tutsis. He wrote a bestselling book that was subsequently made into a movie.

c) This person won the Nobel Peace Prize in 2003 and is the first female judge in her country. She is the founder and leader of the association Support Children's Rights in Iran.

d) This person was a Roman Catholic nun who helped poor, sick and orphaned children in Calcutta, India. She won the Nobel Peace Prize for humanitarian work in 1979, and she was beatified by Pope John Paul II after her death.

e) This person became interested in animals as a child in England. She studied chimpanzees in Gombe Stream National Park in Tanzania, Africa for forty-five years, and became a global leader in the effort to protect chimpanzees.

f) This person was the most famous leader of the American Civil Rights Movement and has a day named after him. His most influential speech starts with the words: "I have a dream."

Task 1 The World Is a Village

"The world is a village" is an expression that means that we are all part of the same community. People from distant places can interact even more since the arrival of airplanes and the Internet. In this task, you will explore how people from different countries, young and old, near and far, are all connected.

1 Find out how we are all connected.

Many of us feel that we can't help people in other countries because they are so far away from us. Understanding how connected we are helps us realize that others' problems are also our problems. In this activity, you will learn how our lives and actions are closely connected with those of other people around the globe.

Pay attention. Try not to be distracted.

Don't panic even if a lot of information is given. Find all the answers you can and try to identify the main message.

> Read the following paragraph about a typical Canadian student's morning.

> *I woke up at 6:30 this morning to the radio on my alarm clock. I walked across the warm carpet in my room to the bathroom. I had a shower, combed my hair and got dressed, choosing my favourite T-shirt and jeans. My dad was making coffee and sliced a banana over my cereal. I also had toast and peanut butter. After breakfast, I grabbed my sweater and backpack and left the house. My friend's mother called me and offered to give us a lift to school. In the car, we listened to our favourite CD and also stopped for gas on the way. Before school started, we played soccer and then headed into school at the bell.*

> Think about how this typical Canadian student's morning connects with the rest of the world.

> Listen to the audio segment and fill out a chart with the help of the example below.

> Identify products you use every morning, the countries involved in bringing them to Canada and what kind of impact they have on the world.

Product	Countries Involved in Bringing the Product to Canada	Impact on the World
Alarm clock	China, Brazil, Greece, Sweden, Liberia, Portugal, …	Not mentioned
Carpet	India	Child labour
Shower products	▬▬▬▬▬	▬▬▬▬▬

> After listening to the audio segment, answer these questions:

1. What was your first impression of this activity?

2. Do you think that you have products in your house that were made in Canada?

Self-**E**valuate

Did I fill in the chart correctly?

Did I stay focused in order to complete the activity?

2 Discover people helping children in war zones.

In this activity, you will learn about a doctor who works for a Canadian charity dedicated to providing assistance to war-affected children around the world. He encouraged others to think differently, making them realize that problems around the globe are everyone's business.

> Read the text below twice.

> While you read the text, take notes on what surprises you.

Boy reads election pamphlet, Kabul, Afganistan, September 9, 2005

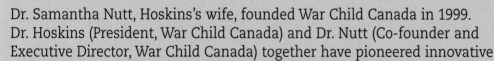

More than a Doctor

Dr. Eric Hoskins is one of the driving forces behind War Child Canada. He is a doctor, an activist and a humanitarian who dedicates his life to promoting human rights and to advancing the cause of peace globally. War Child Canada is a registered charity dedicated to providing urgently-needed
5 humanitarian assistance and long-term development support to war-affected children around the world. War Child Canada also generates awareness, support and action for children's rights everywhere. War Child has held benefit concerts to raise money for their humanitarian programs and these famous music concerts have attracted thousands of young people.

10 Hoskins was brought up in Ontario in a rural community, but he was destined to see the world. When he finished medical school, he worked on several missions in different countries. Over and over again, he saw the terrible impact that war and poverty had on local populations, especially children, but it also made him realize that one person could
15 do extraordinary things. He became an optimist and an idealist through his own work experiences.

Dr. Eric Hoskins

Dr. Samantha Nutt, Hoskins's wife, founded War Child Canada in 1999. Dr. Hoskins (President, War Child Canada) and Dr. Nutt (Co-founder and Executive Director, War Child Canada) together have pioneered innovative
20 ways to support overseas humanitarian projects that have benefited thousands of children affected by war. They have been able to integrate their compassion for civilians with their love for music, and to provide young people with opportunities to become global citizens. They decided to make their target audience youth. They arranged for their first public
25 service announcement to be shown on MuchMusic. After it aired, they received thousands of e-mails and phone calls from people who wanted to do something.

Read the text twice. Skim it the first time you read it and then scan it to find more information.

Dr. Hoskins has already persuaded about 100 000 Canadian students to participate in high school clubs or hold their own benefit concerts in order
30 to contribute to War Child Canada's projects **overseas**. War Child Canada currently provides support to war-torn communities in Iraq, Afghanistan, Sudan (including Darfur and southern Sudan), Uganda, Sierra Leone, Democratic Republic of Congo, Ethiopia, Sri Lanka, Ghana and Georgia. As a result, thousands of Canadian teens have become peace activists.

Words

overseas = in a foreign country

Words

witness = see an event

issue = problem or question

³⁵ Hoskins has **witnessed** first-hand that young people really are interested in international human rights **issues**, and that they are actively looking for ways to help.

War Child Canada not only provides extensive assistance in war-affected regions, but also creates public support and awareness for their cause by ⁴⁰ getting people involved.

Hoskins says that Canada is a middle power with a strong voice. He says that even in remote areas of the world, Canadians are held in high regard. Foreign countries have seen that Canadians have a positive influence in the world. He acknowledges, however, that there is still much to be done.

Children clearing rubble in Karachi, Pakistan, July 26, 2006

> After reading the text, answer these questions with a partner:

① What impressed you most about Dr. Hoskins?

② Explain the title of the article in your own words.

③ How did War Child Canada become popular so quickly?

④ Why are Canadians held in high regard?

⑤ List some of the countries that have received aid from War Child Canada and identify the continents where they are located. Do these countries have something in common?

Talk

It impressed me that …

The title means that …

War Child Canada became popular because …

Sierra Leone is located in …

Go Further

> Practise your pronunciation by giving a paragraph to your partner as a dictation exercise. Then switch roles. Practise spelling the difficult words.

> Do research to find other organizations that help people in foreign countries. Present your findings to the class.

Self-Evaluate

Did I give my personal opinion?

Did I ask for help when I needed it?

3 Create a catalogue for a fundraiser.

Your school can support organizations like War Child Canada by organizing fundraisers. Thousands of Canadian high schools are involved in fundraising each year. In this activity, you will make a catalogue of items that you would like to sell to high school students in order to raise money for a humanitarian organization.

Girl on a Swing, India, 2000, Andrew Macara (1944–)

Step 1 Prepare

> Make a list of ten items to put in the catalogue. Try to be original in your choices. Find other ideas than selling chocolates!

> Look at other catalogues to give you ideas.
> Think about how you want to lay out the catalogue. Do you want to include one item per page or many items? Do you want to use photos or illustrations, black and white or colour? What will be the price range of the items? How will you advertise the catalogue?

Step 2 Produce

> Attract your reader by describing the items, for example:

The first item on the list is a CD compilation. You'll love it! There's a song to please everyone in your family—even your baby brother!

> Are your sentences clear? Ask a partner to read the descriptions.

> Check your grammar, spelling and punctuation.

> Add photos, illustrations, colours and different fonts to make your catalogue stand out.

> Make changes and create the final text.

Step 3 Present

> Exchange your catalogue with a partner. Who has the most original list of items?

> Don't forget: The proceeds of your sales go towards supporting the organization of your choice.

Be **smart**

Self-evaluate your work. Rate the catalogue on a scale of 1 to 10.

Ic**T**

Options

Find photos and pictures online.

Post the catalogue on your blog.

Self-Evaluate

Did I include ten items?

Did I write the descriptions clearly?

Structure

Connectives

People are connected by actions: What one person does can have an effect on others.
Connectives help you to express cause and effect, contrast and conditions for such actions.

Cause and Effect

One action influences another. This is called cause and effect. Connectives help you link one action with another.

- Using **because**, **because of** and **due to**

  Because is followed by a subject and a verb.
  Because the speech was powerful, people decided to help.

  Because of and **due to** are followed by a noun.
  Because of / Due to the powerful speech, people decided to help.

- Using the conjunctions **therefore**, **consequently** and **so**

  Pay attention to punctuation. A comma or a period is usually used immediately in front of a conjunction.
  The humanitarian help didn't arrive on time. **Therefore / Consequently**, people died.
  The humanitarian help didn't arrive on time, **so** people died.

- Using **such … that** and **so … that**

  Such … that is used with an adjective and a noun.
  It was **such** a good idea **that** we copied it.

  So … that is used with an adjective or an adverb.
  The organization is **so** popular **that** it needs ten new volunteers every month.

Contrast

Certain actions have their limits. Connectives help you express a contrast of ideas.

- Using **although**, **but … anyways**, **despite**, **even though**, **however**, **nevertheless**

  Even though it was a great initiative, it didn't work out.
  They raised a lot of money **despite** the problems they encountered.
  Thousands of students participated in the fundraiser. **Nevertheless**, not enough money was raised.

Conditions

Connectives help you express conditions associated with certain actions.

- Using **otherwise** and **or else**

  Otherwise and **or else** are used differently, but have the same meaning.
  I always eat breakfast. **Otherwise**, I can't concentrate.
  I always eat breakfast, **or else** I can't concentrate.

> Use the following connectives in the sentences below. Use each connective only once.

| because | even though | such … that |
| because of | so … that | therefore |

❶ Food supplies didn't arrive on time. ▬▬▬▬, people started without them.

❷ It was ▬▬▬▬ difficult ▬▬▬▬ we didn't make it.

❸ Carl was late ▬▬▬▬ heavy traffic.

❹ Patricia was happy ▬▬▬▬ she had a healthy baby.

❺ It was ▬▬▬▬ a rainy day ▬▬▬▬ the event had to be cancelled.

❻ ▬▬▬▬ you helped, it was too late to reach the goal.

Helping the Physically Challenged

In Task 1, you learned about coming to the aid of children in war zones. There are also people with many different kinds of special needs that you can help.

 1 Read about a phenomenal woman.

In this activity, you will read about a woman who didn't let a handicap stop her from achieving her goals. Sabriye Tenberken was just twenty-six years old and blind when she rode into Tibet on horseback to start a school for blind children, where they could learn to read Braille, speak three languages and take care of themselves.

> Before reading the text, answer the following questions individually and then discuss your answers with your classmates.

  ❶ What do you know about blind people?

  ❷ Do you have any questions about blindness?

  ❸ What do you think a blind person can teach someone? Give examples.

  ❹ Make predictions about the text that you will read.

Plan. Look at the questions to find out what information you will need in order to answer.

Don't be stressed if you don't understand every word. Remember that you don't always know all the words in a French text!

Encourage yourself even if the text is longer than what you are used to reading.

Phenomenal Woman—Sabriye Tenberken

❶ As we **stride** up a narrow street, a little girl sitting on a **stoop** spots Tenberken through the **crowd**, springs to her feet and crows at the top of her lungs, "Xia ze lai le!" A simple Chinese sentence, it means, "Gangway! Here comes an idiot!"

❷ In the seven years Sabriye's spent living in Tibet—and indeed in the twenty-seven in her native Germany before that—she's been the object of this phrase, and worse, countless times. Sabriye Tenberken (pronounced Sah-bree-yah Ten-BURR-ken) single-handedly has brought literacy to the blind people of Tibet. In founding the Lhasa-based Braille Without Borders (BWB), the region's first rehabilitation and training centre for the blind, she has inspired nothing short of a revolution in their status, their thinking, their future. "You cannot insult me with blindness," she says, "because I'm proud to be blind."

❸ Born with a degenerative retinal disease, Tenberken was blind by twelve. Her classmates spurned and taunted her. Determined to fit in, Tenberken denied her blindness to herself and worked overtime to hide it.

❹ Tenberken enrolled at a boarding school for the blind, where among academic subjects the students were taught horseback riding, swimming, white-water rafting, Braille, and above all, self-reliance. "Suddenly, I was one among many," she tells me. "I had friends. I was equal and happy. I thought, 'Okay. I may be ugly and blind, but I have a brain. I can do things.'"

Words
stride = walk with long steps
stoop = porch with steps in front of a building
crowd = large group of people

5 Tenberken majored in central Asian studies at the University of Bonn, the only blind student out of 30 000. There, several professors tried to dissuade her from studying the difficult Tibetan language. There were no Tibetan texts available in Braille. Using the system of rhythmic spelling Tibetans employ to memorize their complex language, Tenberken created her own method of translating the Tibetan language into Braille. She compiled a Tibetan-German / German-Tibetan dictionary, and eventually Tenberken helped to devise a software system that enabled her to transpose entire Tibetan texts into formally printed Braille, a **feat** no one before had ever accomplished.

6 "I developed this system for my own use," she says, "but when I realized that blind people in Tibet could also benefit from it, I got the idea to bring it here and start a school." Rejected by several development organizations, who saw her blindness as too great a **liability**, Tenberken resolved to make the project happen on her own. In 1997, at the age of twenty-six, much to the **dismay** of everyone but her immediate family, she travelled alone to China, took an intensive course in Chinese, then proceeded to Tibet, where she learned that more than 30 000 of Tibet's 2.6 million people are blind—about twice the global rate. While poor diet and unhygienic conditions are factors, Tibet's main cause of blindness is its high elevation; at this altitude, the intensity of the sun's ultraviolet rays causes damage to the unprotected eye.

7 Tenberken discovered a deep prejudice against the blind in Tibet, where blindness is considered punishment for **misdeeds** perpetrated in a past life. For centuries, Tibet's blind have been shunned, vilified and generally treated as subhuman.

8 At the moment, there are thirty-seven students—ranging in age from three to nineteen—in residence at the school, as well as six trained teachers and five staff members, but new students arrive regularly.

9 Tenberken says that when students first arrive at the school, they often object to being asked to learn and participate in school tasks. "They say, 'I'm blind! I can't do that.' But when they see the other kids working hard, they change their views." The students are helping each other, not passively waiting to be told what to do.

10 Upon completing their preliminary education at BWB, students can opt to return to their villages, attend a normal school with sighted children or train for a vocation, such as medical massage, animal husbandry, cheese-making or farming. Tenberken's ultimate goal is to establish an international training centre in Kerala, India, where blind people from all over the developing world can learn the management skills necessary to establish their own schools and training centres for the blind.

Rosemary Mahoney, "Phenomenal Woman—Sabriye Tenberken," *O, The Oprah Magazine*, August 2005, pp. 223–225 and 237–238

> Answer the following questions about each paragraph in the text. Then check your answers with your teacher.

1. Paragraph 1: What negative word is used to describe blind people?

2. Paragraph 2: What is the Lhasa-based Braille Without Borders?

3. Paragraph 3: When did Sabriye become blind?

4. Paragraph 4: Which sports did she learn in school?

5. Paragraph 5: Why did teachers discourage her from learning Tibetan?

6. Paragraph 6: Why was her project rejected by many organizations?

7. Paragraph 7: Is it true that blind people are accepted in Tibetan culture?

8. Paragraph 8: Is it true that the school doesn't accept new students anymore?

9. Paragraph 9: When do students change their attitude towards blindness?

10. Paragraph 10: What is Sabriye's dream?

> Reflect on the following questions, then write your answers.

11. Sabriye has done amazing things in her life. What do you find the most unbelievable?

12. What would be challenging for you if you were blind? Give five examples.

13. What would you find most difficult: being blind, deaf or in a wheelchair? Why?

Self-**E**valuate

Did I answer the questions as completely as possible?
Did I answer all the questions correctly?

Facts

The Braille Alphabet

The Braille Alphabet was based on a method of communication originally developed by Charles Barbier in response to Napoleon's demand for a code that soldiers could use to communicate silently and without light, called "night writing." Barbier's system was too complex for soldiers to learn and was rejected by the military. In 1821, he visited the Royal Institution for Blind Youth in Paris, France, where he met Louis Braille. Braille identified the major failing of the code, which was that the human finger could not hold the whole symbol without moving, and therefore could not move rapidly from one symbol to another. His modification was to use a six-dot cell—the Braille System—which revolutionized written communication for the blind.

Nowadays, Braille computers are a great help to blind people. They include voice recognition software and special keyboards and scanners. Braille computers can translate to and from Braille. Generally, each page of printed material translates into two or three Braille pages.

a	n
b	o
c	p
d	q
e	r
f	s
g	t
h	u
i	v
j	w
k	x
l	y
m	z

 2 Try an experiment.

Blindness is one of the most feared disabilities a person can have. In this activity, you will experience one aspect of what it feels like to be blind. You will examine objects using only your senses of touch and smell in order to guess what they are.

> Choose a partner and blindfold her/him.

> Give your partner three objects to identify.

> Encourage your partner to touch and smell the objects to guess what they are.

> Switch roles and examine the three objects that your partner gives you.

> Answer the following questions after you have both tried the experiment:

1. How did it feel not being able to see? Did you feel uncomfortable, nervous or afraid?

2. Did you identify the objects correctly?

3. What sense did you use to identify the object?

4. What are your general observations from this experiment?

5. Name five things you think you wouldn't be able to do if you were blind.

6. Name the two most common "aids" blind people use.

7. What three questions would you like to ask a blind person?

8. How would feel if you had to perform this experiment for an entire day?

Self-Evaluate

Did I use Smart Talk to help me?

Did I pronounce my sentences clearly?

3 Change your school to help people with special needs.

Are there students in your school who are blind, deaf or in a wheelchair? Do you know about the challenges they face every day? In this activity, you will find ways to change the environment of your school in order to help facilitate their lives.

> Make a list of five ideas to help the physically challenged in your school, for example:

Install a ramp for wheelchairs at the entrance of the school.

> Share your ideas with your classmates.

> Vote for the five best ideas. Have a discussion to determine whether your school is ready to implement the proposed changes.

> What is your community doing to help people with special needs?

Changing the World with Food

You may think that children and teens in communities like the one you live in do not need help, but some do. For example, thousands of children suffer from obesity and health problems due to bad nutrition.

1 Learn about a special chef.

A famous chef in England has changed the lives of students by convincing school cafeterias to make their menus healthier. The schools have to provide at least two portions of fresh fruit and vegetables a day, serve fish at least once a week, remove salt from lunchroom tables, limit fried foods to two servings a week and cut out candy, soda and potato chips. In this activity, you will read about Jamie Oliver, a chef who is trying to change the way children eat.

> Before reading the text, list three strategies you can use to help you before and while you read.

> Think about what you would like to change in your school cafeteria.

> Use the strategies while you read the text.

Jamie Oliver

Jamie Oliver is an English celebrity chef. He is well-known for his role in campaigning against what he believes to be unhealthy, **processed** foods in British schools. Jamie Oliver was born in May 1975 and grew up in Essex, where his parents owned a pub-restaurant. From an early age, Oliver helped
5 in the pub kitchen, and by the time he was eleven, he could chop "like a demon." He remembers that a lot of the boys at his school thought that cooking was a "girlie" thing to do. By the age of sixteen, Oliver knew that he wanted to be a chef, so he attended Westminster Catering College before studying in France.

10 He started a cooking programme called *The Naked Chef*. Of course, he didn't cook naked! By "naked," he meant avoiding complicated recipes and replacing the culinary **jargon** by easy-to-understand steps. He believes in simple, tasty food, starting with ingredients people already have in their **cupboards**, refrigerator or garden. This popular series brought Oliver
15 worldwide fame. He has now written several cooking books that have been translated into many languages.

Oliver wanted to create something positive using his wealth and fame. He came up with the idea of establishing a charity restaurant called Fifteen, where he trains fifteen disadvantaged young people to work in
20 the **hospitality** industry. Following the success of the original restaurant in London, more Fifteens have opened around the globe.

Smart Words

processed = modified

jargon = special words or expressions used in a particular job

cupboard = compartment used to store food, cookware and tableware in the kitchen

hospitality = food, drink and lodging services

Oliver began a formal campaign to ban unhealthy food in British schools in order to encourage children to eat fresh, tasty, nutritious food instead. Oliver's efforts to bring radical change to the school system challenged
25 the junk food culture by showing schools that they could serve healthy meals that children enjoyed eating. Oliver worked with students and was amazed by their diet and lack of knowledge about food. He also worked with parents in order to understand their home food habits and convince them to eat better. He had the challenge of retraining the school cafeteria
30 cooks, and finally he met with government officials to convince them to ban junk food in schools. His actions have impacted every country that has heard of this food **shift**.

> Write down the line number in answer to the following questions. Note that the questions aren't in order.

1. On which line does it say that Oliver was surprised about how children ate?

2. On which line can you find proof that Fifteen has become a success?

3. On which line does it mention when Oliver became a famous chef?

4. On which line is there a hint that Oliver was good with a knife when he was young?

5. On which line does Oliver mention food being bad in school cafeterias?

> Reflect on the following questions:

6. Do you like to cook? If so, what meal do you enjoy preparing? If not, why don't you like to cook?

7. Do you think that it is a good idea to change the food offered in school cafeterias? Do you think that the change will be successful? What obstacles does the plan face?

8. Why is it important for schools to serve nutritious food?

Go Further

> Make a list of good foods and bad foods and then analyze what you eat the most. How can you make a change?

> Write a letter to your school principal asking her/him to change the menu of the school cafeteria.

Self-Evaluate

Did I answer the questions correctly?

Did I give my personal opinion?

2 Watch a video about cafeteria food.

Studies show that eating healthy food helps students learn better. Despite this fact, however, most of the food that is served in school cafeterias fails nutrition tests. What do you think about this? What kind of food is served in the cafeteria in your school?

In the Kitchen, 1893, Gustave-Henri Marchetti (1873–unknown)

> Before watching the video, think about your school cafeteria by answering the following questions:

1. In your opinion, does your school cafeteria offer healthy food choices?

2. What are the most popular choices on the menu?

3. Which choice would get a high mark in a nutrition test? In other words, which choice is balanced, tasty and not too fatty?

4. Which choice would get a low mark in a nutrition test?

5. Do most of the students in your school prefer to bring their own lunch, eat at a restaurant close to the school or eat in the cafeteria?

> Before watching the video, read the following questions.

> After watching the video, answer the questions with complete sentences.

6. What new information did you learn from the video?

7. Do you agree that students are responsible for what they eat, or do you think that it is the school's responsibility to offer students healthy food choices?

8. If you had to summarize the information presented in the video for a friend, what would you say? Write three sentences to summarize what you learned from the video.

9. Most people already know that the way they nourish their body is important, so why do many people eat junk food every day? Give your opinion.

10. Write five words from the video that are new to you. It doesn't matter if you spell them incorrectly.

Even though the video is long, don't panic! Continue watching and trying to understand as much as you can.

Take notes while you are watching to help you understand.

Self-Evaluate

Did I answer all the questions?

Did I give my personal opinion?

3 Discuss your school cafeteria.

School cafeterias offer food, but how is it served: on washable plastic plates or in Styrofoam containers? What about the vending machines? Do they offer only chips and chocolate bars? Discuss what is going on in your school and how you can improve the situation.

> **Sit with a partner and discuss the following questions:**

1. What would your reaction be if you couldn't eat french fries, hamburgers and pizza at your school cafeteria? Would you be glad or angry? Why?

2. How would you react if you saw the following items on the menu board at your school tomorrow: lentil soup, spinach salad, vegetarian lasagna, yoghurt and fruit?

3. Does your cafeteria serve food on Styrofoam plates? If so, do you think that it is a problem? Do you think it is a good idea to bring your own dishes to eat from? Why or why not?

4. Think about the vending machines in your school. Name five products that you can buy from them. Are they healthy choices?

Be smart

Take your time to give your partner a complete answer.

While you are speaking, try to correct any errors that you notice.

5. Did you know that companies with products in vending machines earn a lot of money from your school? Do the vending machines in your school advertise specific beverage companies? Do you think that this is acceptable? Why or why not?

6. Should cooking classes be obligatory in high schools? Do you feel it is your parents' responsibility to teach you how to prepare healthy meals?

7. Some people say that changing food in schools doesn't make a difference because students can bring chips, soda and chocolate bars in their lunch bags. What do you think?

8. Who should you talk to in order to start improving the situation at your school cafeteria: the student council, the teachers, the principal, …?

Smart Talk

First of all, …

I would …

I think it is bad, because …

I agree / disagree with you, because …

What do you think?

S e l f - E v a l u a t e

Did I contribute to the discussion?

Did I persevere even when I made mistakes?

Changing the World with Humanitarian Work

In this task, you will discover another way to help people: by creating programs in other countries and volunteering.

1 Read about Frédérique Vallières's initiative.

Frédérique Vallières, a young woman from the Montréal, Québec region, founded a non-profit organization based on the principle that every human being has the right to proper health care, education, nutrition and shelter regardless of race, gender or religion. Read the interview below to find out more about Frédérique Vallières.

> Before reading, try to guess the answers to the following questions. Then read the interview and check if your predictions were correct.

  ① Why did Frédérique want to go to Kenya?

  ② What were some of the obstacles that she faced there?

Interview with Frédérique Vallières, Co-Founder of Reach Out to Humanity (ROTH)

How did you come up with the idea of starting ROTH?
ROTH came about after my first trip to Africa. My friends and I saw many children suffering from extreme poverty—children eating out of garbage cans, children walking around without shoes, children whose parents
5 couldn't **afford** to send them to school. My friends and I wanted to change this, so we decided to form our own group to make a difference.

How did you get people involved to help you with ROTH?
I'm the co-founder along with three of my best friends. We actually met while travelling through Kenya during my first visit to Africa. The great
10 thing is that we're all from different places. I'm currently living in Québec, Alannah lives in Toronto, Paul is from Ireland and Aaron is from England. The goal is to be able to represent ROTH all over the globe.

Why did you want to go to Kenya?
After I graduated from university, I was ready to do some travelling. I always
15 wanted to go to Africa and I'd heard so many great things about Kenya. The people are wonderful, there are great sites to see, with many animals around and most importantly, it is a safe place to travel.

If young people want to get involved in helping people abroad, what advice would you give them?
20 I'd say choose an organization that fits in closely with their own personal beliefs. I'd advise them to pick charities and non-profit organizations that maintain the same beliefs that they do, and to get involved in projects or activities that they enjoy.

Be Sm^art

Plan. Review question word formation in the Smart Reference section (page 272).

Ask for help if you have any questions.

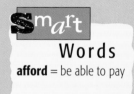

Sm^art
Words
afford = be able to pay

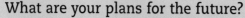

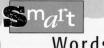
Words
slum = district inhabited by very poor people
wealthy = rich

What are your plans for the future?

25 I hope to carry on with ROTH as long as I can. I'd love to keep travelling and building more projects. However, I know that I'll have to go back to school eventually. I'd like to gain more expertise in international development so that I can take ROTH even further.

Had you done voluntary work before?

30 When I was in secondary school, I used to go to Tijuana, Mexico and build houses in the **slums**. That's when I first fell in love with volunteering and helping others, and that's when I realized how little it actually takes to make a difference in the world.

Would you say that your living conditions in Kenya are dangerous?

35 They aren't exactly dangerous, but you have to be aware of your surroundings. We come from what others perceive to be a very **wealthy** nation—which we are—and when you are travelling in places where you automatically come off as a foreigner, you have to be careful where you go and at what time. You have to be smart and respectful of other cultures 40 when you travel.

Which obstacles were in your way and how did you overcome them?

The biggest obstacles were finding some of the resources in Kenya that are so readily available in Canada. For the most part, we were able to find everything, but sometimes we had to order them from Nairobi—the capital 45 city—and we had to wait on our materials for a few days, which put us behind on our timeline.

What impact is ROTH having here in Québec?

ROTH is having a positive impact here in Québec. Most of our volunteers come from Québec, and over twenty-five Québécois were present for 50 the construction of the Piave Maternity Ward and Counselling Centre in Kenya during the summer of 2007.

> Write five questions for an interview with someone who wants to join ROTH.
> Use the questions in the interview with Frédérique Vallières as a model.
> Exchange questions with a partner and take turns answering each other's questions.
> When you answer the questions, think about the qualities needed in order to be a good volunteer candidate.

Self-Evaluate

Did I formulate the questions correctly?
Did I give relevant answers?

2 Change passions into help.

Be smart

Take your time to find original ideas.

If you had to choose one way to change the lives of others, what would you decide to do? What saddens you about the world today? What are you willing to do to create a change? Think about hobbies that you have. What makes you the happiest? Doing what you love is often the best way to help others, because you are having fun at the same time!

> With a partner, make a list of six talents or interests you could use to help make the world a better place.

> For each talent or interest, write and discuss three different ways it could help other people. For example:

Art: Make public places more beautiful, teach young children how to use colour and decorate the walls of a children's hospital.

> Share your answers with the class. Are you surprised by some of your classmates' ideas?

smart
Talk

I think that …
That's a great idea!
My hobby is … and
I think that it could …
We need to find
more ideas.

Sentence Starters

1. If you love sports, …

5. If you are a good cook, …

2. If you have good computing skills, …

6. If you love to read, …

3. If you love math, …

7. If you like to organize parties and events, …

4. If you like to be outdoors, …

8. If you play a musical instrument …

The Artist's Studio, circa 1665–1666, Johannes Vermeer (1632–1675)

Self-Evaluate

Did I find ideas for each talent or interest?
Did I listen to my partner's ideas?

Facts

The Benefits of Volunteering

Studies demonstrate that two hours volunteering per week helps promote good health. Volunteers report that the satisfaction and pride they experience gives them energy and enthusiasm in all aspects of their life. Other important benefits of volunteering are that it helps you develop valuable personal contacts and looks great on a resumé! Decide how many hours you wish to contribute each week and in which field (the welfare of children, health care, the environment, the arts, music, politics, …). You will gain new strengths and skills, build self-confidence and enjoy the satisfaction of making a difference!

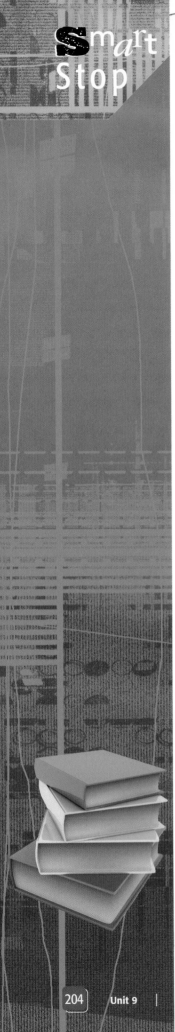

How to Avoid Plagiarism

When you write different types of texts, you look for sources in magazines and books and on the Internet to make your text more credible. To avoid copying someone else's words, here are a few tips:

- Highlight the important information in the source.

- Take point-form notes while you are reading the source (see the Smart Reference section, page 290). Don't write complete sentences when taking notes.

- Use your own words. Avoid making only slight variations in the language and then thinking that it is your own.

- Let the reader know the source of the information.

- Indicate which passages are taken directly from the source by putting them in quotation marks.

- At the end of your text, indicate the references for the sources in a bibliography as described below.

How to Write a Bibliography

The following information should be included when indicating references for your sources in a bibliography:

Books
Author's last name, author's first name. Book title (*in italics*), city of publication: name of publisher, year published, pages used. For example:

Canfield, Jack. *Chicken Soup for the Teenage Soul*, Deerfield Beach: Health Communications Inc.,1997, pp. 232–235

Magazine Articles
Author's last name, author's first name. Title of article (in quotation marks), name of magazine (*in italics*), volume number (where applicable), date of issue, pages used. For example:

Mahoney, Rosemary. "Phenomenal Woman—Sabriye Tenberken," *O, The Oprah Magazine*, August 2005, pp. 223–225 and 237–238

Internet Sites
Author's last name, author's first name (if unavailable, write "unknown"). Title of article or web page (in quotation marks), site name (*in italics*), date of article or date site was accessed, site address (URL). For example:

Author unknown. "Get Involved," *Student Action*, May 16, 2008, http://www …

Note: The Internet is an amazing tool that allows easy access to information without leaving home. However, you must be careful when using Internet sources, because some sites contain false information. Always consult at least two websites on the same topic to confirm that the information is correct.

Helping Communities

We can make a difference, one step at a time. Research projects that are helping people in your community or in a community elsewhere in the world.

Describe projects making an impact.

Option A

Produce a news report on a project that is helping to improve people's lives.

Option B

Make a class magazine about outstanding local initiatives.

Option A

Produce a news report on a project that is helping to improve people's lives.

Options

Use a video camera to prepare the news report. Edit the film and add titles, subtitles, sound effects and colour to make the news report more interesting.

Step 1 **Prepare**

> Find team members and assign roles. Decide who will be in charge of writing the text, who will be in charge of filming and who will be in charge of editing.

> Brainstorm for ideas. Research the Internet, read magazines and books, and talk to people you know to find a project idea. Use the categories in Smart Start to inspire you.

> Write down all your reference sources. Use Smart Stop on page 204 to help you.

Step 2 **Produce**

> Write the text. Give details. Who is the hero of the news report? Who is the person helping and how? What are the strong points of the project? How can more people participate? Does the project face any obstacles?

> Present your report to another group and ask for feedback.

> Revise: Is your message clear? What can you add or remove to make it better?

> Check the spelling and grammar. Did you use connectives correctly?

> Think of props that you will need: a suit, eyeglasses, a desk, …

> Make changes and create a final version of the media text.

> Film the news report or prepare to present it in class.

Step 3 **Present**

> Present the news report to the class.

> Vote on the best news report. Which group came up with the most interesting idea? Which group presented the news report in the most original way? Which group spoke the best English?

Options

Use computer software to make the article professional-looking.

Make a class magazine about outstanding local initiatives.

Step 1 Prepare

> Think about the kind of article you want to write for the class magazine. Read English magazines and newspapers to give you ideas.

> Research the Internet, read magazines and books, and talk to people you know to find ideas. Use the categories in Smart Start to inspire you.

> Write down all your reference sources. Use Smart Stop on page 204, to help you.

Step 2 Write

> Write a draft of the article. Give details. Who is the hero of the article? What are the strong points of the project? How can more people participate? Does the project face any obstacles?

> Include an introduction, the main body of the text and a conclusion.

Step 3 Revise

> Is your message clear? What can you add or remove to improve the article?

> Ask a classmate to read the article and make suggestions.

> Make changes to the article.

Step 4 Edit

> Check the spelling and grammar. Did you use connectives correctly?

> Write a final copy.

Step 5 Publish

> Put the article together with those of your classmates to create a class magazine.

> Make a copy of the magazine for every student in the class.

> Be proud of the work that you did!

Words

REVIEW

1. afford
2. crowd
3. cupboard
4. dismay
5. feat
6. hospitality
7. issue
8. jargon
9. liability
10. misdeed
11. overseas
12. processed
13. shift
14. slum
15. stoop
16. stride
17. transparent
18. waste
19. wealthy
20. witness

Self-Evaluate

Did I follow all the steps?

Did I refer to ideas from the unit to help me create the text?

Did I write correct sentences?

Did I use resources to help me identify reference sources and did I use connectives properly?

Reflection

1. Which activity did you like the most? Why?
2. Which activity was the most challenging for you?
3. Name two strategies that you learned to use in this unit.
4. If you had to do this unit over again, what would you do differently?
5. What are your goals for the next unit? What would you like to improve?

Corneille: A Man of This World

Biography of Corneille

Corneille Nyungura was born March 24, 1977 in Germany. He spent most of his childhood in his country of origin, Rwanda. In 1994, his parents and family members were killed in the Rwandan genocide, and Corneille was forced to flee to Germany
5 where he lived with friends of his parents.

Corneille's interest in music started very young. When he was sixteen years old, Corneille made his first recording and was selected as a finalist in a popular music contest in Rwanda. In 1997, he moved to Montreal to go to university, but soon focused on his music career instead. Today, Corneille uses his popularity to raise awareness
10 about children who are victims of war and to fight AIDS.

Corneille's lyrics are about issues that are important to him. In his song "A Man of This World," Corneille presents his struggle for identity after persecution in his native land and discrimination elsewhere in the world.

Smart Words

flesh = skin

roots = family history or origin

dwell = live

fuss = unnecessary or unwelcome attention

spit = force liquid out of one's mouth

A Man of This World

15 I was born black and free
I was born in the cold
Cold was home to me
Until I was told
I was really from the South
20 So I traveled closer to the sun
But you see
Flesh burning beat
Got me crossing the sea
Back to the cold again
25 So here I am
Here I am
I'm a stranger
Anywhere I run to
Yes I am
30 A stranger
And I just can't seem to
Find a race I could claim
The **roots** to my name
But who I am
35 Is a man of this world
This is my second shot

Winter's smiling at me
I'm taking this shot
To be all I can be
40 So the next place I stop
Will be the land of the free
A place where a million of colours and
dreams **dwell**
Sounds like a place to me, where
45 someone might understand
Just who I am, who I am
Now there's this **fuss** about colour
And everybody needs to belong
But take a minute to consider my
50 perspective
You see, black kicked me out once
And white took me in
But white looked at me once
And nearly **spat** at my skin
55 I'm so confused, I'm so confused
About who I should hate
I figure I'll just love them all

Corneille Nyungura, *A Man of This World*, Corneille's website

Try Living on $2 a Day

Poverty is hunger. Poverty is lack of shelter. Poverty is being sick and not being able to see a doctor. Poverty is not having access to school and not knowing how to read. Poverty is not having a job. Poverty is losing a child to illness brought about by unclean water. Poverty is powerlessness, lack of representation and freedom.

Nearly three billion people—half the world—live on less than two dollars a day. Nearly a billion people entered the twenty-first century unable to read a book or sign their names. Less than one per cent of what the world spent every year on weapons was needed to put every child into school by the year 2000 and yet it didn't happen.

One billion children live in poverty (one in two children in the world). Six hundred and forty million live without adequate shelter, 400 million have no access to safe water, and 270 million have no access to health services. Ten point six million died in 2003 before they reached the age of five.

All over the world, **disparities** between rich and poor, even in the wealthiest of nations, are rising sharply. Fewer people are becoming increasingly "successful" and wealthy while a disproportionately larger population is also becoming even poorer.

There are many issues involved when looking at global poverty and inequality. It is not simply enough or correct to say that the poor are poor due to their own or their own government's bad governance and management. In fact, you could say that the poor are poor because the rich are rich and have the power to enforce unequal **trade agreements** that favour interests more than the poorer nations.

People are hungry not because of lack of availability of food, or "over" population, but because they are too poor to afford the food. Politics and economic conditions have led to poverty and dependency around the world.

Addressing world hunger therefore implies addressing world poverty as well. If food production is further increased and provided to more people while the **underlying** causes of poverty are not addressed, hunger will still continue because people will not be able to purchase food.

Poverty is a disaster. I can make a change and so can you. If we all join hands and put our minds to what we believe in, anything is possible. Everywhere we go, poverty is faced. Poverty is increasing, by a large amount. We need to make a difference, and we need to do it now.

How much longer can we watch these young and old people on the streets suffering? Not much longer, because they are dying. They need help and they need it as soon as possible. Maybe this statistic will be an **eye-opener**, and we can try to make a difference.

One point four million people die each year from lack of access to safe drinking water and adequate sanitation.

Saudia Mohamed, "Try living on $2 a day," North Bay, Ontario, Young People's Press website, July 17, 2006

Smart Words

disparity = unfair difference

trade agreement = contract between countries regulating buying and selling goods

underlying = most important, but not easily noticed or identified

eye-opener = surprising, new learning experience

I Spy

In this unit, you will discover the differences and similarities between real-life and movie versions of spy jobs and gadgets. You will also learn about the kinds of people that intelligence agencies recruit. You will complete a job application form, find out how to read body language and learn about a real-life Canadian spy story.

WHAT QUALITIES DO YOU NEED TO BE A SPY?

Final Task

Recruit potential spies or report a spy incident.

Option A

Write a job description and application form for an intelligence service.

Option B

Write a news report about an international spy scandal.

Smart Start

Have you ever watched a spy movie and dreamed of becoming a spy? Spies in movies have lives filled with danger, excitement and heroism. They also seem to have an interesting collection of high-tech gadgets to help them save the world. Is the life of a spy really like in the movies?

Be smart

Use the descriptions to help you while you are speaking.

Listen to yourself while you are talking and correct any errors you make.

C1 1 Discuss spy gadgets.

One of the most interesting things about being a spy in the movies is the surveillance and intelligence equipment that spies use. Of course, movies exaggerate—real-life spies don't drive million-dollar cars or billion-dollar planes—but some of the gadgets that you see in the movies actually exist. In this activity, you will decide which items are really used in the intelligence business.

> Look at the pictures and descriptions below.
> With a partner, decide which items are real and which ones are fake.
> Share your ideas with your classmates.

A cellphone with software that can break into electronic locks and emit an electric shock of 12 000 volts

A subminiature portable camera that can take high-quality, spontaneous pictures

A pen filled with acid to dissolve metal

A hollow silver dollar used for hiding film and other secret documents

A credit card containing a concealed lock-pick and X-ray glasses

A fake eyeball that releases a small amount of acid when improperly opened, thereby destroying the film hidden inside

Smart Talk

I think that … is real, because …

What do you think?

That's a good idea!

We had a hard time deciding if … was real, because …

Self-Evaluate

Did I take a risk and try to explain my ideas even if I wasn't sure?

Did I try to listen and correct the errors I made when speaking?

2 Imagine a spy's typical workday.

What does a spy do during a typical day at work: sneak into government buildings, receive information about important officials, …?

> With a partner, write down six tasks that a spy might do during a typical workday, for example:

Follow suspects and take pictures to see where they go and whom they meet.

> Decide what tools your spy will need for each task. Write them down beside each task. For example:

A camera, binoculars

> Decide how to present the tasks:

- As a schedule: two events in the morning, two in the afternoon or evening, two at night?

- As a checklist / to-do list?

> Show your results to your classmates.

S e l f - **E** v a l u a t e

Did I share six ideas?

Did I choose an effective way to present the tasks?

Pandora's Box, 1951, René Magritte (1898–1967)

Sm**a**r**t** Talk

I think a spy might …

Do you think a spy would …?

I think that is unrealistic, because …

What else do you think a spy might do?

Sm**a**r**t** Facts

Famous Spy Authors

Ian Fleming, one of the world's most famous spy authors, had a life very similar to that of his hero, James Bond. He was born into a rich family and loved to gamble and entertain women. He also worked as a journalist reporting on spy trials, and served as an officer in the British Navy. He lived on and off in Jamaica, the setting of many James Bond films.

Frederick Forsythe is another famous British spy novelist who was a journalist and a pilot in the British Navy. His books are extremely realistic and well researched. In fact, the details he provides about obtaining false identities and putting microphones in unusual places are often ones that the British government has used in its intelligence services!

TAsk 1 Recruiting Intelligence Officers

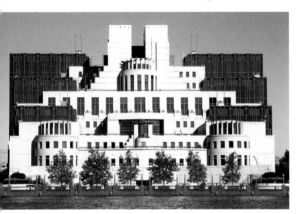

For many years, the British government wouldn't admit having an intelligence agency, and Canada and the United States made sure that the activities of CSIS (the Canadian Security Intelligence Service) and the CIA (Central Intelligence Agency) were as discreet as possible. Recently, there has been a major change since intelligence agencies are now using the Internet to recruit intelligent and skilled people into their service.

MI6 Secret Intelligence Service
Headquarters, London, England

C2 1 Listen to an interview.

MI6, the branch of the British government that deals with foreign intelligence, is actively looking for people, especially women, to join its service. You will listen to an interview with someone who used to work for MI6 about the kinds of people they are trying to recruit.

> Before listening to the interview, write a list of qualities that a good spy should have, including education, special skills and languages.

> Think about why an intelligence agency might want to hire women specifically. What special skills do women offer?

> After listening to the interview and taking notes, answer the questions below.

1. What is MI6 doing to **attract** women?

2. What must an MI6 agent be able to do?

3. Why does the reporter believe that not many women worked for MI6 in the past?

4. What is Leslie's response to this reason?

5. Why does MI6 want to recruit women?

6. Are female spies required to seduce men as part of their job? Explain.

Self-Evaluate

Did I use the notes I took to help me answer the questions?

Did I answer all the questions clearly and completely?

How to Take Notes

Notes are a useful reminder of what you read, listened to, watched or thought about. Here are important rules to remember when taking notes:

1 Determine the purpose of the notes. What will you use them for: to help you study for a test, to answer questions, to compare two texts? The purpose of the notes will help you decide how to organize them (point form, Venn diagram, chart, …).

2 Keep it simple. Try to use only a few words or important ideas.

3 Use your own words to avoid plagiarism and to help you understand the notes later on.

4 Use symbols whenever you can, for example:

# = number		:) = funny idea	
+ = additional information		!!! = important	
@ = at		? = not understood / not clear	
* = essential information		≠ = not equal	

5 Don't worry about spelling and grammar.

6 Use different coloured pens and highlighters to help you remember things, for example, blue for ordinary, red for important:

The spies did their training at a secret location in northern Québec.

7 Write words on different parts of the page. Spread out your ideas and use arrows and lines to connect them.

Here are different ways to take notes quickly and efficiently and to organize ideas on a page:

Point Form
This is the most common form of note-taking. Summarize your ideas in a few words and use bullets to separate your ideas.

Diagrams and Word Webs
A Venn diagram allows you to compare ideas. In a Venn diagram, you put ideas that are different in the separate parts of the circles and ideas that are the same in the parts of the circles that overlap.

A word web is helpful when you have to answer many questions at once. It allows you to organize the information according to the question asked, quickly and easily.

Charts
You can use a simple chart to help you organize your ideas into lists and then compare ideas.

Idea / Question	Text A	Text B
Formats for notes	Point form	Venn diagram Chart

You can also use a KWL chart to reflect on what you already **K**now, what you **W**ant to know and what you have **L**earned about a topic (see Unit 6, page 120).

2 Read frequently asked questions.

One of the ways that websites give you quick access to important information is by providing a frequently asked questions (FAQ) page. In this activity, you will look at the features of two different FAQ pages.

> Read the information from the two FAQ pages found on pages 215 and 216.

> While reading the FAQ pages, use a Venn diagram, a chart or another kind of graphic organizer to take notes and compare the information from the two websites.

> After reading the FAQ pages, write your own FAQs for people looking for information about how to apply for a job at an intelligence agency. Using the information from the websites on the following pages, think of three questions and three answers that could appear on your FAQ page.

> Using your notes and the MI6 and CIA websites, answer the following questions with complete sentences. Once you have finished, compare your answers with a partner.

1. Which FAQs do both websites answer?

2. Are you allowed to tell people that you are applying to become a spy? Were you surprised by the answer given on the website? Why or why not?

3. According to the CIA website, what are the benefits you will receive if you work for them? Are there any benefits offered that you think are not necessary? Are there any others that you feel should be offered?

4. Which FAQ from either website is the most useful to a person looking for a job in this field? Explain your answer.

5. Give one very important FAQ that is not given on either website. Why do you think it is an important FAQ that should be included? Explain your answer.

6. After reading the two websites, would working for either agency interest you? Why or why not?

Go Further

> Write another question for either the MI6 or CIA FAQ page and ask a partner to answer it.

> Check if CSIS has an FAQ page. Write an e-mail to CSIS recommending that they add an important FAQ to their website. Use the features of a letter to help you (see page 155).

Be Smart

Use ideas from the texts to help you write FAQs.

Use a graphic organizer to help you organize your notes.

ICT

Options

Research information on another intelligence agency website to use in your FAQs.

Use software to create an imaginary FAQ page for another intelligence agency.

Self-Evaluate

Did I incorporate important ideas from the texts in my notes?

Did I use features of the FAQ websites to help me create FAQs for an intelligence agency?

Frequently Asked Questions—MI6

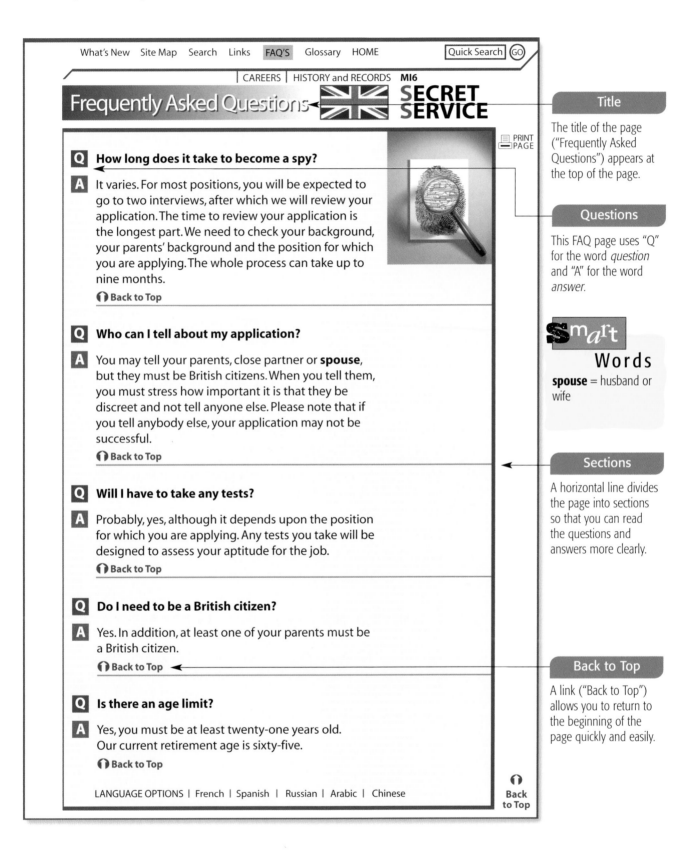

What's New   Site Map   Search   Links   **FAQ'S**   Glossary   HOME

Quick Search GO

| CAREERS | HISTORY and RECORDS   **MI6**

Frequently Asked Questions

SECRET SERVICE

🖶 PRINT PAGE

Q **How long does it take to become a spy?**

A It varies. For most positions, you will be expected to go to two interviews, after which we will review your application. The time to review your application is the longest part. We need to check your background, your parents' background and the position for which you are applying. The whole process can take up to nine months.

🎧 **Back to Top**

Q **Who can I tell about my application?**

A You may tell your parents, close partner or **spouse**, but they must be British citizens. When you tell them, you must stress how important it is that they be discreet and not tell anyone else. Please note that if you tell anybody else, your application may not be successful.

🎧 **Back to Top**

Q **Will I have to take any tests?**

A Probably, yes, although it depends upon the position for which you are applying. Any tests you take will be designed to assess your aptitude for the job.

🎧 **Back to Top**

Q **Do I need to be a British citizen?**

A Yes. In addition, at least one of your parents must be a British citizen.

🎧 **Back to Top**

Q **Is there an age limit?**

A Yes, you must be at least twenty-one years old. Our current retirement age is sixty-five.

🎧 **Back to Top**

LANGUAGE OPTIONS | French | Spanish | Russian | Arabic | Chinese

🎧 **Back to Top**

Title

The title of the page ("Frequently Asked Questions") appears at the top of the page.

Questions

This FAQ page uses "Q" for the word *question* and "A" for the word *answer.*

S**m**a**r**t Words

spouse = husband or wife

Sections

A horizontal line divides the page into sections so that you can read the questions and answers more clearly.

Back to Top

A link ("Back to Top") allows you to return to the beginning of the page quickly and easily.

Frequently Asked Questions—CIA

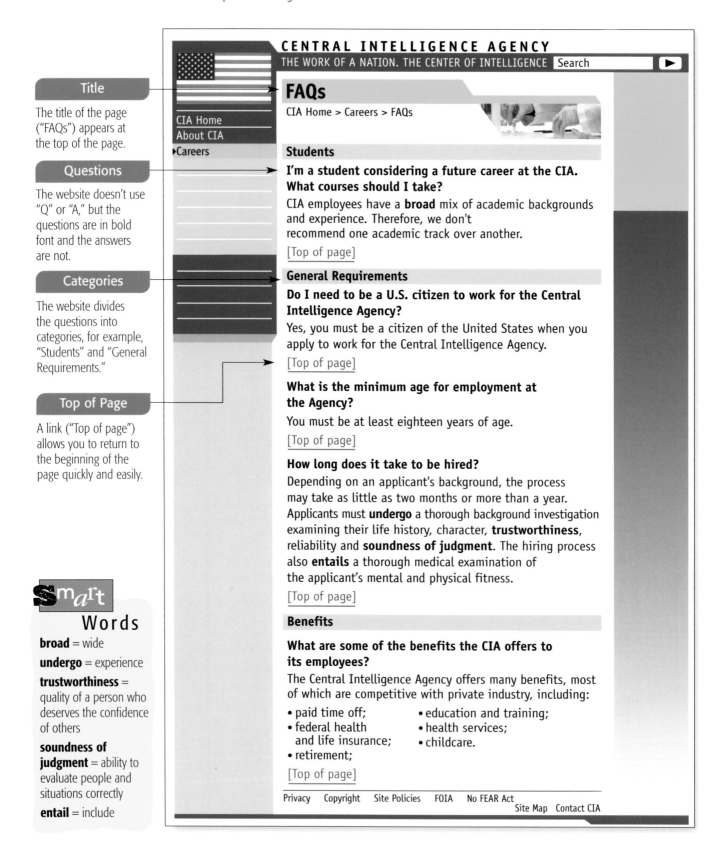

3 Interview an intelligence officer.

You have listened to an interview with an intelligence officer and you have read questions people ask when applying for a job at an intelligence agency. Now it is your turn to think of questions to ask an intelligence officer.

> With a partner, create a dialogue between a reporter and a spy.
> Write at least five questions and five answers.
> Try to think of questions and answers that are interesting and creative.
> Follow the steps below or adapt them with your partner.
> Once you have finished, perform the interview in front of the class or a small group.

Step 1 **Prepare**

> Brainstorm with your partner. Think of ideas and questions you want to ask. Which intelligence service does the agent work for? Why are you interviewing the agent?
> Plan. Write an outline of questions and answers for the interview.
> Read through the outline. Do the questions make sense? Are they interesting?

Step 2 **Write**

> Write a draft using the outline you created.
> Add dialogue to introduce the participants and end the conversation.
> Add actions for the actors to do, such as: *(laughs)*, *(nods)*, …

Step 3 **Revise**

> Read the script with your partner. How does it sound when you read it out loud?
> Ask someone to listen to you and your partner reading the script and give you feedback.

Step 4 **Edit**

> Look carefully at the script. Do you see any spelling and grammar mistakes?
> Make the necessary corrections.
> Write a final copy.

Step 5 **Publish**

> Perform the script in front of a small group or the class.
> Hand in the script to your teacher.
> Reflect on what you wrote.

Self-Evaluate

Did I write a realistic dialogue?

Did I use correct spelling and grammar?

Magritte and the Spies, 1971, The Cronica Group

T^Ask 2 On the Job with Intelligence Officers

You now have a good idea why intelligence agencies are recruiting people and what kinds of people they are looking for. Before considering a possible future career as a spy, find out what exactly spies do on the job.

1 Read descriptions of real-life spy jobs.

The interesting thing about working for an intelligence agency, or any other government agency or corporation, is that there is more than one type of job available. In this activity, you will read job descriptions posted on the CSIS website and decide whether they may be suited to you.

Office of Imagery Analysis, Central Intelligence Agency, Virginia, U.S.A.

Pay attention to the features of the job descriptions. Look at the title of each section.

Scan. Read the job descriptions again to find the answers to the questions.

> Before you read the job descriptions, ask yourself:
>   • What education and skills would I need to become a spy?
>   • How much money would I earn?
>   • What would I like to do?
>   • What would I not like to do?

> While reading the job descriptions, take notes. Use a Venn diagram to help you compare and contrast the job postings.

> After reading the job descriptions, answer the following questions:

1 Which jobs require you to understand more than one language?

2 Which jobs require you to work well as part of a team?

3 Which jobs require you to work at night? What phrases in the text support this answer?

4 How much does each job pay? Do you think that the pay is suitable for the job? Why or why not?

5 Which job seems like the most stereotypical spy job? Support your answer with an example.

6 Which job are you most interested in? Why?

7 What characteristics do you have that make you a good candidate for one of the jobs? Explain your answer.

8 What surprised you about the job descriptions?

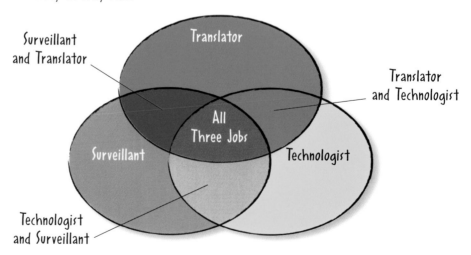

Français	Contact Us	Help	Search	Canadian Site
About CSIS	Priorities	Publications	News Room	Public Safety
Home	FAQ	A-Z Index	Site Map	Careers

Sm**a**r**t**
Words

conduct = carry out

detail = list or give all the facts or information

undergraduate degree = first degree at college or university

dexterous = having good manual skills

Who We Are
What We Offer
Become an Intelligence Officer

How to Apply

🖨 PRINT VIEW

Immediate Career Opportunities

Surveillant

Summary:

In a team environment and under the direction of a team leader, the surveillant is responsible for:
• **conducting** discreet surveillance;
• researching and analyzing information;
• writing regular operational reports **detailing** exact movements and activities.

Requirements:

The applicant must:
• be in good physical health;
• be able to adapt quickly to a variety of settings and situations;
• be able to work effectively during periods of high intensity and stress;
• display initiative, motivation and discretion;

• be able to work a flexible schedule;
• have a university **undergraduate degree** or a minimum of a two-year community college diploma;
• have no criminal record, be drug free and be able to obtain a Top Secret security clearance.

Salary: $52 690 to $64 110 per year

Technologist

Summary:

The technologist is responsible for:
• installing and maintaining varied and complex technical equipment;
• providing advice on technology matters;
• evaluating equipment.

Requirements:

The applicant must:
• be dexterous;
• have an aptitude in electronics, mechanical engineering, computer sciences or imaging disciplines;
• be able to work effectively as part of a team;
• be willing to travel on short notice;
• be fluent in English;

• have a university undergraduate degree in electrical and/or mechanical engineering or a minimum of a three-year community college diploma in electrical and/or mechanical engineering technology;
• have no criminal record, be drug free and be able to obtain a Top Secret security clearance.

Salary: $59 540 to $82 340 per year

Translators / Interpreters

Summary:

You will translate and interpret documents and oral communications of foreign languages into English or French.

Requirements:

The applicant must:
• be prepared to travel;
• be prepared to give testimony in court as an expert witness;

• have a university degree in languages or equivalent work experience.

Salary: $46 640 to $56 750 per year

Self-**E**valuate

Did I complete the Venn diagram?

Did I answer the questions as completely as possible?

Be Smart

Repeat what your partner says to show you understand.

Use gestures when speaking.

Cooperate. Share ideas with your partner.

Smart Talk

What qualities did you list for being a spy?

I didn't include that one, because …

Would you be a good spy?

Why? Why not?

Can you give me an example?

I think I'd be a good spy, because …

C1 2 Think about whether you could be a spy.

You have had a chance to read descriptions of jobs available in the secret service. In this activity, you will determine whether you could become a spy.

> Copy the chart below.

> List the qualities you need to be a spy and then list your personal qualities. Determine whether you would make a good spy. Why or why not?

> Use information from the previous activity to help you.

> Share your conclusions with a partner.

Qualities Needed to Become a Spy	My Qualities
Must like to travel	I speak three languages: French, English and Spanish

Self-Evaluate

Did I use examples to support my ideas?

Did I speak clearly and without hesitating?

C2 3 Complete a job application form.

Did you find a job that interests you in the secret service? All of the secret services (CSIS, MI6, CIA) have online job application forms. In this activity, you will complete one of them.

> Think about the position for which you are applying.

> Read through the application form carefully and then fill it in.

> Feel free to invent information.

Go Further

> Find another job application form online or in your community. Fill it in for extra practice.

> Write a cover letter to submit along with the online application form. Introduce yourself, mention the position for which you are applying and explain why you are a good candidate for the job.

1. CONTACT DETAILS	
Title: ❏ M. ❏ Mrs. ❏ Ms.	Residential Address:
Names (including middle name):	Address (2nd line):
Family Name:	City / Town:
Home Phone No.:	Country:
Work Phone No.:	Postal Code:
Cellphone No.:	Place of Birth:

2. EDUCATION

Please enter the names of the schools, colleges and/or universities you attended.

Secondary Education

Name and address of school	Start Date	End Date

Post-Secondary Education

Name and address of college / university	Start Date	End Date

3. INFORMATION TECHNOLOGY

Provide details of your IT skills and competency.

4. OTHER ACHIEVEMENTS

Provide details (including dates) of other achievements (e.g. positions of responsibility, prizes, awards and scholarships, sports, volunteer work, ...).

5. GENERAL QUESTIONS

A Motivation

Explain why you are interested in the position of _____ and what your expectations are. Limit your answer to twenty-five words.

B Working with Others

Describe a situation (outside of formal education) where you joined a new group. How did you integrate within the group? Limit your answer to twenty-five words.

C Self-Portrait

This is your opportunity to tell us about yourself and your plans for the future. Limit your answer to twenty-five words.

Self-Evaluate

Did I persevere and fill in every section of the application form?

Did I include relevant information?

 # T^A_sk 3 Intelligence Training

Once you enter the secret service, you will learn many skills to help you in your new profession. You will need to be able to analyze both information and people's characters.

 ## 1 Learn to read body language.

A good spy must be able to determine when people are telling the truth and when they are lying. Intelligence and police officers have developed techniques to help them decide whether the person they are interviewing is stating a fact or giving false information. In this activity, you will read a summary of ways to read body language to determine whether a person is telling the truth or not.

Be smart

Use the illustrations to help you understand the text.

> Before reading the text below with a partner, write down as many ways of telling whether someone is lying as you can, for example:

A person is lying if she/he doesn't look at you when talking.

> Read the text using the illustrations to help you understand.

> Think about each behaviour as you read. Do you do these things?

The Body Language of Lies

How can you tell when a person is lying? It isn't always easy. The police and other law enforcement agents spend hours learning to read body language in order to tell whether someone is lying or not. Here are some of the clues they rely upon:

5 **Gestures:** People who are lying keep their hands and arms close to their body, while people who are telling the truth often spread their hands apart and keep their palms open and facing upwards. In addition, they often unconsciously touch their heart or chest.

Avoiding eye contact: This is one type of body language that we know about 10 instinctively. People who are lying avoid eye contact as much as possible. They would rather look down or to one side than look you directly in the eye while speaking. Liars are uncomfortable facing their questioners, so they usually turn their head or body away whenever they can.

Speaking: People who are lying have to think more carefully about what 15 they are saying, so they tend to speak more slowly and use full sentences rather than contractions. For example, they might say, "I did not take your lunch!" instead of "I didn't take it!"

Position in the room: Liars want to place as much distance between you and them as possible, which means that they won't sit too close to you. 20 Sometimes they even unconsciously place objects, such as a book or a coffee mug, between themselves and you.

Details: When people are telling lies, they don't voluntarily provide many details; instead, they give you a general idea. For example, they might say, "I saw her when I was downtown yesterday" instead of "I saw her standing 25 on the corner of De Maisonneuve and Guy last night at around ten o'clock." When you ask people who are lying to tell you the order of events again, they don't add extra details, unlike people who are telling the truth and who elaborate on their information quickly and easily.

Changing the topic: When people are lying, they try to change the topic 30 quickly. If you aren't sure whether a person is lying or not, a good trick is to watch how they react when you change the subject while they are talking. If the person seems **relieved** or enthusiastic about the new topic, she/he might have been lying to you.

Words

relieved = not feeling distressed or anxious anymore

Physical discomfort: One important thing to remember is that when people 35 are lying, they exhibit physical discomfort. In other words, they are more likely to move around, sweat and breathe irregularly when talking to you. They often shift in their seat or wipe their hands on their clothes (because they are sweating). If you take the pulse rate of someone who is lying, you may find that it is higher than normal.

40 **A final word of caution:** Be careful! Before you rush out to try these techniques on your girlfriend or little brother, be aware that just because people exhibit one or more of these signs, doesn't necessarily mean they are lying. Remember that the above behaviours should be compared to the person's normal behaviour whenever possible.

> After reading the text, answer the following questions individually with complete sentences. Share your answers with a partner or a small group.

1 Look at the list again. Do you display any of these behaviours when you lie? If so, which ones?

2 Do you recognize any of these behaviours in your parents or friends when they are lying? If so, which ones?

3 Do you think that this list of behaviours will help you detect whether someone is lying? Why or why not? Who will you try to use these techniques on first?

Self-**E**valuate

Did I use the illustrations to help me understand the text?

Did I write complete sentences giving my personal opinion?

Facts

More on Body Language

Your body sends messages that are independent of what you are saying. Here are a few common body language gestures and how people interpret them:

Non-Verbal Behaviour	Interpretation
Standing with hands on hips	Readiness, aggression
Sitting with legs apart	Open, relaxed
Arms crossed on chest	Defensiveness
Touching, slightly rubbing nose	Rejection, doubt, lying
Rubbing the eye	Doubt, disbelief
Hands clasped behind back	Anger, frustration
Rubbing hands	Anticipation
Hands clasped behind head and legs crossed	Confidence, superiority
Open palm	Sincerity, openness
Tapping or drumming fingers	Impatience
Tilted head	Interest
Biting nails	Insecurity, nervousness

Pay careful attention to body language when your partner is speaking.

Use what you learned about body language in the previous activity.

Relax! Have fun with this activity.

Talk

Can you tell me where ...?

Who ...?

When ...?

What do you mean by ...?

I think that ... is a lie, because ...

2 Test your skills.

It is time to put the information you just learned about lying to use. Try this fun game with a partner or a small group.

> Think of three qualities about yourself, or experiences that you have had, that would make you an excellent spy.

> Think of two statements that are true and one that is false. For example:

  I have travelled to many countries. (True)

  I learned to speak Cantonese when I was five. (False)

  I won the science fair when I was twelve. (True)

> Write the three statements.

> Write four sentences to explain each statement. Add details such as the time, place, smells, people you were with, feelings, ...

> Take turns playing the game with one or two partners:

  1 Give each statement to your partner.

  2 Your partner will ask you questions to test you.

  3 Ask your partner: Which statement is the lie?

Self-Evaluate

Did I find three statements?

Did I use verb tenses correctly?

Structure

Direct and Indirect Speech

Have you ever noticed when reading newspapers (or watching the news on TV or on the Internet), that reporters often tell you what other people said? This is called reported or indirect speech. Here is what you have to do when changing direct speech to indirect speech.

1 Start your sentence by reporting what was said. Common expressions used are:
said that, reported that, mentioned that, …

2 Change the verb tense:

Direct Speech	Indirect Speech
"I **am** scared of terrorists."	Mr. Singh said that he **was** scared of terrorists.
If the verb tense is the …	**Change it to the …**
Simple present (I **walk**.)	Simple past (He **walked**.)
Simple past (I **walked**.)	Simple past (He **walked**.)
The simple past usually stays the same in reported speech, but it is sometimes changed to the …	Past perfect (He **had walked**.)
Future (I **will walk**.)	Conditional (He **would walk**.)
Present progressive (I **am walking**.)	Past progressive (He **was walking**.)

3 Change the pronoun:

Direct Speech	Indirect Speech
"**I** am scared of terrorists."	Mr. Singh said that **he** was scared of terrorists.
Change the subject pronoun in the first person …	**To the third person:**
I We	He, she They

4 Change the time reference:

Direct Speech	Indirect Speech
Mr. Singh: I am scared of terrorists **now**.	Mr. Singh said that he was scared of terrorists **at that moment**.
If the person says …	**Change it to …**
this evening today / this day these days now yesterday a week ago last weekend here next week tomorrow	that evening that day those days at that moment the day before a week before the weekend before / the previous weekend there the following week the next day / the following day

3 Watch an interview with a real-life mole.

In June 2006, a group of young men, including five teenagers, were arrested in Ontario for planning to bomb various locations in Canada. The arrest came after two moles (or spies) infiltrated the terrorist organization and provided authorities with the information necessary to stop the attacks. In this activity, you will listen to an interview with Mubin Shaikh, one of the moles involved in the case.

Listen carefully. Don't be distracted.

Plan. Read the questions before watching the video.

Take notes while you watch.

> Before watching the video, read the questions below.
> Take notes while you watch using one of the techniques in Smart Stop (page 213).
> After watching the video, use your notes to answer the questions.
> Discuss your answers in a small group or as a class.

1. How many people were involved in the bomb plot?
2. Who did Shaikh contact when he heard Momin Khawaja had been arrested?
3. Why did he contact this organization?
4. What other organization was Shaikh working for?
5. Name two things Shaikh did as a spy.
6. Why does Shaikh think he is the best person for the job?
7. What characteristics does Shaikh have that allowed him to infiltrate the group?
8. What did the group use to attract members?
9. What surprised you about the video?
10. Would you offer to spy on an organization to protect your country even if it put you and your family in danger? Why or why not?

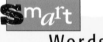

Words

acquaintance = person you know

plot = secret plan

conspicuous = standing out

Self-Evaluate

Did I use an effective note-taking technique to help me answer the questions?

Did I answer the questions clearly and completely?

Facts

Canadian Security Intelligence Service

Canada hasn't always had CSIS to gather intelligence. In fact, until the 1960s, it was the Royal Canadian Mounted Police (RCMP)—the federal government's police officers—who were in charge of domestic and international security.

In the 1960s, international politics became more complicated as the Cold War between the Soviet communists and the American capitalists intensified. In 1970, a terrorist group called the Québec Liberation Front (or FLQ) was involved in the kidnapping and murder of Québec minister Pierre Laporte. The Canadian government realized that they needed a new agency to deal with foreign and domestic threats. In August 1981, they announced that they would create a security intelligence service separate from the RCMP. CSIS began its formal existence on July 16, 1984.

Becoming a Spy

You may have all the qualities required to become an excellent intelligence officer, but maybe the life of a spy isn't for you after all. Prepare to use what you have learned either to recruit others or to create a spy story of your own.

Recruit spies or report a spy incident.

Option A

Write a job description and application form for an intelligence service.

Option B

Write a news report about an international spy scandal.

Option A

Write a job description and application form for an intelligence service.

Step 1 **Prepare**

> Brainstorm: What particular position are you advertising? What qualities are required in order to do this job?

> Research the Internet for more information. Use job application forms and advertisements from your community as models.

> Organize your ideas into an outline for the job description and application form.

> Think about the features of each: Where will you put the information? How much space will you leave for people to write in?

> Reflect: Look over your ideas again. Do you need to add anything?

Step 2 **Write**

> Write a draft job description and application form.

> Use the information in this unit to help you.

Step 3 **Revise**

> Reread the drafts. Are they clear?

> Fill in the application form to see if it works.

> Ask someone to look at your work and give you feedback and suggestions.

> Make changes.

Step 4 **Edit**

> Check your spelling and grammar with the help of a dictionary and other resources.

> Write a final copy.

Step 5 **Publish**

> Hand in the job description and application form to your teacher.

> Publish the texts in the class newspaper or on the class website.

Options

Record the news report and add titles, sound effects and music using recording equipment or computer software.

Publish the news report as a podcast on your blog.

Write a news report about an international spy scandal.

Step 1 Prepare

> Brainstorm to find ideas: Who does the scandal involve? Where does it take place? What are the consequences?

> Research real-life spy scandals. Check facts and details in your story to make it more believable.

> Plan: Create an outline of the news report, including an introduction and a conclusion. Think about the features of a radio or TV news broadcast.

> Look over your ideas again: Is there anything you missed? Should you discard any ideas?

Step 2 Produce

> Write a draft of the news report.

> Include direct and indirect speech.

> Reread the news report: Do your ideas make sense?

> Show your work to your peers and ask them to give you suggestions and feedback.

> Use a dictionary to check your spelling.

> Make sure that you used direct and indirect speech correctly.

> Make changes to the news report.

> Add in cues for sound effects.

> Create a final copy.

Step 3 Present

> Hand in the news report to your teacher or perform it in front of the class.

Smart Words
REVIEW

1. acquaintance
2. attract
3. broad
4. conduct
5. conspicuous
6. daycare
7. deal with
8. detail
9. hire
10. plot
11. relieved
12. spouse
13. trustworthiness
14. undercover
15. undergo

Self-Evaluate

Did I follow and adapt the steps?

Did I make sure that the ideas in my text were relevant?

Did I form sentences appropriately?

Did I use a dictionary to verify my spelling?

Reflection

1. Which activity did you like the most? Why?
2. Which activity was the most challenging for you?
3. Name two strategies that you learned to use in this unit.
4. If you had to do this unit over again, what would you do differently?
5. What are your goals for next year? What would you like to improve?

Big Brother Is Watching You!

Are you being watched while you work? Is someone recording your every move while you babysit? Spying equipment is becoming **commonplace** with employers today, including everything from nanny cams in teddy bears to cameras in the staffroom at your **retail** job. Should employers be required to tell you that they are spying on you?

5 Seventeen-year-old Lisa Gold and Robin Setters disagree on the matter. "I have been babysitting since I was fourteen years old. If you are going to **trust** me with your children and your home, then trust me. Don't spy on me," says Lisa. "I'm a good sitter and I enjoy my job. The children like me. If I look at your clothes or try on your jewellery, there is no harm in that."

10 "I'm a bit of a computer nut and I was trying to figure out a way to find more babysitting jobs. I started researching on the Internet and found that many professional nannies were providing their own nanny cams. I have a laptop and a webcam that I take to each job. Parents can go online and see what we are doing. I have been booked every weekend since," says Robin. "Parents want control and need to know that the person
15 who is caring for their child is loving and giving. I have nothing to **hide**."

Spying on employees is nothing new. One sixteen-year-old who works at a convenience store where there are video cameras says, "The cameras are there for our security, but they also record everything we do. I have seen people get fired because they were **stealing**. The camera is there and I know it is recording my every move. I'm not going
20 to do something stupid like steal a chocolate bar."

Sixteen-year-old Janet Wood works in retail. Not only are there cameras all over the store where she works, but at the end of each shift, a manager checks her bag to make sure she hasn't taken anything. "Many retail stores do bag checks. It would be really easy for someone to put a sweater in their backpack during their break. We know
25 where the cameras are. I understand why the store requires us to have our bags checked. When I think about it, though, it does make me feel like they don't trust me," says Wood.

With the rapid changes in technology and spying equipment becoming smaller and undetectable, more and more employers will protect themselves by using spying
30 equipment. What can you do about it? Smile! You may be on camera …

Sm**a**rt Words

commonplace = not unusual; happening in many places

retail = shop that sells products

trust = believe someone is honest and will not do anything wrong

hide = keep something secret from others

steal = take something without permission or without paying for it

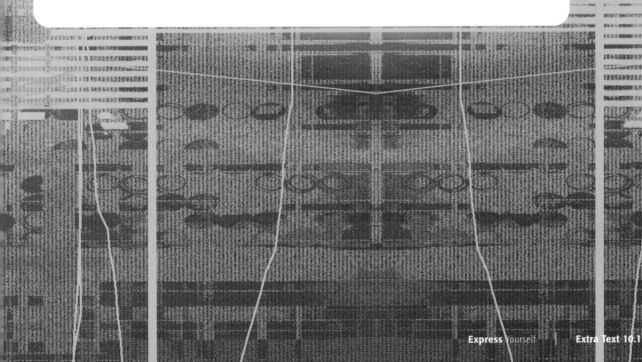

Poisoned Spy Puzzle a Real-Life Murder Mystery

It's a murder mystery filled with intrigue **reminiscent** of the Cold War—there's a retired Russian spy poisoned by a radioactive substance, a secret dossier, a [5] **slain** investigative journalist and a shadowy fugitive billionaire.

But the story of the agonizing death of Alexander Litvinenko is an up-to-the-minute tale of politics, power and [10] betrayal. And the final chapter of this spy thriller has not yet been written.

The most crucial questions remain unanswered: Was Litvinenko's death murder? Who killed him? Where did they [15] get the poison?

Most intriguingly, who might have ordered his death?

The tale began after Litvinenko, a former Russian intelligence officer, met with [20] Mario Scaramella, an Italian security expert, in a London sushi bar Nov. 1. Scaramella passed Litvinenko a secret file **purportedly** showing that both men were on a hit list of Kremlin opponents.

[25] Both men somehow **ingested** polonium-210, a substance normally produced in nuclear reactors.

Litvinenko fell ill and died, blaming Russian President Vladimir Putin. [30] Scaramella was exposed to a smaller amount and showed no signs of illness, doctors said Saturday.

Investigators have found traces of radiation at least a dozen sites across [35] London, including two British Airways jetliners. Litvinenko's wife was also contaminated with trace amounts of the poison, a friend said Friday, although she was not hospitalized.

[40] Litvinenko told a reporter in June that a new Russian law would permit authorities to target its opponents abroad. He feared he was among them.

Another former Russian intelligence [45] officer, Mikhail Trepashkin, wrote in a letter delivered Friday by human rights activists in Moscow that the Federal Security Service, or FSB, the main successor agency to the Soviet KGB, had [50] created a **hit squad** to kill Litvinenko and other Kremlin foes.

Trepashkin, who is serving a four-year sentence for **divulging** state secrets in a prison in Yekaterinburg, said he warned [55] Litvinenko of the **threat** during a meeting in August 2002.

The Kremlin has dismissed the accusations as fantasy.

But the *Guardian* newspaper Friday [60] reported that British intelligence sources suspect Litvinenko was the victim of a plot by "rogue elements" in the Russian state. Investigators suspect that several Russian agents may have entered Britain [65] with a crowd of Moscow soccer fans shortly before Litvinenko met Scaramella, the newspaper reported.

Litvinenko's friends, meanwhile, have little doubt that Russian authorities were [70] somehow involved.

"These latest developments only reinforce our thinking that it was the Russian government or some element of [Russia's] political landscape that was [75] behind this," said Alex Goldfarb, Litvinenko's friend and spokesman.

Goldfarb and others suspect he was targeted because he was investigating the death of Anna Politkovskaya, a [80] Kremlin critic shot to death in her apartment building in October.

This is not the first time the Kremlin has been accused of using drugs and poisons against critics. Suspicion fell on Russian [85] authorities in 2004 when Ukrainian President Viktor Yushchenko was poisoned with dioxin.

That same year, Ivan Rybkin, a former speaker of the Russian parliament, [90] disappeared during his race against Putin for the Russian presidency. He later said he had been drugged.

In each case, Moscow has denied the accusations.

"Poisoned spy puzzle a real-life murder mystery," Associated Press, CTV News website, December 2, 2006

Smart Words

reminiscent = which reminds us of something

slain = killed

purportedly = supposedly, apparently

ingest = take food or other substances into the body

hit squad = group of criminals employed to kill someone

divulge = give secret information

threat = declaration of an intention to cause harm or trouble if someone doesn't do what is asked

You have made a lot of progress this year. How much do you remember since the last review?

Words Review

Read over the vocabulary selection from each unit and try to remember what each word means.

Unit 6	Unit 7	Unit 8	Unit 9	Unit 10
bid	apologize	crowded	afford	attract
complain	awkward	cruise	aware	acquaintance
counterpart	bucket	measure up	dismay	conduct
deserve	casual	neat	feat	daycare
drop out	lung	pace	issue	deal with
gimmick	messy	payoff	liability	hire
lack	pitfall	ponder	overseas	plot
opponent	shout	rate	slum	relieved
thigh	tidy	sleek	waste	spouse
unusual	wedding	wave	witness	undercover

Here are two ways to help you remember the meanings of the words.

1 Use flash cards.

> On one side of the flash card, write the vocabulary word. On the other side, write a definition in your own words.

> Work with a partner and use the flash cards to quiz each other. Give the word and ask your partner for the definition, or give the definition and ask your partner for the word and its correct spelling. You can also ask each other to use the word in a grammatically correct sentence.

> Another idea: Make picture flash cards. Draw or find illustrations of some of these words. Put them up on your classroom walls. A visual reminder will help you learn the words quickly!

2 Compete in a challenge.

> Your teacher will write the Smart Words on strips of paper and stick them to the board.

> Divide the class into two teams.

> When your teacher reads out a definition, run to the board and grab the strip of paper with the appropriate word written on it. Note that only one student from each team should compete at a time.

> Repeat the challenge for the next definition.

> After the teacher has read out all the definitions, count the strips of paper in each team's possession. The team with the most strips of paper wins the challenge.

Structure Review

Review the Smart Structures in each unit.

Unit 6	Unit 7	Unit 8	Unit 9	Unit 10
Comparative and Superlative Adverbs Karen writes **quickly**. Paul writes **more quickly** than her. Kelly write **the most quickly**. Exceptions: He works **harder** than her. They run the **farthest**.	**Modals** I **might** stop smoking. She **could** leave. You **shouldn't** eat junk food. **Must** we follow the rules? **Future Tense** They **will** take turns. She **is going to** learn German. We **won't** leave early.	**Passive Voice** Traffic accidents **are caused** by people. (passive voice) People **cause** traffic accidents. (active voice)	**Connectives** Cause and effect: **Because of** him, the world changed. **Therefore**, children's health improved. Contrast: They raised money **despite** the problems. **Although** the car is old, it is fuel efficient. Conditions: I always get up early. **Otherwise**, I can't go jogging.	**Direct and Indirect Speech** Direct speech: Mr. Singh said, "I am scared of terrorists." Indirect speech: Mr. Singh said that he was scared of terrorists.

Your Turn to Practise!

> **Complete the following exercise.**

1 What is the adverb form of the adjective "careful"?

2 Write a sentence using the comparative form of the adverb "slowly."

3 Write a sentence using the superlative form of the adverb "quietly."

4 Write a sentence in the negative form expressing possibility. (modals)

5 Write a polite question asking for help. (modals)

6 Decide if these sentences are written in the active or passive voice.

a) Mopeds are driven in many countries.

b) Hybrid cars help the environment.

7 Change this sentence from active voice to passive voice.
Jules rides a bike to work.

8 Find the connective in each example.

a) I would like to travel the world. However, I'm afraid of flying.

b) Many students eat junk food despite the fact that it is unhealthy.

9 Change these sentences from direct to indirect speech.
Kim said, "I want to join the CIA." Tim responded, "I will help you."

10 Change these sentences to the future tense.

a) I travelled to New York last week.

b) Maria is not playing in the swimming pool right now.

Cut
by Bob Greene

Facts

Bob Greene is an American journalist who has written for several prestigious newspapers and magazines, such as *Sports Illustrated* and *Esquire*. He is known for writing human-interest stories because he feels that he should tell stories about experiences that we all share.

"Cut" is an essay describing a personal story of how not making a high school sports team affected the author and his friend as adults. The English word *cut* often refers to a negative action or behaviour.

Before You Read

Part A Vocabulary

If you understand the important words before you read a text, you will enjoy
the story even more. Become familiar with the new vocabulary first.

> Read the definitions below.

> Use the definitions to help you fit the words into the paragraph below. Think
> about the kind of word you will need for each blank: a noun, an adjective,
> an adverb or a verb.

1. **altered** = changed

2. **face** = accept

3. **overachiever** = someone who works hard
   to be successful

4. **pleaded** = asked for something in
   an emotional way

5. **sob** = cry

6. **stared** = looked continuously without moving

7. **tacked** = attached to a surface with a pin

8. **tried out for** = made an effort to qualify for

9. **vividly** = very clearly

10. **worthy** = deserving

I'm an ▬▬▬. I remember ▬▬▬ the time in Secondary 4 when I ▬▬▬
a part in a play, but didn't get it. I felt terrible—I wanted to ▬▬▬ loudly in front
of everyone! I ▬▬▬ with the teacher to give me the part. She told me that
I needed to ▬▬▬ the fact that I couldn't be the best at everything. I was really
angry, so I ▬▬▬ a note to her door that said, "I'm a mean teacher!" I ▬▬▬
at it for a moment and then walked away. When I went home and thought about it,
I ▬▬▬ my ideas and phoned my teacher to apologize. I told her that I was sorry
and that she was ▬▬▬ of more respect from me.

Part B Strategies

Strategies can help you understand a text in a second language. Here are
two strategies for you to use:

> Guess. Predict what the main ideas of the text will be, by using the illustrations
> throughout the story and what you already know about competition, pressure
> and sports.

> Skim. Read the text quickly to get a general idea of what it is about the first time
> you read. Do not stop reading if you find difficult words or passages you don't
> understand.

While You Read

Now you are ready to read the text.

> While you read, decide whether your predictions about the story were correct.

- Did you guess what the illustrations were about?

- Did you realize how hard it can be to qualify for sports teams?

Cut

I remember **vividly** the last time I cried. I was twelve years old, in the seventh grade, and I had **tried out for** the junior high school basketball team. I walked
5 into the gymnasium; there was a piece of paper **tacked** to the bulletin board. It was a cut-list. The seventh-grade coach had put it up on the board. The boys whose names were on the list were still on
10 the team. They were welcome to keep coming to practices. The boys whose names were not on the list had been cut. Their presence was no longer desired. My name was not on the list.

15 I had not known the cut was coming that day. I stood and I **stared** at the list. The coach had not composed it with a great deal of subtlety. The names of the very best athletes were at the top of the sheet
20 of paper, and the other members of the squad were listed in what appeared to be a descending order of talent. I kept looking at the bottom of the list, hoping against hope that my name would
25 miraculously appear there if I looked hard enough.

I held myself together as I walked out of the gym and out of the school, but when I got home I began to **sob**. I couldn't stop.
30 For the first time in my life, I had been told officially that I wasn't good enough. Athletics meant everything to boys that age. If you were on the team, even as a substitute, it put you in the desirable
35 group. If you weren't on the team, you might as well not be alive.

I had tried desperately in practice, but the coach never seemed to notice. It didn't matter how hard I was willing
40 to work. He didn't want me there. I knew that when I went to school the next morning, I would have to **face** the boys who had not been cut—the boys whose names were on the list, who were still on
45 the team, who had been judged **worthy** while I had been judged unworthy.

All these years later, I remember it as if I were still standing right there in the gym. And a curious thing has happened.
50 In travelling around the country, I have found that an inordinately large proportion of successful men share that same memory—the memory of being cut from a sports team as a boy.

55 I don't know how the mind works in matters like this. I don't know what went on in my head following that day when I was cut. But I know that my ambition has been enormous ever since then.
60 I know that for all of my life since that day, I have done more work than I had to be doing, taken more assignments than I had to be taking, put in more hours than I had to be spending. I don't know if
65 all of that came from a determination never to allow myself to be cut again— but I know it's there. And apparently it's there in a lot of other men, too.

Bob Graham, thirty-six, is a [lawyer] in Chicago. "When I was sixteen, baseball was my whole life," he said. "I had gone to a relatively small high school, and I had been on the team. But then my family moved, and I was going to a much bigger high school. All during the winter months, I told everyone that I was a baseball player. When spring came, of course, I went out for the team."

"The cut-list went up. I did not make the team. Reading that cut-list is one of the clearest things I have in my memory. I wanted not to believe it, but there it was."

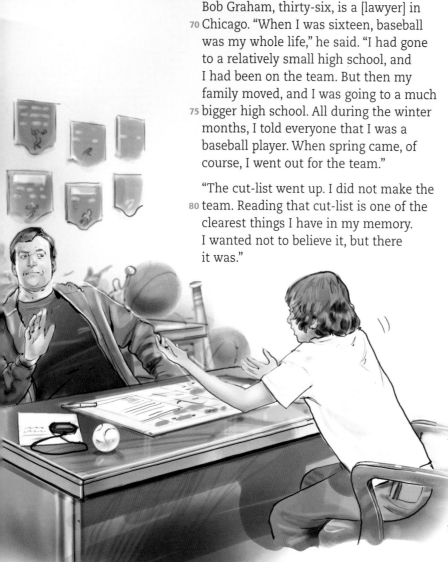

"I went home and told my father about it. He suggested that maybe I should talk to the coach. So I did. I **pleaded** to be put back on the team. He said there was nothing he could do. He said he didn't have enough room."

"I know for a fact that it **altered** my perception of myself. My view of myself was knocked down; my self-esteem was lowered. I felt so embarrassed. My whole life up to that point had revolved around sports, and particularly around playing baseball. That was the group I wanted to be in—the guys on the baseball team. And I was told that I wasn't good enough to be one of them."

"I know now that it changed me. I found out—even though I couldn't articulate it at the time—that there would be times in my life when certain people would be in a position to say 'You're not good enough' to me. I did not want that to happen ever again."

"It seems obvious to me now that being cut was what started me in determining that my success would always be based on my own abilities, and not on someone else's perceptions. Since then, I've always been something of an **overachiever**. When I came to the law firm, I was very aggressive ... I never wanted to be left behind."

"Looking back, maybe it shouldn't have been that important. It was only baseball. You pass that by. Here I am. That coach is probably still there, still a high school baseball coach, still cutting boys off the baseball team every year. I wonder how many hundreds of boys he's cut in his life."

Bob Greene, "Cut," *Cheeseburgers*, Markham, Simon & Schuster Canada, 1985, pp. 41–46

After You Read

Step 1 Explore the text—What did you understand?

> Answer the questions below with complete sentences.

> Compare your answers with a partner or your class.

1 What two sports did the boys try out for? Do people play these sports at your school? Are they competitive sports or just for fun?

2 How old was Bob Greene when he tried out? How old was Bob Graham? Are sports more important for teenagers than they are for adults or children? Why or why not?

3 In which order did the coach put the names on the cut-list?

4 What does it mean if your name isn't on the list?

5 What effect did being cut have on Bob Greene?

6 How did being cut affect both boys' friendships at school?

7 What advice did Bob Graham's father give him when he was cut? Did the advice work?

8 How were both boys affected by their cut in their adult life?

Step 2 Establish a personal connection with the text—Reflect.

> Answer these questions using complete sentences.

> Share your opinions with a partner or your class.

1 Have you ever tried to do something and failed? If so, what happened? If not, how do you think that you would feel if you were cut from something important to you? Explain your answer.

2 Imagine that you are the coach of a high school athletic team. You need to make a decision about how you are going to form your team. Are you going to have people try out and then cut them? Or are you going to keep everyone who turns up to practice? Explain your answer.

3 How would high school sports teams be different if they accepted everyone that wanted to play rather than doing tryouts and cutting people?

4 Both men say that being cut from a team when they were young motivated them to work harder than everyone else in order to be more successful later in life. Do you think that being cut was a positive or negative experience for the men overall? Do you think that fear of failure is a good motivator? Why or why not?

5 Have you had a negative experience in your life that has affected you in a positive way? Describe the situation and the positive effect it had on you. Is it more common for a negative situation or a positive situation to have a good effect on your life? Why?

6 What strategy did you use to help you understand the text? Did it work? What would you do differently next time?

Step 3 Generalize beyond the text—Take the story further.

This short story relates to Unit 1, as it talks about the connection found in our culture between achievement and rejection in sports. In the text, two very successful men explain how failing at sports when they were young motivated them to achieve more when they became adults. In the assignments below, you will think about the connection between early failure and later success.

Follow the steps that you use in the Final Task for the Writing Process: Prepare, Write, Revise, Edit and Publish.

> Choose one of the following assignments.
> Write at least one hundred words.
> Use the Smart Reference section (pages 268–280) to check verb tenses and other Smart Structures.

1 Write a story. Tell the story of someone who tried out for a team and was cut. Describe the setting, who is there, how the person is feeling at every minute …

> Include a clear beginning, middle and end to your story.
> Use the simple past and past progressive tenses.

2 Write a dialogue to give advice. Imagine that your child comes home from school one day, crying, and tells you that she/he has been cut from a sports team. What advice would you give your child? How would you comfort her/him?

> Write a dialogue between you and your child.
> Use modal auxiliaries.

3 Write a short essay. Do you think that competition is a healthy part of our culture? Why or why not? What does it teach us? Write a short essay explaining your point of view and giving concrete examples.

> Follow a clear structure: Provide an introduction that introduces the topic and your point of view, body paragraphs that state your reasons, and a conclusion that summarizes your argument.
> Use the simple present tense.

4 Make a pamphlet. Imagine that you are the director of a large school. Each year, many students try out for the school's athletic teams. However, not everyone can make the teams. Explain to parents what they should say to, or do for, their children if they don't make the cut. Here are a few ideas: how to prepare for tryouts; how to train; how to accept being cut; how to be a good team member.

> Include the features of a pamphlet (see the Smart Stop on page 16 of the Student Book).
> Use modal auxiliaries.

5 Write a journal. Describe the decision-making process that the coach in the story had to go through and why it was difficult. Describe the different athletes that came to the tryouts. Discuss their strengths and weaknesses. Separate your journal into different dates or days of the week.

> Use the simple past tense.

Already Perfect
by Elisa Donovan

Facts

"Already Perfect" is a story from the popular series *Chicken Soup for the Teenage Soul*. The short stories in this collection are written by teenagers like you. The series' topics include relationships, friendship, family, love and more.

The author of this story is Elisa Donovan, an American actress who decided to speak about her battle with anorexia in order to help other teenage girls and boys. Anorexia is a disease characterized by low body weight and body image distortion with an obsessive fear of gaining weight. It can lead to serious medical conditions.

Before You Read

Part A **Vocabulary**

If you know the important words before you read a text, you will understand the text even better. Do you recognize the definitions of the words below?

> Look at the words in the left-hand column and try to guess what they mean.
> Read the definitions in the right-hand column.
> Match as many definitions to words as you can. Check the dictionary definition of the word when you aren't sure.

1. struggle
2. strive
3. grow up
4. failure
5. thrive on
6. praise
7. skip
8. crumb
9. shrink
10. recovery

a) expression of admiration
b) getting better after an illness or injury
c) become smaller in size
d) very small amount
e) miss
f) need
g) not a success
h) get older
i) work very hard
j) fight

Part B **Strategies**

Strategies can also help you understand when you read a story in a second language. Guessing is a good strategy to use.

> Read the title of the story again and look at the picture that illustrates an important scene in the story. With this information, predict what the story will be about.
> Write down your guesses to the following questions:

1. Did Elisa feel perfect when she was in front of the cameras?
2. Did people know that Elisa had an anorexia problem?
3. Did Elisa become anorexic because she was overweight?

While You Read

Now you are ready to read the text.

> While you read, take notes. Write the sentences that prove anorexia is a disease. Find the symptoms and the warning signs.

Already Perfect

Everyone can identify with the need to fit in. Each one of us **struggles** with self-esteem and self-worth to some degree. I spent much of my time **striving**
5 to achieve perfection in every aspect of my life. What I did not realize was that in my desperate need to be perfect, I sacrificed the very body and mind that allowed me to live.

10 I was a happy kid with lots of friends and a supportive family. But **growing up** was really hard and even scary sometimes.

During my childhood, I was constantly
15 involved in something that included an audience viewing my achievements or my **failures**. I was into acting by age seven, and progressed to training for and competing in gymnastics, horseback
20 riding and dance—all of which required major commitment, discipline and strength. My personality **thrived on** the high energy required to keep up. I wanted everyone's **praise** and acceptance, but
25 I was my own toughest critic.

After I graduated from high school and moved out on my own, my struggles with self-esteem and happiness increased. I began to put pressure on myself to
30 succeed in the adult world. Meanwhile, I was feeling very inadequate and unsuccessful. I started to believe that my difficulties and what I perceived to be my "failures" in life were caused by my

35 weight. I had always been a thin-to-average sized person. Suddenly, I was convinced that I was overweight. In my mind, I was FAT! Slowly, my inability to be "thin" began to torture me. I found
40 myself involved in competition again. But this time, I was competing against myself. I began to control my food by trying to diet, but nothing seemed to work. My mind became obsessed with
45 beating my body at this game. I slowly cut back on what I ate each day. With every portion I didn't finish or meal I **skipped**, I told myself that I was succeeding, and in turn, I felt good about
50 myself.

Thus began a downward spiral of my becoming what is known as anorexic. The dictionary defines it as "suppressing or causing loss of appetite, resulting in
55 a state of anorexia." When taken to an extreme, anorexia can cause malnutrition and deprive the body of the important vitamins and minerals that it needs to be healthy.

60 In the beginning, I felt great—attractive, strong, successful, almost super-human. I could do something others couldn't: I could go without food. It made me feel special, and that I was better than
65 everyone else. What I didn't see was that I was slowly killing myself.

People around me began to notice my weight loss. At first they weren't alarmed; maybe some were even
70 envious. But then the comments held a tone of concern. "You're losing too much weight." "Elisa, you're so thin." "You look sick." "You'll die if you keep this up." All their words only reassured
75 me that I was on the right path, getting closer to "perfection."

Sadly, I made my physical appearance the top priority in my life, believing that it was the way to become successful and accepted. As an actress, I am constantly being judged by my appearance. The camera automatically makes people appear heavier than they are. So I was getting mixed messages like, "Elisa, you 85 are so skinny, but you look great on camera."

I cut back on my food more and more, until a typical day consisted of half a teaspoon of nonfat yogurt and coffee 90 in the morning, and a cup of grapes at night. If I ate even a bite more than my allotted "crumbs" for the day, I hated myself and took laxatives to rid my body of whatever I had eaten.

95 It got to the point where I no longer went out with my friends. I couldn't—if I went to dinner, what would I eat? I avoided their phone calls. If they wanted to go to the movies or just hang out at home, 100 I couldn't be there—what if food was around? I had to be home alone to eat my little cup of grapes. Otherwise, I thought I was failing. Everything revolved around my strict schedule of 105 eating. I was embarrassed to eat in front of anyone, believing that they would think I was gluttonous and ugly.

My poor nutrition began to cause me to lose sleep. I found it hard to concentrate 110 on my work or to focus on anything for any length of time. I was pushing myself harder and harder at the gym, struggling to burn the calories that I hadn't even eaten. My friends tried to help me but 115 I denied that I had a problem. None of my clothes fit, and it was hard to buy any, since I had shrunk to smaller than a size zero!

Then one night, like so many nights 120 before, I couldn't sleep, and my heart felt as though it might beat its way out of my chest. I tried to relax, but I couldn't.

The beating became so rapid and so strong that I could no longer breathe. 125 The combination of starving myself and taking pills to get rid of anything that

I did eat caused me to nearly have a heart attack. I stood up, and immediately fell down. I was really scared, and I knew 130 I needed help. My roommate rushed me to the hospital, beginning the long road to my recovery. It took doctors, nurses, nutritionists, therapists, medications, food supplements ... and most 135 important, a new sense of what was really true about myself to get back on track with reality.

Recovering from what I did to my body and reprogramming the way I think 140 about myself has been a very slow and extremely painful process. I still struggle with the effects of anorexia every day. Although it has been a couple of years since that hospital visit, it is by no 145 means over for me. I must be honest with myself and stay committed to being healthy.

I had used my anorexia as a means of expression and control. I used it as my 150 gauge for self-esteem and self-worth. It was my identity. Now I realize that the way to success lies in my heart, mind and soul, rather than in my physical appearance.

155 I now use my intelligence, my talents and acts of kindness to express myself. This is true beauty, and it has nothing to do with the size of my body. With my experience of trying to be "perfect" on the outside, 160 I had sacrificed who I was on the inside. What I know now is, we are—each and everyone of us—already perfect.

Elisa Donovan, "Already Perfect," *Chicken Soup for the Teenage Soul II*, ed. J. Canfield, M.V. Hansen & K. Kirberger, Deerfield Beach, Florida, Health Communications, Inc., 1998, pp. 135–138.

After You Read

Step 1 Explore the text—What did you understand?

> Answer the questions below with complete sentences.

> Compare your answers with a partner or your class.

1. Elisa wanted to feel praised and accepted. Who judged her the most?

2. How did she feel at the beginning when she started losing weight?

3. What can anorexia cause?

4. What did she eat on a typical day?

5. Why did she not go out with her friends anymore?

6. Why couldn't her friends help her?

7. Why was she rushed to the hospital?

8. How does she express herself now?

Step 2 Establish a personal connection with the text—Reflect.

> Answer these questions using complete sentences.

> Share your opinions with a partner or your class.

1. What did you learn from the story? What surprised you?

2. Have you ever had to deal with a weight problem? Do you know someone who eats very little in order to stay thin? What advice do you have for this person? How could you help a friend who is anorexic?

3. Write what you know about this topic. Make a list.

4. Give your opinion on these statements:
   a) The fashion industry is responsible for young girls becoming anorexic.
   b) Boys never have this type of problem.
   c) If parents can get their daughters to start eating again, the problem of anorexia will be resolved.
   d) Most anorexics recover from this disease once they receive treatment.

5. Decide whether these statements are true or false:
   a) Anorexics eat food in huge quantities.
   b) A physical consequence to anorexia is weight gain.
   c) Anorexics and bulimics share one thing: they purge food.
   d) Brain shrinkage can be a result of anorexia.
   e) It is easy for anorexics to talk about their problem.

6. What other problems do teens face? What do you find difficult about being a teen? How do you solve these problems?

Step 3 Generalize beyond the text—Take the story further.

This short story is related to Unit 3, which focuses on beauty standards. Our culture is obsessed with weight and thinness, and the media portrays this image over and over again. The message behind the image is that if you want to be successful, loved and valued, you must be thin.

> Choose one of the following assignments.
> Write 100–150 words.
> Use the Smart Reference section (pages 268–280) to check verb tenses and other Smart Structures.

1 Write a newspaper article about how anorexia affects young girls as a result of the images they see in the media.

> Include different opinions of a teenage girl or boy, a parent and a doctor.
> Use direct and indirect speech.

2 Pretend that you are an ethics teacher preparing a class to inform students about anorexia and bulimia. Write a list of symptoms and a description of the treatment related to each disease.

> Do research to complete the lists and find pictures to add.
> Use modals and the future tense.

3 Write a journal. Pretend that the journal belongs to a person battling with anorexia (a teen or an adult). Explain the person's everyday actions and emotions.

> Use the simple present tense.

4 Write a dialogue and act it out. Choose a situation involving Elisa and her dad, a friend or a teacher. Find questions to help understand the disease and provide solutions.

> Use question words and question formation.

5 Write about a person you know who suffers from anorexia or bulimia and describe her/his story. How did it start? How bad was the problem? Did the person receive help? How is the person now? You can also decide to invent a story.

> Include emotion words.
> Use the simple present or simple past tense.

Wisdom for Sale
A traditional folktale

Facts

A folktale is a traditional story that has been passed on orally from person to person over the years. For centuries, stories were told around campfires at night and were never written down. The story that you are about to read may be very different from its original version. In fact, we often have no idea who the author of a folktale was.

Folktales can be happy, sad, funny, wise or exciting, but there is usually an important lesson about life and relationships to be learned from them. They have remained popular because everyone loves a good story. Most of the time, they have happy endings and support the idea that good behaviour is always rewarded.

Before You Read

Part A Vocabulary

It helps to know some of the difficult words before reading a story. Here are ten words from the story that may be new to you.

> Look at the words listed below to determine whether you know their meaning. How many do you understand without consulting a dictionary?

begged	crowd	forgiveness	guilt	mess
odd	rupee	thief	tiny	waved

> Now read the following pairs of sentences and decide whether each word is being used correctly in sentence a) or in sentence b).

1 odd
- a) It was very *odd* to see him with purple hair.
- b) It is very *odd* that my parents care for me.

2 tiny
- a) You have *tiny* feet—You're a size five!
- b) You have *tiny* feet—You're a size twelve!

3 rupee
- a) In India, I paid for the merchandise in *rupees.*
- b) In Paris, I always use *rupees* to pay.

4 thief
- a) This woman is very generous—She's a *thief.*
- b) He stole my money—He's a *thief.*

5 crowd
- a) There was a *crowd* of two people in my hospital room.
- b) There was a *crowd* at the show.

6 mess
- a) He is in such a *mess*—The situation is very complicated.
- b) My teacher is very tidy—She loves the *mess* we make.

7 begged
- a) Christian is very good in English—He *begged* his teacher to help him with his homework.
- b) My dad said "No," so I *begged* him to change his mind.

8 forgiveness
- a) Her son asked for *forgiveness* for the bad things he had done.
- b) Her son asked for *forgiveness* for the good things he had done.

9 waved
- a) I *waved* my hand to introduce myself.
- b) I *waved* my hand to say hello.

10 guilt
- a) I felt the *guilt* of lying to my parents.
- b) I felt the *guilt* of being a nice person.

Part B **Strategies**

"Wisdom for Sale" is the longest story in your Student Book. Here are a few strategies to help you understand the story.

> Separate the text into three sections.

> Take notes while you are reading to help you understand. Use a legend to take notes, for example:

   ! = This part surprises me.

   ? = I don't understand this part.

   S = Here is a summary of this part.

   ♡ = I like this part.

   ☆ = I am proud because I understood this part.

While You Read

Now you are ready to read the text.

> While you read, fill out a character map for four of the characters portrayed in the story. For example:

Character name:	Character trait:	Supporting detail:
Brahman boy	Intelligent and fair	He gave the money back to ...

> Decide whether these statements are true or false:

 1 The Brahman boy did not have a house.

 2 At first, people on the street laughed at the Brahman boy.

 3 The merchant was very happy that his son received advice from the Brahman boy.

 4 The merchant paid 500 rupees the second time he saw the Brahman boy.

 5 The king wanted to meet the Brahman boy because he was an orphan.

 6 The king also paid the Brahman boy 500 rupees.

 7 The Queen tried to poison the Brahman boy.

 8 The Brahman boy returned on the streets after helping the king.

Wisdom for Sale

A poor Brahman[1] boy lost his parents in a terrible flood. He was left alone, an orphan with no home and no job. He didn't know what he would do or how
5 he would live. But he was a very smart boy and had learned many things from his father, so it didn't take him long to think of a great idea. One day, he walked into town, hired the smallest, cheapest
10 place he could find in the marketplace and opened a store. He spent the little money he had on paper, ink and a pen. Over his store, he put a sign saying: "Wisdom for Sale."

15 All around him in the busy marketplace, merchants owned large, attractive stores selling things that people needed, like cloth, meat, fruit and vegetables. The Brahman boy stood outside his little
20 store all day, calling out, "Wisdom for sale! Good prices! Wisdom of all kinds! Wisdom!"

People passing his store, who had come to buy supplies for their homes and
25 families, thought he was **odd** but amusing, too. Instead of buying his wisdom, they crowded around, laughing at him and shouting.

"If you're so wise, boy, why do you have
30 such a **tiny** store, and why do you wear such old dirty clothes?"

"Oh wise one, can you make my wife stop telling me what to do?"

But the boy was patient.

35 One day, a merchant's son was walking through the marketplace and heard the boy shouting, "Wisdom! Get it here! Good prices!" He followed the boy's voice through the colourful, noisy crowds until
40 he came to his tiny store. This merchant's son was very rich, but also very stupid. He didn't understand what the boy was selling. He thought it was something he could eat or hold. He asked
45 the Brahman boy the price per kilo.

The Brahman boy answered. "I don't sell wisdom by weight. I sell it by quality."

So the merchant's son put down a **rupee** and said, "All right. I'd like a rupee's
50 worth of wisdom, please."

The boy's face suddenly became very serious. He put the rupee in his pocket and told the merchant's son to sit down. Then he also sat down. He looked
55 carefully at the merchant's son's face for a moment, then up at the sky. Then he took out a piece of paper, closed his eyes, took a deep breath, opened his eyes and wrote. When he had finished, he folded
60 the paper, waved his hand over it three times, stood up and gave it to the

---

1 Brahman: the highest social level of followers in the Hindu religion

merchant's son. On the paper were the words, "It is not wise to stand and watch two people fighting."

65 The boy told him in a serious voice, "Keep this with you always."

The merchant's son was very excited. He quickly went home and ran into the house, shouting, "Father, you won't 70 believe what happened to me today. Come quick and see what I've bought!"

When his father read the paper, he couldn't believe his eyes. He screamed at his son, "You stupid boy! I can't believe 75 my son paid a rupee for this nonsense! Everyone knows you shouldn't stand and watch two people fighting! Who sold you this garbage?"

His son then told him about the boy and 80 his little store.

The father immediately went to the store.

"Aha! There you are!" he shouted when he entered the tiny store and saw 85 the Brahman boy.

"Yes, here I am," replied the boy. "And who are you?"

"I'm the father of the fool who bought this piece of nonsense from you!" 90 He threw the piece of paper at the boy. "You're a **thief** and you've cheated my son! Yes, he's a fool, but you're a thief! Return the rupee he paid you or I'll call the police!"

95 The Brahman boy read the paper and said, "If you don't like my goods, you can return them. Give me back my goods and I'll return your money."

"I've just returned your goods. Now give 100 me my son's rupee or I'll call the police!"

"Sir, you have not returned my goods. You've only returned the piece of paper. If you want your money, you must return my wisdom. You must sign a document 105 saying that your son will never use my advice, that he will always stand and watch two people fighting."

"What? You must be joking!" shouted the angry merchant.

110 But by now a **crowd** had gathered around to watch the argument and they agreed with the boy.

"He's right, you know. The man's only returned the paper."

115 "Yes, who do you think you are? Trying to frighten a poor storekeeper!"

So the father agreed to sign the document and the Brahman boy then returned his money. The merchant was 120 secretly thankful that it had been so easy to get his silly son out of this **mess**.

The king of this region had two queens. These two queens were extremely jealous of each other and they argued 125 about everything. Their maids supported them, of course, and argued as bitterly as their queens. One day, each queen sent her servant to the marketplace. By chance, both maids went to the same 130 store at the same time and unfortunately wanted to buy the same melon. An argument developed.

"Excuse me, but I was just going to buy that melon."

135 "Oh, what a pity. I got it first."

"Yes, but you got it first because you pushed in front of me."

"Excuse me, I didn't push in front of you."

"You did! My hand was just reaching out 140 to pick it up and you pushed in front."

"I didn't !"

"You did!"

"I didn't!"

"You did!"

145 "Did not!"

"Did!"

"Did not!"

They began to argue so loudly that the store owner ran away in fear. The 150 two girls fell out of the store onto the ground, pulling each other's hair and hitting each other.

The merchant's son was passing, heard the maids fighting and stopped to 155 watch them, as his father had instructed him to. One of the maids noticed the merchant's son and ordered him to be her witness.

"You saw that! She hit me!"

160 The other maid interrupted. "No, she hit me! You saw her, didn't you! You're my witness."

They continued fighting until suddenly one of them said, "Oh dear! Look at 165 the time. My queen's expecting me."

They both immediately picked themselves up, shook the dirt from their dresses, gathered their shopping and hurried back to the palace.

170 When the two maids returned to the palace, they told their queens all about the argument. The queens were naturally very angry and complained to the king. The maids had also told their 175 queens about the witness who had seen everything. Each queen ordered the merchant's son to be her maid's witness or have his head cut off. The king sent a messenger to the merchant's house 180 with his queens' commands.

The merchant and his son were very worried when they received these commands.

"We need to see the Brahman boy 185 immediately and ask him what to do," said the father.

They rushed to the little store and told the Brahman boy the whole story. He thought for a moment and said, "This 190 is a difficult situation. I can help you, but it will cost 500 rupees."

The merchant happily paid this. The boy's face became very serious. He took a deep breath, closed his eyes for 195 a moment, opened his eyes and said, "When they call you to the palace, pretend to be crazy. Pretend that you don't understand anything."

The next day, the king called 200 the merchant's son to the palace as a witness. The boy behaved as the Brahman boy had instructed him to. Eventually the king lost patience with this madman and ordered him out of 205 the palace. The merchant's son was

delighted with this success and told everyone about the Brahman boy's great wisdom. The Brahman boy was soon well-respected in the marketplace.

210 But the merchant wasn't happy. His son would now have to pretend to be crazy for the rest of his life or the king would find out and cut off his head. So the merchant and his son went back to
215 the Brahman boy for more wisdom. For another 500 rupees, the Brahman boy advised them to go back to the king at a carefully chosen time and tell him the whole story.

220 He told them, "If you approach him at the right time, when he's relaxed and in a good mood, he'll think it's funny and forgive you. But choose your time well. Make sure he's in a good mood."

225 The merchant's son followed his advice. He went to the palace on a beautiful warm evening as the sun was setting. He felt that no one could be in a bad mood on a beautiful evening like this. It
230 was after dinner and he knew the king had eaten well because kings always eat well. The guards presented him to the king. He was right. The king was in a very good mood.

235 The merchant's son told him the whole story and **begged** for the king's **forgiveness** for doing such a silly thing. The king thought the story was very funny and forgave him. He told him not

240 to worry as everyone makes mistakes sometimes.

When the merchant's son had left the palace, the king sat alone, thinking about the story. He was very curious
245 about this Brahman boy and his special talent. So he sent for the boy and asked him if he had any more wisdom to sell.

The Brahman boy said, "Of course. I have plenty to sell, especially to a king. But my
250 wisdom isn't cheap. It will cost you 100 000 rupees."

The king didn't hesitate. He paid him 100 000 rupees and the Brahman boy followed his usual routine. He sat, he
255 thought, he looked carefully at the king's face and then at the sky above. Then he took a deep breath, closed his eyes, opened them again and wrote on a piece of the king's special paper. When he had
260 finished writing, he folded the piece of paper, **waved** his hand over it three times and gave it to the king. On the piece of paper, the king read the words, "Think deeply before you do anything."
265 The king thought this advice was very wise and he had it written in gold letters on all his royal plates and cups and sewn on his fine pillows and sheets so he would never forget it.

270 Some months later, the king became very sick. He didn't realize that one of his queens and his minister were planning his murder. As part of their plan, they

had paid the king's doctor to put poison into his medicine. One night, when the king was taking his medicine, he lifted his golden cup up to his lips and just before he started to drink, he noticed the words he had had written on the cup: "Think deeply before you do anything." Without suspecting anything, the king thought about the words, lowered his cup and looked at the medicine in it.

The doctor, who was standing there watching this, became very nervous. He was full of **guilt** and fear, certain that the king had guessed that his medicine was poisoned.

While the king was lying there thinking, the doctor suddenly threw himself at his feet and cried, "Forgive me, my king!"

Before the king could say anything, the doctor told him what the queen and the minister were planning and how they had involved him. He then began to cry and begged again to be forgiven.

The king was completely shocked at first, but as soon as he had recovered, he called his guards and had the doctor locked up. He then sent for his minister and his wife. When the guards brought them into his room, the king told them what had just happened and that he had put the doctor in prison.

His wife immediately said, "Oh, I'm so pleased! I always knew that man was crazy, but this wild story he's invented is proof."

"Crazy, you say? Wild story, you say?" answered the king. "Let's see who's telling the truth. Drink my medicine."

The queen immediately fell at the king's feet, admitted her guilt and begged for his forgiveness. The minister just stood there silently looking very depressed. The king ordered his guards to take them both away and cut off their heads.

The Brahman boy was then sent for by the king. When the guards brought the boy into his room, the king thanked him for saving his life. He made the boy his new minister and arranged for him to live in the palace. A fine apartment and beautiful clothes were prepared for him. The boy lived happily in the palace as a wealthy man of honour and remained the king's most trusted adviser for the rest of his life.

"Wisdom for Sale," *World Folktales*, Edinburgh Gate, Pearson Education Limited, 2003, pp. 36–42.

After You Read

Step 1   Explore the text—What did you understand?

> Answer the questions below with complete sentences.

> Compare your answers with a partner or your class.

1. What is the first piece of advice described in the story?

2. Do you understand why the merchant is upset that his son paid for the piece of advice? Explain.

3. What happens when the merchant's son doesn't follow the advice?

4. The Brahman boy advises the merchant's son to pretend to be crazy when he goes to the palace. What is the problem with this advice?

5. Why does the king want to meet the Brahman boy?

6. What advice does the Brahman boy give the king?

7. How does this advice save the king?

8. How much money does the Brahman boy earn from his "wisdom store" in the story?

Step 2   Establish a personal connection with the text—Reflect.

> Answer these questions using complete sentences.

> Share your opinions with a partner or your class.

1. Many people read their horoscope in the paper every day. Often they are looking for wisdom that will help them make better decisions. What questions do people want answered when they read their horoscope?

2. Can you name five jobs that exist today where people are paid for the advice they give to others?

3. Read the following pieces of advice and decide whether they are good or bad and explain why, for example:

   - You should go to bed before midnight if you want to feel more rested.
   - You should always keep the door of your house locked even when you are inside.
   - You should never eat ice cream because it is fattening.
   - You should move to an English-speaking city if you want to learn English quickly.
   - You should always answer your cellphone—no matter the circumstances.
   - You should work out two or three times a week to stay in good physical condition.

4. Folktales are loved by many people because they give good advice and make us think about our lives. Name the lessons that you learned in the following folktales:

   Hansel and Gretel   *The Three Little Pigs*
   Beauty and the Beast   *Little Red Riding Hood*

Step 3 **Generalize beyond the text—Take the story further.**

"Wisdom for Sale" is related to Unit 9, which focuses on people improving the lives of others around the world. In this short story, the Brahman boy helps others by using his talent and passion.

Follow the steps that you use in the Final Task for the Writing Process: Prepare, Write, Revise, Edit and Publish.

> Choose one of the following assignments.
> Write 100–150 words.
> Use the Smart Reference section (pages 268–280) to check verb tenses and other Smart Structures.

1 Make a list describing:
  a) Advice that you received in your life—Explain which advice was good, which was bad, and why; or
  b) Advice that you would give to someone who wants to become bilingual in English.

  > Use direct and indirect speech.

2 Write a role play in pairs. One student is the Brahman boy and the other is the customer. The customer should think of ten problems that the Brahman boy will solve.

  > Perform the role play in front of the class so that your classmates can decide whether the Brahman boy's advice is good or bad.
  > Use modals and the future tense.

3 Interview the Brahman boy about his life with the king after the end of the story. Invent the rest of the story, but make it more realistic. Folktales almost always end with the sentence: "... and they lived happily ever." However, in real life, problems arise from time to time.

  > Use question words and question formation.

4 Summarize a folktale that you like or write a folktale of your own. Make sure that the folktale teaches a lesson and has a happy ending. Read the folktale to your class.

  > Include a problem and a solution, and add illustrations.
  > Use the simple past tense.

5 Transpose "Wisdom for Sale" to today's world. What would the Brahman boy sell today? Who would replace the role of the king? How would the story end?

  > Use the simple present tense.

After Twenty Years
Based on a story by O. Henry

Facts

O. Henry is the pen name of American author William Sydney Porter (1862–1910). He wrote around four hundred short stories and is best known for his ability to write "twist" endings. Most of his stories are set in New York City in the early part of the twentieth century and deal with ordinary people, such as police officers, servers and store owners.

"After Twenty Years" is set on a dark New York City street on a wet and windy night. "Silky" Bob is waiting for his childhood friend Jimmy. They made a promise twenty years earlier to meet on this night on this particular street corner. A passing police officer questions Bob about what he is doing there on such a miserable night. Bob explains the strange meeting and the police officer, satisfied with his story, leaves Bob to wait for his pal. Finally Jimmy arrives, or at least Bob thinks that the man is Jimmy ...

Before You Read

Part A Vocabulary

If you understand the important words before you read a text, you will enjoy the story even more. Become familiar with the new vocabulary first.

> Read the definitions below. Then find the words in bold type in the story that match these definitions.

> Write out the definitions and their matching words. For example:
> Definition: *light rain* Word: *drizzle*

Definitions

1. pulled
2. equipment for the home and garden
3. thick, heavy stick
4. shine from a very bright light
5. light rain
6. very small amount or sign of something
7. restaurant
8. permanent mark on the skin
9. sudden strong movements of air
10. having a square-shaped jaw

Part B Strategies

Strategies can help you understand when you read a story in a second language. Here are two strategies you can use when reading this story:

> Focus. Don't be distracted.
> Use the pictures as clues to help you guess what the story is about.
> Decide whether the statements below are true or false. Explain which clues helped you predict the answers.

1. The story takes place during a winter night.
2. The two men portrayed in the story are best friends.
3. One of the men goes to jail at the end of the story.
4. The story is about an event that happened a few years ago.

While You Read

Taking notes while you read will help you understand what is happening in the story.

> Make a story map by writing down important information about the story in note form.

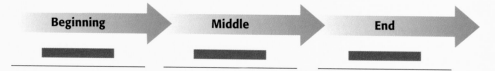

Beginning	Middle	End

After Twenty Years

The police officer on the beat moved up the avenue. The time was barely ten o'clock at night, but chilly **gusts** of wind with a **hint** of rain kept people off
5 the streets.

The neighbourhood was one that kept early hours. Now and then you might see the lights of a cigar store or of an all-night **diner**; but the majority of
10 the doors belonged to businesses that had long since been closed.

About halfway down the block the police officer suddenly slowed his walk. In the doorway of a darkened **hardware**
15 store a man leaned, with an unlighted cigar in his mouth. As the police officer walked up to him, the man spoke up quickly.

"It's all right, officer," he said. "I'm just
20 waiting for a friend. It's an appointment made twenty years ago. Sounds a little funny to you, doesn't it? Well, I'll explain if you'd like to make certain everything is OK. About that long ago there used to be
25 a restaurant where this store stands—Big Joe Brady's restaurant."

"Until five years ago," said the police officer. "It was torn down then."

The man in the doorway struck a match
30 and lit his cigar. The light showed a pale, **square-jawed** face with keen eyes, and a little white **scar** near his right eyebrow.

"Twenty years ago tonight," said the man, "I ate here at Big Joe Brady's with Jimmy
35 Wells, my best friend, and the finest friend in the world. He and I were raised here in New York, just like two brothers, together. I was eighteen and Jimmy was twenty. The next morning, I left for the
40 west to make my fortune. You couldn't have **dragged** Jimmy out of New York; he thought it was the only place on Earth. Well, we agreed that night that we would meet here again exactly twenty
45 years from that date and time, no matter what our conditions might be or from what distance we might have to come. We figured that in twenty years, each of us ought to have our destiny worked out
50 and our fortunes made—whatever they were going to be."

"It sounds pretty interesting," said the police officer. "It's been a long time. Haven't you heard from your friend since
55 you left?"

"Well, yes, for a time we corresponded," said the other. "But after a year or two, we lost track of each other. But I know Jimmy will meet me here if he's alive,
60 for he always was the truest friend in the world. He'll never forget. I came a thousand miles to stand in this door tonight, and it's worth it if my old partner turns up."

65 The waiting man pulled out a handsome watch decorated with small diamonds.

"Three minutes to ten," he announced. "It was exactly ten
70 o'clock when we parted here at the restaurant door."

"Did pretty well out west, didn't you?" asked the police officer.

"You bet! I hope Jimmy has done half as
75 well. He was kind of slow, though, but a nice fellow. I've had to compete with

some of the people in my business. A man gets comfortable in New York. It takes the west to put a razor-edge
80 on him."

The police officer twirled his **club** and took a step or two.

"I'll be on my way. Hope your friend comes around all right. Are you going
85 to wait for him if he's late?"

"Yes!" said the other. "I'll give him half an hour at least. If Jimmy is alive on Earth, he'll be here by that time. So long, officer."

90 "Good night, sir," said the police officer, continuing along his beat, trying doors as he went.

There was now a fine, cold **drizzle** falling, and the wind had risen. The few
95 people passed quickly and silently with coat collars turned high and their hands in their pockets.

About twenty minutes he waited, and then a tall man in a long overcoat, with
100 collar turned up to his ears, hurried across from the opposite side of the street. He went directly to the waiting man.

"Is that you, Bob?" he asked, doubtfully.

105 "Is that you, Jimmy Wells?" cried the man in the door.

"Bless my heart!" he exclaimed, grasping his friend's hands with his own. "It's Bob, sure as fate. I was certain I'd find you
110 here if you were still alive. Well, well, well! Twenty years is a long time. The old gone, Bob; I wish it had lasted, so we could have had another dinner there. How has the west treated you, old man?"

115 "It has given me everything I asked it for. You've changed lots, Jimmy. I never thought you were so tall."

"Oh, I grew a bit after I was twenty."

"Doing well in New York, Jimmy?"

120 "Moderately. I have a position in one of the city departments. Come on, Bob;

we'll go around to a place I know of, and have a good long talk about old times."

The two men started up the street, arm
125 in arm. The man from the west, his egotism enlarged by success, was beginning to outline the history of his career. The other, covered by his overcoat, listened with interest.

130 At the corner stood a drugstore, brilliant with electric lights. When they came into this **glare**, each of them turned simultaneously to gaze upon the other's face.

135 The man from the west stopped suddenly and released his arm.

"You're not Jimmy Wells," he snapped. "Twenty years is a long time, but not long enough to change a man's nose."

140 "It sometimes changes a good man into a bad one," said the tall man. "You've been under arrest for ten minutes, 'Silky' Bob. Chicago thought you may have come our way and contacted us. Now, before
145 we go to the station, here's a note I was asked to hand you. You may read it here at the window. It's from Officer Wells."

The man from the west unfolded the little piece of paper handed him. His
150 hand was steady when he began to read, but it trembled a little by the time he had finished. The note was rather short.

"Bob: I was at the meeting place on time. When you struck the match to light your
155 cigar, I saw it was the face of the man wanted in Chicago. Somehow I couldn't do it myself, so I went around and got a plainclothes man to do the job. Jimmy."

After You Read

Step 1 Explore the text—What did you understand?

> Answer the questions below with complete sentences.

> Compare your answers with a partner or your class.

1. What promise did Jimmy and Bob make to each other?

2. How old is Jimmy in the story? How old is Bob?

3. Did Jimmy and Bob keep in touch over the years? Which sentence proves this?

4. Who is the police officer?

5. How did the police officer know Bob had "made his fortune"?

6. How do the weather and the time of day help the police arrest Bob?

7. How does Jimmy finally arrest Bob?

8. Name two physical characteristics that describe Bob.

9. Why didn't Bob realize that the man who came to meet him wasn't his friend Jimmy?

10. Henry was known for his "twist" endings. What is the twist at the end of this story?

Step 2 Establish a personal connection with the text—Reflect.

> Answer these questions using complete sentences.

> Share your opinions with a partner or your class.

1. Do you think that Patrolman Wells made the right decision by turning in his friend? Why or why not? What would you do if you were a police officer and your best friend was a known criminal? What is more important— obeying the law or being loyal to a friend? Explain your answers.

2. Have you made plans with a friend to meet in the far future? What do you think your life will be like then? What do you think your friend's life will be like? How do you think you and your friend will change in the future? Explain your answers.

3. Think of reasons why Bob was arrested. What types of crimes could he have committed?

4. Which strategies did you use to help you understand the story? Did they help you? Why or why not? Which ones would you use next time? Did you predict the meaning of the illustrations correctly?

5. What did you enjoy about this story? Do you enjoy reading stories with "twist" endings, or do you prefer other kinds of stories? Explain your answers.

Step 3 Generalize beyond the text—Take the story further.

In Unit 10, you learned about spies and about what it takes to be a great spy. In this story, the police officer uses spying techniques to help him catch a criminal.

> Choose one of the following assignments.

> Write 150–200 words.

> Use the Smart Reference section (pages 268–280) to check verb tenses and other Smart Structures.

1 Write a front page news article about the capture of "Silky" Bob to explain the events of the story.

> Include pictures of "Silky" Bob, Patrolman Wells and New York City in the early 1900s.

> Use direct and indirect speech.

2 Rewrite the story as a play using dialogue.

> Write a script with dialogue for each of the three characters in the story.

> Find two other people and perform your version of the story. Dress up in costumes and use props to enhance the performance.

3 Make a travel pamphlet of New York in the early 1900s.

> Describe interesting places that people would want to visit in the city and include early pictures of the places.

> Use the features of a pamphlet (see the Smart Stop on page 16 of the Student Book).

4 Do research on this author or another author you really enjoy. What is special or surprising about her/his life? Which short stories or novels did she/he write?

> Find information in magazines or on the Internet.

> Use the simple past tense.

> Add an illustration of the author.

5 Transform the story into a comic book.

> Rewrite the story using dialogue.

> Use the comic strip in Unit 5 (pages 102–103) as a model.

> Illustrate the story and bind it so that it looks like a comic book.

Talk

Words Review

Structures

Texts

Strategies

Processes

Ideas to Improve Your English

Talk

These short sentences or sentence starters will help you when speaking English.

Greetings, Identification, Leave-Taking

Good morning / Good afternoon / Good evening
What's your name?
Nice to see you again.
Pleased to meet you.
I would like you to meet Steph.
Nice talking to you.
See you later.
Goodbye.
Sorry, I have to go.

Take care.

Telephone Talk

Hello, this is Cara speaking.
I'll call you back later.
She is not here at the moment.
Would you like to leave a message?
How do you spell your name?
Could you ask him to call me back?

Who is calling?

Fillers and Discourse Markers

Just a moment …
I mean …
First of all, …
On the other hand, …

Wait a minute.

Feelings, Interests, Tastes, Preferences, Opinions

My favourite is …
I prefer …
I think that …
I disagree …
In my opinion, …
I don't mind.
I enjoy …

I like …

Teamwork, Encouragement, Feedback

It's my turn.

Let's do it together.
Whose turn is it? Who's next?
Who wants to do the first part?
Do you want to …?
Let's divide the work.
We should try …
What do you suggest?
We did a great job.
We worked well together.
I would like to work with you next time.

Apologies

I'm sorry.

Please forgive me.
Excuse me.

Warnings

Watch out!

Be careful.
You should not …
It's not a good idea.
Danger!
Watch your step!

Capabilities

I can do that!

I know how to …
Do you know how to …?
I think we can do this …

Permission

Could you ...?

Is it alright if I ...?
Can I /May I?

Requests for Help / Information / Clarification

How do you say ...?
Can you explain this again?
What do you mean?
Can you repeat that please?
Is it okay if ...?
Can I help you?

Can you help me?

Suggestions

Let's ...

Would you like to ...
What do you say we ...
Do you want to ...

Goal Setting

I need to improve ...
Next week, I will ...
Our team wants to ...

My goal is to ...

Reflecting

My strong point is ...

I understand this text.
I used this strategy ...
This was difficult for me because ...
I participated very well.
I need to focus on ...

 **Smart**

Words Review

 A

achieved = accomplished

acquaintance = person you know

afford = be able to pay

amp = piece of electronic equipment used to make sounds louder

annoyed = not happy

apologize = express regret

appeal = attraction

at the end of the day = finally

attract = make someone interested

awkward = embarrassing

B

backdrop = painted cloth hung at the back of a stage

ban = prohibition

barely = almost not at all

bid = attempt

bleak = cold and without comfort

borough = area or section of a city

broad = wide

bucket = container

C

carpooling = travelling in a car together and sharing the costs

casual = not formal

chill out = relax

clog = block

commute = travel to and from a job each day

compelling = important

complain = protest, criticize

complexion = colour, texture and appearance of a person's skin

conduct = carry out

conspicuous = standing out

counterpart = someone with an equivalent job

coverage = attention given to a story in the media

cover song = song written, performed and made famous by other bands

cozy = warm and comfortable

crease = line in the eyelid

crooked = not straight

crowd = large group of people

crowded = occupied by many people

cruise = travel at a constant speed

crushed = feeling terrible because you failed at something

cupboard = compartment used to store food, cookware and tableware in the kitchen

 D

dabble = do or be involved in something, but not in a serious way

daycare = childcare service

dead-end street = situation that offers no advantages

deadline = date by which something should be done

deal with = do what is necessary to solve a problem or situation

deserve = merit

detail = list or give all the facts or information

dexterous = skilled with the hands

dismay = surprise

drawn into = pulled or guided into

dread = fear

drool = let saliva run from the mouth

drop out = leave

E

encounter = meet

 F

feat = achievement requiring great courage

field = area

flunk = fail

flustered = confused

foreign = relating to a country that isn't your own

forgiveness = when someone stops being angry with another person

fossil fuels = oil, gas or coal

freckles = small patches of light brown colour on the skin

frugal = buying only what is necessary

fuel-efficient = consuming little energy

G

gather = bring together

gig = concert where musicians and bands play

gimmick = trick to attract attention

gleaming = shiny

glove = covering for the hand

go cold turkey = stop suddenly

grades = points for an exam or work

grassroots = ordinary people who promote something they believe in or enjoy

greenhouse gases = chemicals that cause the earth's temperature to rise

ground floor = first floor

H

hang out = spend time

harbour = contain

heal = become healthy again

heap = pile

high-ranking = very important

hire = employ

hospitality = food, drink and lodging services

huddle = curl up in a small space

I

issue = problem or question

J

jargon = special words or expressions used in a particular job

jarring = shocking

jive = get along

K

kinesthetic = related to body movement

knickers = underwear

L

lack [verb] = miss, need

leisurely = in a slow and relaxed way

lessen = diminish

liability = disadvantage

lineup = line of people waiting

link = connection to another website

live and learn = discover from your experiences

low-cut = showing a lot of skin

lung = organ used to breathe

lyrics = words in a song

M

mall patron = person who shops at a shopping centre

mate = someone with whom you work or do an activity

mean = not nice

measure up = be good enough

messy = dirty

mind-blowing = amazing

misdeed = illegal or immoral act

N

neat = clever and useful

network = meet and talk to people who may be useful to your work

novel = book

O

opponent = person or team you are playing against

outgoing = friendly and sociable

outrage = strong reaction

overlook = ignore

overseas = in a foreign country

P

pace = speed

PA system = equipment that makes someone's voice loud enough to be heard by a group of people (short for "public address" system)

payoff = return on an investment

perpetrator = person who does something illegal

pitfall = danger or difficulty

plagued = irritated

plot = secret plan

ponder = think about

practitioner = person who practises a tradition

processed = modified

prod = push quickly
purchase = buy
puzzle = confuse

R

rail-thin = very thin
rate = speed
recipient = person who receives something
refrain = stop
rehearsal = practice
reliable = dependable
relieved = not feeling distressed or anxious anymore
rod = straight metal bar
run into = meet by chance

S

scapegoat = person blamed for mistakes or faults of another
self-talk = talking to yourself
shift = change
shout = talk very loudly
skein = tangled piece
slanted = prejudiced
sleek = smooth and attractively shaped
slum = district inhabited by very poor people
spouse = husband or wife
spread the word = pass on a message
springboard = diving board
stick up for = defend
stoop = porch with steps in front of a building
strength = quality or ability
stride = progress
stride = walk with long steps
surgeon = doctor who operates
sustainable = used without destroying the environment

T

thigh = part of the leg between the hip and the knee
thin = fall out
thoughtful = serious and quiet
throw = make an object move through the air
tidy = neat
touch base = talk with a person for a short time
transparent = open to public observation

trial = examination of evidence by a judge and/or jury to decide guilt
trustworthiness = quality of a person who deserves the confidence of others

U

unclad = without clothes
undercover = working secretly
undergo = experience
unencumbered = unrestricted
unusual = different, strange
upset = angry

V

voucher = coupon

W

waif-like = very skinny
waste = material that goes in the garbage
wave = move your hand and arm in the air
weak = not strong
wealthy = rich
wedding = marriage
well-being = feeling of being healthy and happy
widespread = happening in many places
wiki = collaborative website that allows people to add, remove and edit content
witness = see an event
wrap things up = finish
wrench = tool used for turning a bolt

Structures

Present Tenses

<table>
<tr><td colspan="2">

Simple Present Tense

Monday Tuesday Wednesday Thursday   Friday   Saturday Sunday

*I **play** my guitar every day.*

</td><td colspan="2">

Present Progressive Tense

now

*I **am playing** my guitar right now.*

</td></tr>
</table>

Simple Present	Present Progressive
Use the simple present	**Use the present progressive**
• For actions that occur every day or express a routine *We **have** band practice every Monday.* *He **practises** every day.* • For a general truth *Amps **are** heavy.* *My father **plays** guitar in a band.* • For likes and dislikes *I **love** heavy metal music.* *She **doesn't like** jazz.*	• To describe an action taking place right now *I **am enjoying** the show.* *He **is playing** drums now.* *They **are missing** band practice.* • To describe an action that will take place in the near future *I **am singing** in a band tonight.* *Mary **is doing** an audition soon.* *Sam **is playing** a guitar solo soon.*
Rules for the simple present • Add *-s* for the third person singular. • Add *-es* for words ending in *sh*, *ch*, *s*, *x* and *o*. • Subject + verb + rest of sentence *He **wants** to be famous.* *She **watches** music videos.* *It **gets** crowded at concerts.*	**Rules for the present progressive** **Affirmative** • Subject + verb *to be* + main verb + *ing* *I **am singing**.* *You **are watching** TV.* *She/He **is trying** to perform.* *We/They **are rehearsing** on stage.*
• Pay attention to the verb *to be*. *I **am** (**I'm**) happy to perform.* *You **are** (**You're**) a good singer.* *She/He/It **is** (**She's**/**He's**/**It's**) nice.* *We **are** (**We're**) good musicians.* *They **are** (**They're**) very skilled.*	**Negative** • Subject + verb *to be* + *not* + main verb + *ing* *I **am not going**.* *You **are not buying** the tickets.* *She/He **is not listening** to the music.* *We/They **are not dancing**.*
Key Words: every day, all the time, usually, sometimes, often, never	**Key Words:** now, at this moment, today, tonight, soon, Look! Listen!

Past Tenses

Simple Past and Past Progressive Tenses

yesterday now

*Yesterday I **talked** to my teacher about LOVE.* (simple past; action completed)
*Yesterday I **was talking** to my teacher when a journalist came into the classroom.* (past progressive; action in progress)

Simple Past	Past Progressive
Use the simple past	**Use the past progressive**
• For actions that began and ended in the past *I **talked** to a friend yesterday.* *He **did not use** his car last week.* ***Did** she **send** her poem in November?* Remember that there are two categories of verbs: regular and irregular. Regular verbs end in *ed.* *I **explained** the situation.* Irregular verbs vary (see page 270 of the Smart Reference section). *I **understood** the problem.*	• To describe an action that took place in the past during a specific time frame *Yesterday, I **was playing** hockey between 4:30 and 6:30 p.m.* *I **wasn't trying** to be rude during the meeting.* ***Were** you **crying** at the end of the movie?* • To describe a longer action that was taking place in the past when it was interrupted by a shorter action *I **was speaking** to my mom when my dad came into the room.* Remember to form the past progressive with: the verb *to be* in the past + the main verb + *ing.* *I **was helping** my mom in the kitchen.*
Key Words: last night, yesterday, two minutes ago, today, last month	**Key Words:** between … and …, during, when, while

Present Perfect Tense

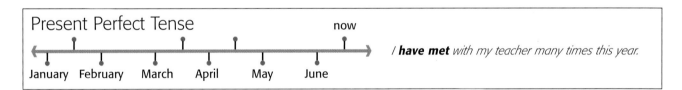

now

*I **have met** with my teacher many times this year.*

January February March April May June

Present Perfect
Use the present perfect
• When an action happened at an unspecified time *He **has** already **been** to Japan.* • When an action started in the past and continues in the present *I **have** only **lived** here for a year.* • When several actions occurred in the past at different times *Gangsters **have disturbed** us many times over the years.* Remember to form the present perfect with the auxiliary *to have* in the present + the past participle (see the irregular verb chart on page 270 of the Smart Reference section). *I **have thought** about it.*
Key Words: already, for the past few days, once, twice, yet, many times, before, since

List of Irregular Verbs

Base Form	Simple Past	Past Participle
1. **awake**	awoke	awoken
2. **be**	was, were	been
3. **beat**	beat	beaten
4. **become**	became	become
5. **begin**	began	begun
6. **bend**	bent	bent
7. **bet**	bet	bet
8. **bid**	bid	bid
9. **bite**	bit	bitten
10. **bleed**	bled	bled
11. **blow**	blew	blown
12. **break**	broke	broken
13. **bring**	brought	brought
14. **build**	built	built
15. **burn**	burnt	bunt
16. **buy**	bought	bought
17. **catch**	caught	caught
18. **choose**	chose	chosen
19. **come**	came	come
20. **cost**	cost	cost
21. **cut**	cut	cut
22. **deal**	dealt	dealt
23. **dive**	dove	dove
24. **do**	did	done
25. **draw**	drew	drawn
26. **dream**	dreamt	dreamt
27. **drink**	drank	drunk
28. **drive**	drove	driven
29. **eat**	ate	eaten
30. **fall**	fell	fallen
31. **feed**	fed	fed
32. **feel**	felt	felt
33. **fight**	fought	fought
34. **find**	found	found
35. **fly**	flew	flown

Base Form	Simple Past	Past Participle
36. **forbid**	forbade	forbidden
37. **forget**	forgot	forgotten
38. **forgive**	forgave	forgiven
39. **freeze**	froze	frozen
40. **get**	got	gotten
41. **give**	gave	given
42. **go**	went	gone
43. **grow**	grew	grown
44. **hang**	hung	hung
45. **have**	had	had
46. **hear**	heard	heard
47. **hide**	hid	hidden
48. **hit**	hit	hit
49. **hold**	held	held
50. **hurt**	hurt	hurt
51. **keep**	kept	kept
52. **know**	knew	known
53. **lead**	led	led
54. **leave**	left	left
55. **let**	let	let
56. **lie**	lay	laid
57. **lose**	lost	lost
58. **make**	made	made
59. **mean**	meant	meant
60. **meet**	met	met
61. **pay**	paid	paid
62. **put**	put	put
63. **read**	read	read
64. **ride**	rode	ridden
65. **ring**	rang	rung
66. **run**	ran	run
67. **say**	said	said
68. **see**	saw	seen
69. **sell**	sold	sold
70. **send**	sent	sent

Base Form	Simple Past	Past Participle
71. **set**	set	set
72. **shake**	shook	shaken
73. **shoot**	shot	shot
74. **shut**	shut	shut
75. **sing**	sang	sung
76. **sit**	sat	sat
77. **sleep**	slept	slept
78. **slide**	slid	slid
79. **speak**	spoke	spoken
80. **spend**	spent	spent
81. **split**	split	split
82. **spread**	spread	spread
83. **stand**	stood	stood
84. **steal**	stole	stolen
85. **stick**	stuck	stuck

Base Form	Simple Past	Past Participle
86. **sting**	stung	stung
87. **stink**	stank	stunk
88. **swear**	swore	sworn
89. **sweep**	swept	swept
90. **swim**	swam	swam
91. **take**	took	taken
92. **teach**	taught	taught
93. **tell**	told	told
94. **think**	thought	thought
95. **throw**	threw	thrown
96. **understand**	understood	understood
97. **wake**	woke	woken
98. **wear**	worn	worn
99. **win**	won	won
100. **write**	wrote	written

Pronouns and Possessive Adjectives

Subject Pronoun	Object Pronoun	Reflexive Pronoun	Possessive Pronoun	Possessive Adjective
Acts as the subject	Acts as an object	Refers to the subject	Acts as a marker of possession and defines ownership	Indicates ownership
I	Me	Myself	Mine	My
You	You	Yourself	Yours	Your
He, she, it	Him, her, it	Himself, herself, itself	His, hers	His, her, its
We	Us	Ourselves	Ours	Our
You	You	Yourselves	Yours	Your
They	Them	Themselves	Theirs	Their
She *saved my life.*	*She saved* **me**.	*He repaired it* **himself**.	*The idea is* **yours**.	*The community rewards* **its** *heroes.*

Prepositions

about	among	beneath	except	into	on top of	since	until
above	around	beside	for	like	onto	through	up
across	at	between	from	near	out of	to	upon
after	before	by	in	of	outside	toward	with
against	behind	down	in front of	off	over	under	within
along	below	during	inside	on	past	underneath	without

Questions

Question Word	Refers to	Example
Who?	a person	**Who** speaks English?
What?	an object, a thing, a name	**What** city do you want to see?
Where?	a place	**Where** do you live?
When?	a time or a date	**When** were you born?
Why?	a reason	**Why** do you like to speak English?
Whose?	a belonging	**Whose** father speaks English?
Which?	a distinction	**Which** city do you prefer?
How?	a way, a manner	**How** are you today?

How can be used together with many adjectives:
How far? How big? How long? How interesting? How many?

How many is used for things you can count (friends, desks, people):
How many classmates watch English programs on TV?
How many video games do you have?

How much is used for things you can't count (sugar, coffee, money):
How much English do you speak?
How much money do you have?

Information Questions

There are two ways to form information questions using question words:

question word	verb "to be"	rest of question		
What	are	coins?		
Where	is	Australia?		

question word	auxiliary	subject	verb	rest of question
Where	do	you	want	to travel?
Why	does	the teacher	speak	so fast?

Yes/No Questions

There are two ways to form yes/no questions:

verb "to be"	subject	adjective	answer	
Are	you	bilingual?	Yes, I am.	
Is	your mother	American?	No, she isn't.	

auxiliary	subject	verb	rest of question	answer
Do	you	understand	Chinese?	Not really.
Does	she	speak	Greek?	Yes, she does.

Modals

Function	Modal	Example
Possibility	**may, might**	*I **might** take your advice.*
Capability	**can, could**	*I **could** lower my tone of voice.*
Permission	**may, can**	***Can** I forward this e-mail?*
Suggestion or advice	**should**	*You **shouldn't** eat with your fingers.*
Obligation	**must, have to**	*You **have to** follow these rules.*
Intention or promise	**will**	*I **will** try to change my behaviour.*
Politeness	**would, could**	***Would** you help me, please?*

Future Tense

Will and *Be Going To*		
Use **will** or **be going to** to express the future tense.		

	Will	**Be Going To**
Affirmative	*Claudia **will** use the right fork.*	*He **is going to** eat with his fingers.*
Negative	*Claudia **will not** use the right fork.*	*He **is not going to** eat with his fingers.*
Question	***Will** Claudia use the right fork?*	***Is** he **going to** eat with his fingers?*

Use **will** or **be going to** to express a prediction.
*We **will** invent new etiquette rules.*   *We **are going to** invent new etiquette rules.*

Use **be going to** to express a plan.
*I **am going to** learn etiquette rules.*

Use **will** to express an intention.
*I **will** answer the phone.*

You will often hear people using the informal pronunciation of **going to**: "**gonna**." Even though it is technically incorrect, you can use **gonna** when speaking. However, you shouldn't use it when writing:

incorrect *I'm **gonna** help with these new rules.*   correct *I'm **going to** help with these new rules.*

Key Words:
tomorrow, later, next week, today

Conditional Form

Would
Use would
• For general situations *I* **would** *help you, but I don't have the time.*
• For polite requests **Would** *you help me, please?*
• For a repeated action in the past *When I lived in Québec, I* **would** *go to soccer practice every week.*
• For preference when combined with the word *rather* *I* **would** *rather go to the cinema than stay at home.*
Contracted form
• I **would**–I'**d** I **would not**–I **wouldn't**

Could
Use could
• For capability *I* **could** *help you tomorrow.*
• For polite requests **Could** *you do this for me, please?*
• For expressing certainty in the negative form *Charles-Alexandre* **could not** *have failed the exam.*
• For suggestions *We* **could** *go to the next tournament.*
Contracted form
• She **could not**–she **couldn't**

Should
Use should
• For advice *You* **should** *come early so that we have enough time to do our homework.*
• For suggestions *You* **should** *talk to the art teacher about your project.*
• For high probability *Maika* **should** *do well in her driving exam.*
Contracted form
• She **should not**–she **shouldn't**

Intensifiers

Intensifiers are adverbs that enhance other adverbs and adjectives. In English, they come before the words that they modify.

Mr. Bessette, our English teacher, is **really** *busy right now.*   (*really* modifies the adjective *busy*)
I'm a **little** *tired today.*   (*little* modifies the adjective *tired*)
You performed **extremely** *well..*   (*extremely* modifies the adverb *well*)

Pay attention when you use the intensifier **very**.

• **Very** cannot modify a verb.

   incorrect   *I* **very** *like competition.*   correct   *I am* **very** *competitive.*

• You can use **very much** to modify a verb.

   incorrect   *I* **very much** *like competition.*   correct   *I like competition* **very much**.

Here are more examples of intensifiers:

too, very, really, fairly, rather, little, enough, totally, extremely, definitely

Comparative and Superlative Adverbs

Adverbs

An adverb is an adjective that used to describe a verb.
She writes **quickly**. (The adverb *quickly* describes the verb *writes*.)

An adverb is formed by adding *-ly* to the end of an adjective.
quiet → **quietly**

If the adjective ends in *-y* (for example, *happy*), you change the *y* to an *i* and then add *-ly*.
happy → **happily**

Exceptions:
Some adjectives stay the same when they become adverbs, for example: **fast**, **hard**, **early** and **far**.

Forming Comparative and Superlative Adverbs			

For adverbs ending in *-ly*, add the word *more* to form the comparative and the words *the most* to form the superlative.

Adjective	Adverb	Comparative Adverb	Superlative Adverb
quiet	quietly	more quietly	the most quietly
careful	carefully	more carefully	the most carefully
happy	happily	more happily	the most happily

Adjective → *Jeff is* **quiet**
Adverb → *Jeff works* **quietly**.
Comparative adverb → *Jeff works* **more quietly** *than Steve.*
Superlative adverb → *Jeff works* **the most quietly** *of all the students.*

Pay attention: Usually the comparative adverb is followed by *than*.

Exceptions			

For most exceptions, add *-er* to form the comparative and *-est* to form the superlative.

Adjective	Adverb	Comparative Adverb	Superlative Adverb
hard	hard	harder	the hardest
fast	fast	faster	the fastest
early	early	earlier	the earliest
good	well	better	the best
bad	badly	worse	the worst
far	far	farther	the farthest

Adjective → *Karen is a* **fast** *runner.*
Adverb → *Patricia runs* **fast**
Comparative adverb → *Mary runs* **faster** *than John.*
Superlative adverb → *Mary runs* **the fastest** *of all the runners on the team.*

Count and Non-Count Nouns

Count Nouns (Nouns That Can Be Counted)

There is a singular and a plural form of count nouns.
*A **gift** / two **gifts***
*An **hour** / two **hours***

Use *there is* when a singular noun follows.
***There is** one gift on the table.*

Use *there are* when a plural noun follows.
***There are** two gifts on the table.*

To indicate a small quantity, use *a few*, or *many* in the negative form.
*There are **a few** posters.*
*There are**n't many** posters.*

To indicate a large quantity, use *many* or *a lot of*.
*There are **many** gifts under the tree.*
*There are **a lot of** presents given at Christmas.*

Non-Count Nouns (Nouns That Can't Be Counted)

Groups of objects
Equipment, furniture, hair

Masses
Rice, sand, sugar

Fluids
Milk, gasoline, water

Abstract ideas
Happiness, love, sadness

Usually non-count nouns have no plural form.
*I need **sunshine** in my garden. (*not *sunshines)*

Non-count nouns don't take articles (*a, an, the*).
*I need to do **homework** tonight. (*not *a homework)*

To indicate a small quantity, use *a little* or *much* in the negative form.
*There is **a little** ice cream left.*
*There is**n't much** ice cream left.*

To indicate a large quantity, use *much* or *a lot of*.
*Will it take **much** time?*
*There is **a lot of** money in my wallet.*

Expressions of Quantity (Used with Both Count and Non-Count Nouns)

Some
*There are **some** cookies in the jar.* (count noun)
*I hope there is **some** sunshine this afternoon.* (non-count noun)

Any
*Do you have **any** presents for me?* (count noun)
*Is there **any** coffee left?* (non-count noun)

Enough
*I don't have **enough** potatoes to make the soup.* (count noun)
*We have **enough** money to buy a car.* (non-count noun)

Plenty of
*There are **plenty of** mountains in Switzerland.* (count noun)
*She has **plenty of** money in the bank.* (non-count noun)

No
*There were **no** squirrels in the park today.* (count noun)
*We have **no** time left to finish the project.* (non-count noun)

A piece of
*I had **a piece of** apple and a muffin for a snack.*
*Julia has **a piece of** furniture for sale that would look great in your room.*

Articles

Definite Article (the)

Use the
- When talking about something we have already talked about
  *Do you remember **the** e-mail hoax I told you about?*
- When there is only one of it in the world
  ***the** Internet,* ***the** sky,* ***the** Earth*
- In front of an important title
  ***the** Prime Minister of Canada*
- In front of newspaper names, buildings, hotels
  ***the** Gazette,* ***the** CN Tower,* ***the** Château Frontenac*

Indefinite Articles (a, an)

Use a / an
- In front of nouns that you can count
  (*apples, dogs,* …)
  *I read **a** webpage. She read **an** e-mail.*
- In front of professions (dentist, teacher, …)
  *He is **a** computer technician.*
- When giving the rate or pace of something
  *fifty megabytes (MB) **a** second*

Gerunds

Gerunds
Gerunds are verbs (verb + *ing*) that have the same function as a noun.
A gerund can be the subject of a sentence. **Swimming** *transforms your body.*
A gerund can be the object of a sentence. *Katherine is always **dieting**.*
Certain verbs are followed by a gerund, for example: *admit, appreciate, avoid, consider, enjoy, finish, imagine, practise, risk, suggest* *I imagine **changing** my body.*
Some verbs are followed by the infinitive, for example: *agree, appear, ask, choose, decide, expect, hope, learn, promise, wish* *I decided **to stay** the way I am.*
Be careful—Some verbs can be followed by either a gerund or an infinitive, for example: *begin, continue, forget, hate, like, love, prefer, remember, start, try* *Andrew hates **to see** his friend sad.* *Andrew hates **seeing** his friend sad.*

Rules for Forming Gerunds
If the verb ends in *e*, drop the *e* and add *ing*. *phone* → **phoning**
If the verb ends with a single consonant, double this final consonant. *plan* → **planning**
If you use the negative form, put *not* before the gerund. *We talked about **not getting** a tattoo this year.*

Punctuation

Punctuation	When to Use It	Example
Period (.)	To finish a sentence	*We decided to form a band.*
Question mark (?)	At the end of a question	*How are you today?*
Comma (,)	To list items To separate two phrases	*I bought a computer, a CD, a CD player and pens.* *Before you take the plane, call me.*
Apostrophe (')	In contractions To show possession	*I'm going downtown.* *Simone's daughter wants to go to Africa.*
Colon (:)	Before a list Before an explanation	*I need the following ingredients: eggs, fruit, sugar and butter.* *There is only one solution: Take it easy.*
Semi-colon (;)	To join related sentences into one sentence	*My father did not want to go to the beach; it was too hot.*
Hyphen (-)	For compounds words For numbers For some prefixes	*Science-fiction* *Thirty-eight* *Ex-boyfriend*
Quotation marks (" ")	To indicate quoted or spoken language	*My father said, "Be careful tonight."*

Passive Voice

Passive Voice	
Use the passive voice • To be more polite. • To appear more objective (fact-based rather than expressing an opinion). • When you don't know who is doing the action.	**Compare:** *People cause traffic accidents.* (active voice) *Traffic accidents are caused by people.* (passive voice)

To make an active sentence passive, follow these steps:

1 Move the object of the sentence into the subject position (at the beginning of the sentence).
People *cause* **traffic accidents.** → **Traffic accidents** *are caused by* **people.**
Subject   Object

2 Change the main verb to the past participle. (See irregular verb list, page 270.)
People **cause** *traffic accidents.* → *Traffic accidents are* **caused** *by people.*

3 Add the verb *to be* to the original verb and conjugate it correctly.
Make sure to use the same verb tense as in the original sentence.
People cause traffic accidents. → *Traffic accidents* **are** *caused by people.*

4 If necessary, add the preposition *by*.
People cause traffic accidents. → *Traffic accidents are caused* **by** *people.*

Examples

Simple present tense:
Car accidents **kill** *pedestrians every year.*
(active voice)
Pedestrians **are killed by** *car accidents every year.*
(passive voice)

Simple past tense:
They **introduced** *two new hybrid cars on the market.*
(active voice)
Two new hybrid cars **were introduced** *on the market.*
(passive voice)

Capitalization

Rule	Example
1 The first letter in a sentence	**S**he is my best friend.
2 The pronoun "I"	**I** think **I** will go to bed early.
3 Days and months	**M**onday, **F**riday
4 Places	**M**exico, **L**ac **S**t-**J**ean
5 Events	**T**he **O**lympics
6 Holidays	**N**ew **Y**ear's **D**ay, **M**other's **D**ay
7 Languages	**S**panish, **G**erman
8 Organizations	**T**oronto **P**olice **D**epartment
9 Planets	**E**arth, **M**ars
10 In titles (the first and last words, all the nouns, adjectives, verbs and adverbs)	**L**ittle **R**ed **R**iding **H**ood

Direct and Indirect Speech

Here is what you have to do when you change direct speech to indirect speech:

1 Start your sentence by reporting what was said. Common expressions used are: *said that, reported that, mentioned that, …*

2 Change the verb tense:

Direct Speech	Indirect Speech
*I **am** scared of terrorists.*	*Mr. Singh said that he **was** scared of terrorists.*
If the verb tense is the …	**Change it to the …**
Simple present (*I **walk**.*)	Simple past (*He **walked**.*)
Simple past (*I **walked**.*)	Simple past (*He **walked**.*)
The simple past usually stays the same in reported speech, but it is sometimes changed to the …	Past perfect (*He **had walked**.*)
Future (*I **will walk**.*)	Conditional (*He **would walk**.*)
Present progressive (*I **am walking**.*)	Past progressive (*He **was walking**.*)

3 Change the pronoun:

Direct Speech	Indirect Speech
"***I** am scared of terrorists.*"	*Mr. Singh said that **he** was scared of terrorists.*
Change the subject pronoun in the first person …	**To the third person:**
I We	He, she They

4 Change the time reference:

Direct Speech	Indirect Speech
*Mr. Singh: I am scared of terrorists **now**.*	*Mr. Singh said that he was scared of terrorists **at that moment**.*
If the person says …	**Change it to …**
this evening *today / this day* *these days* *now* *yesterday* *a week ago* *last weekend* *here* *next week* *tomorrow*	*that evening* *that day* *those days* *at that moment* *the day before* *a week before* *the weekend before / the previous weekend* *there* *the following week* *the next day / the following day*

Connectives

Cause and Effect

One action influences another. This is called cause and effect. Connectives help you link one action with another.

- Using **because**, **because of** and **due to**

  Because is followed by a subject and a verb.
  Because *the speech was powerful, people decided to help.*

  Because of and **due to** are followed by a noun.
  Because of / Due to *the powerful speech, people decided to help.*

- Using the conjunctions **therefore**, **consequently** and **so**

  Pay attention to punctuation. A comma or a period is usually used immediately in front of a conjunction.
  The humanitarian help didn't arrive on time. **Therefore / Consequently**, *people died.*
  The humanitarian help didn't arrive on time, **so** *people died.*

- Using **such ... that** and **so ... that**

  Such ... that is used with an adjective and a noun.
  It was **such** *a good idea* **that** *we copied it.*

  So ... that is used with an adjective or an adverb.
  The organization is **so** *popular* **that** *it needs ten new volunteers every month.*

Contrast

Certain actions have their limits. Connectives help you express a contrast of ideas.

- Using **although**, **but ... anyway**, **despite**, **even though**, **however**, **nevertheless**

  Even though *it was a great initiative, it didn't work out.*
  They raised a lot of money **despite** *the problems they encountered.*
  Thousands of students participated in the fundraiser. **Nevertheless,** *not enough money was raised.*

Conditions

Connectives also help you express conditions associated with certain actions.

- Using **otherwise** and **or else**

  Otherwise and **or else** are used differently, but have the same meaning.
  I always eat breakfast. **Otherwise**, *I can't concentrate.*
  I always eat breakfast, **or else** *I can't concentrate.*

Texts

Internal and External Features of Texts

When you read, listen to or view a text, you have to notice the internal and external features.

Internal Features	External Features
• What is the topic of this text? • What type of language is used? • What are the text components?	• What is the goal of the text? To express feelings and opinions? To inform? To direct or influence? • Who is the audience? • What culture does the text refer to?

Here is an example from a newspaper article.

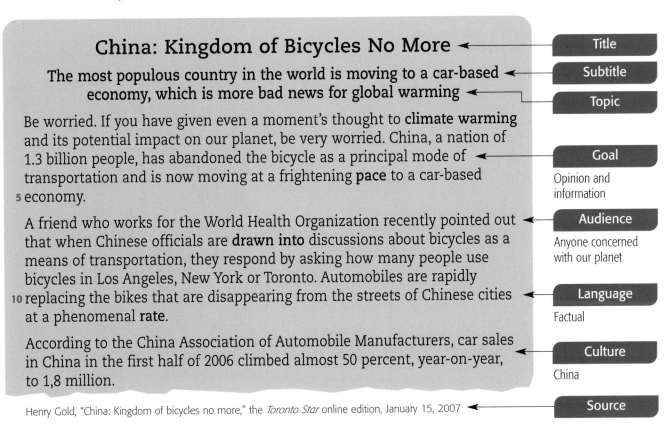

China: Kingdom of Bicycles No More ← Title

The most populous country in the world is moving to a car-based ← Subtitle
economy, which is more bad news for global warming ← Topic

Be worried. If you have given even a moment's thought to **climate warming** and its potential impact on our planet, be very worried. China, a nation of 1.3 billion people, has abandoned the bicycle as a principal mode of ← Goal transportation and is now moving at a frightening **pace** to a car-based
5 economy.

Opinion and information

A friend who works for the World Health Organization recently pointed out ← Audience that when Chinese officials are **drawn into** discussions about bicycles as a means of transportation, they respond by asking how many people use bicycles in Los Angeles, New York or Toronto. Automobiles are rapidly
10 replacing the bikes that are disappearing from the streets of Chinese cities ← Language at a phenomenal **rate**.

Anyone concerned with our planet

Factual

According to the China Association of Automobile Manufacturers, car sales ← Culture in China in the first half of 2006 climbed almost 50 percent, year-on-year, to 1,8 million.

China

Henry Gold, "China: Kingdom of bicycles no more," the *Toronto Star* online edition, January 15, 2007 ← Source

Features of a Poster or an Ad

Headline

The **headline** is noticed by 30 percent of the people who see the poster. It reinforces the poster's message.

Tips and tricks: Make it short (fewer than five words). Play on emotion: Make people laugh, feel angry or think.

Visual

The **visual** part of a poster is the picture or photograph. It is noticed by 70 percent of the people who see it. It is the most important part because it establishes the message of your poster.

Tips and tricks: Use photographs because people are more attracted to realistic images. Choose the colours in your images carefully to attract people.

Body / Text

The **body / text** is noticed by only 5 percent of the people who see the poster. For this reason, there isn't always text on a poster. When there is text, it comes under the headline. The sentences making the point of the poster and giving arguments appear here.

Tips and tricks: Keep the text short and simple. Use facts and statistics if you can.

Signature

The **signature** is noticed by 15 percent of the people who see the poster. It refers to the brand name, the logo or the name of the organization, company or creator.

Tips and tricks: Use bright or contrasting colours to make the signature stand out.

60 Watt Bulb, Stony and friends

present

The Food Bank Benefit Concert

Saturday, February 18
Doors open at 8 p.m.
Tickets: $12 at the door; $10 with a can of food
Legion Hall Café, 873 Greenwood

A Moore Musick Production

Internal Features	External Features
Things to include	**Things to think about**
• An interesting visual • A clear topic / idea • Simple language • A clear headline • Important information	• Who is looking at the poster • What they need to know • What colours will attract attention • Where to put the poster so that it will be seen

Features of a Letter

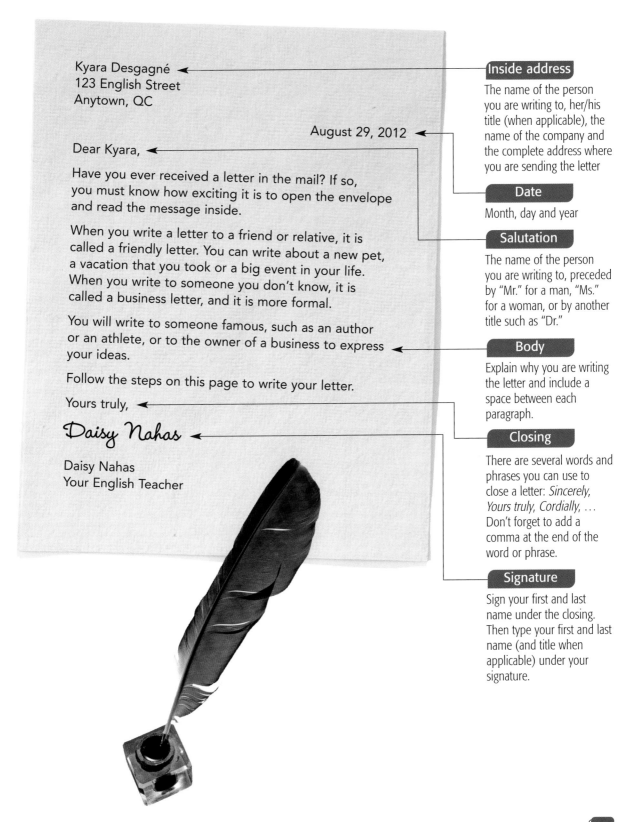

Kyara Desgagné
123 English Street
Anytown, QC

August 29, 2012

Dear Kyara,

Have you ever received a letter in the mail? If so, you must know how exciting it is to open the envelope and read the message inside.

When you write a letter to a friend or relative, it is called a friendly letter. You can write about a new pet, a vacation that you took or a big event in your life. When you write to someone you don't know, it is called a business letter, and it is more formal.

You will write to someone famous, such as an author or an athlete, or to the owner of a business to express your ideas.

Follow the steps on this page to write your letter.

Yours truly,

Daisy Nahas

Daisy Nahas
Your English Teacher

Inside address

The name of the person you are writing to, her/his title (when applicable), the name of the company and the complete address where you are sending the letter

Date

Month, day and year

Salutation

The name of the person you are writing to, preceded by "Mr." for a man, "Ms." for a woman, or by another title such as "Dr."

Body

Explain why you are writing the letter and include a space between each paragraph.

Closing

There are several words and phrases you can use to close a letter: *Sincerely, Yours truly, Cordially, …* Don't forget to add a comma at the end of the word or phrase.

Signature

Sign your first and last name under the closing. Then type your first and last name (and title when applicable) under your signature.

Features of a Form

Hospital logo →

🌲

SNOWY HILL HOSPITAL

FAMILY MEDICAL CENTRE

Personal information →

Name:		Age:	Sex: ❑ M ❑ F	Birth Date:
Street Address:		City:		Postal Code:
Mailing Address: ❑ Same as above ❑ Other		City:	Postal Code:	Religion:
Home Phone:		Work Phone:		Ext: / Dept:
Employer:		Address:		How Long?:
Medicare? ❑ Yes ❑ No	Medicare No.:	Social Insurance No.:		Referred by:

Personal information
Patient's parent or spouse →

FATHER or HUSBAND

Name:		Legal Guardian: ❑ Yes ❑ No		Birth Date:
Street Address:		City:		Postal Code:
Home Phone:	Work Phone:		Ext: / Dept:	Social Insurance No.:
Employer:	Address:			How Long?:

MOTHER or WIFE

Name:		Legal Guardian: ❑ Yes ❑ No		Birth Date:
Street Address:		City:		Postal Code:
Home Phone:	Work Phone:		Ext: / Dept:	Social Insurance No.:
Employer:	Address:			How Long?:

Emergency information
Person to contact in case of emergency →

In Case of Emergency (Friend or Relative Not Listed Above. ONE MUST BE LOCAL)

Name (1):		Address:	
Home Phone:	Work Phone:		Relation:
Name (2):		Address:	
Home Phone:	Work Phone:		Relation:

List Any Immediate Family Member(s) Already Under the Dr.'s Care

Name:	Relation:	Name:	Relation:

Insurance information →

INSURANCE INFORMATION (A Copy of All Insurance Cards Is Required for Filing Purposes.)

Primary Insurance:	Name of Insuree & Social Insurance No.:
Group No.:	Insuree's DOB:	Other Insurances (cont'd on back):

Authorization →

I hereby assign to Snowy Hill Hospital all payments for medical services rendered to myself or my dependants. I understand that I am responsible for any amount not covered by insurance. The above registration information is correct to the best of my knowledge and I understand and accept the above payment policy.
I hereby authorize Snowy Hill Hospital to provide information to my insurance carriers concerning my medical care and that of my dependants.

Signature →

_____   _____
Date   Signature of patient (or parent / legal guardian if patient is a minor)

Features of Video Media

Camera Shot: The camera shot dictates what you will—and will not—see.

	Close-up	Medium Shot	Long Shot
Shot:	• Usually focuses on a person's face	• Shows a person from the waist up	• Shows an entire scene (several people, a room, etc.)
Effect:	• Used for interviews • Shows details	• Used for interviews • Shows a person in her/his surroundings	• Shows the context of what is happening

Tilted Angle, Close-up Shot

Camera Angle: The camera angle is the direction and height from which the camera shoots the scene.

	Tilted	High	Low
Angle:	• The camera films from at least a forty-five degree angle	• The camera is above the person or object being filmed	• The camera is beneath the person or object being filmed
Effect:	• Makes a banal shot look more interesting	• Makes the person or object being filmed look less important	• Makes the person or object being filmed look important or even threatening

High Angle, Medium Shot

Transition Techniques: A sequence of shots in a scene that are joined together.

Transition Technique	Used for
Pan left / right Moving from one part of the set to another	• Giving the viewers the impression that they are in the room and seeing the story through their own eyes
Cut Ending one shot and immediately starting another	• Ending one storyline and starting another • Changing the focus to another character • Changing the location of the storyline
Fade in / out Gradually showing / ending a shot	• Indicating the end of a sequence or the end of the movie • Indicating death or the afterlife
Dissolve Turning one shot into another	• Signalling the passing of time • Signalling a change in the location of the storyline

Low Angle, Long Shot

Features of a Brochure

A brochure is a pamphlet containing pictures and information about a product or service.

Panel 1:

On the front cover, there is the title, topic or idea and maybe a logo or something to surprise the reader.

Panels 2, 3, 4:

On the three inside panels, there is a lot of information and text.

Panel 5:

On the right-side panel, there is a summary of the information found on the three other inside panels.

Panel 6:

On the back cover, there is information about the author, such as the author's name, address, telephone number and e-mail address, as well as a website address to visit for more information.

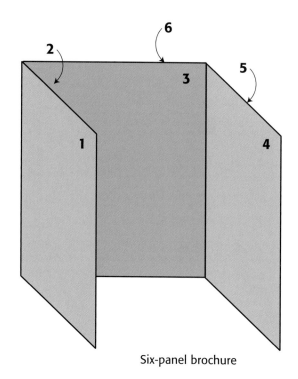

Six-panel brochure

Features of a Pie Chart

Impaired Driving in Canada

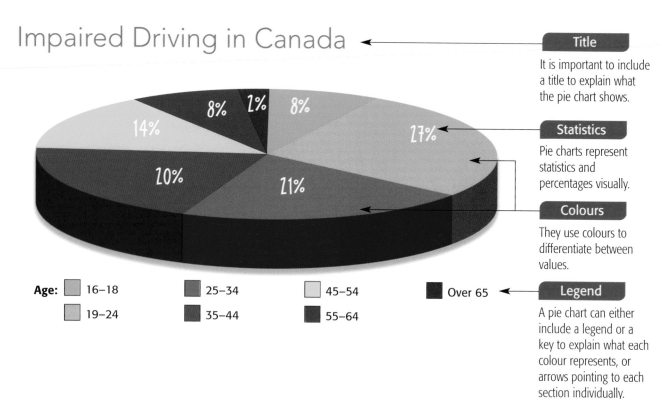

Age: 16–18 · 19–24 · 25–34 · 35–44 · 45–54 · 55–64 · Over 65

Title

It is important to include a title to explain what the pie chart shows.

Statistics

Pie charts represent statistics and percentages visually.

Colours

They use colours to differentiate between values.

Legend

A pie chart can either include a legend or a key to explain what each colour represents, or arrows pointing to each section individually.

Features of a Sticker

Picture

This bumper sticker includes a picture that matches the slogan.

Slogan

This bumper sticker uses a simple slogan to get its message across clearly.

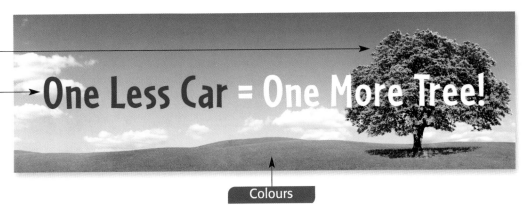

One Less Car = One More Tree!

Colours

This bumper sticker uses bright colours to attract your attention.

Features of a Blog

Blog Entry Title **Blog Title** **Blog Entry Date**

From the Garage

Getting Started
January 20, 2008

I started taking guitar lessons when I was in grade three, but I didn't like my teacher, so I stopped. In grade nine, my friend Bruce introduced me to a great guitar teacher named Elliot. Bruce and I both took guitar lessons from Elliot for a few years.

Then, in grade ten, I got together with a few other kids from my school and decided to form a band to play at the school talent show. Bruce played keyboards and I played guitar. We were really into '60s and '70s rock.

We practised hard for that show. The day before, we thought we were great and we were really excited. The show was a disaster. Our first song was terrible. I remember shaking so badly that I could hardly play. I was completely confused because all the notes I was playing sounded wrong, but I had practised them and they were supposed to be right! After the show, we learned that one of the guitarists had tuned the guitars and bass to the wrong key. We actually played through the entire song that way and then played one more song before getting off the stage. We were so inexperienced. I was **crushed**. **Live and learn**, I guess. I was upset for a while, but then I started thinking about next year ...

I didn't give up, but kept on playing in bands. We used to jam in the basement at my parents' house. Most of my neighbours hated the noise so much that they moved!

Since then, I have played in at least twenty bands, toured the country several times, played in Europe, released a dozen or so albums and recorded a few hundred songs.

I started teaching music five years ago and I love it. One of the best things I do is to encourage young musicians to find other people to play in a band with. When you have a goal like performing together at a show, it really motivates you to practise a lot and get better.

Teaching music is part of my whole experience with music. Music is my life.

Photo

Age: 38
Gender: Male
Occupation: Professor of Stringology*
Location: Montréal, Canada

Profile

Interests		Favourite Music			
Teaching guitar and bass	Coaching bands	Rock	Metal	Punk	Ska
Playing and writing songs	Cycling	Funk	Acid jazz	Electro	
Producing and recording music					

*Stringology isn't a real word in English—it is a joke. The suffix *-ology* is the study of something. For example, psychology is the study of the psyche (or mind). Jon made up this word as a joke because many musical instruments, such as guitars, have strings.

How to Find the Main Idea

When you read a text, it is important to be able to identify its message. Are you able to find the main idea, or do you remember only the details?

Imagine that your friend asks you about the movie you saw last night. Can you tell your friend the main message of the movie in one sentence?

The main idea in a text is normally found in the introductory paragraph. In a paragraph, the main idea is usually the first sentence.

How to Write a Paragraph

Paragraphs usually include three types of sentences:

1 The topic sentence describes the main idea.

2 The supporting sentences provide more information and prove, explain and give examples about the topic sentence. These sentences often start with:

First, Second, Third, …

3 The closing sentence repeats the main idea of the paragraph in different words.

A tattoo is a fashionable thing to have. (Topic sentence with the main idea)

Teenagers all over the world are getting them done. (Supporting sentence)

They can choose from thousands of designs. (Supporting sentence)

A tattoo costs about … (Supporting sentence)

In my class, five students have tattoos because tattoos are fashionable. (Closing sentence)

Example:

Tattoos Are In

Tattoos are a fashionable thing to have. Teenagers all over the world are getting them. If you visit a tattoo shop, you can choose from thousands of designs, suited to every taste. The demand for tattoos has increased dramatically in the last few years and so have the prices. You should know that the price of a tattoo depends on its size. I interviewed all the students in my class—Five students have one. They decided to get a tattoo because it was a fashionable thing to do.

How to Avoid Plagiarism

When you write different types of texts, you look for sources in magazines and books and on the Internet to make your text more credible. To avoid copying someone else's words, here are a few tips:

- Highlight the important information in the source.
- Take point-form notes while you are reading the source. Don't write complete sentences when taking notes.
- Use your own words. Avoid making only slight variations in the language and then thinking that it is your own.
- Let the reader know the source of the information.
- Indicate which passages are taken directly from the source by putting them in quotation marks.
- At the end of your text, indicate the references for the sources in a bibliography as described below.

How to Write a Bibliography

The following information should be included when indicating references for your sources in a bibliography:

Books
Author's last name, author's first name. Book title (*in italics*), city of publication: name of publisher, year published, pages used. For example:

Canfield, Jack. *Chicken Soup for the Teenage Soul*, Deerfield Beach: Health Communications Inc.,1997, pp. 232–235

Magazine Articles
Author's last name, author's first name. Title of article (in quotation marks), name of magazine (*in italics*), volume number (where applicable), date of issue, pages used. For example:

Mahoney, Rosemary. "Phenomenal Woman—Sabriye Tenberken," *O, The Oprah Magazine*, August 2005, pp. 223–225 and 237–238

Internet Sites
Author's last name (if unavailable, write "unknown"), author's first name. Title of article or web page (in quotation marks), site name (*in italics*), date site was accessed, site address (URL). For example:

Author unknown. "Get Involved," *Student Action*, May 16, 2008, http://www …

The Internet is an amazing tool that allows easy access to information without leaving home. However, you must be careful when using Internet sources, because some sites contain false information. Always consult at least two websites on the same topic to confirm that the information is correct.

How to Take Notes

Notes are a useful reminder of what you read, listened to, watched or thought about. Here are important rules to remember when taking notes:

1 Determine the purpose of the notes. What will you use them for: to help you study for a test, to answer questions, to compare two texts? The purpose of the notes will help you decide how to organize them (point form, Venn diagram, chart, …).

2 Keep it simple. Try to use only a few words or important ideas.

3 Use your own words to avoid plagiarism and to help you understand the notes later on.

4 Use symbols whenever you can, for example:

# = number	:) = funny idea
+ = additional information	!!! = important
@ = at	? = not understood / not clear
* = essential information	≠ = not equal

5 Don't worry about spelling and grammar.

6 Use different coloured pens and highlighters to help you remember things, for example, blue for ordinary, red for important:

The spies did their training *at a* secret location in northern Québec.

7 Write words on different parts of the page. Spread out your ideas and use arrows and lines to connect them.

Here are different ways to take notes quickly and efficiently and to organize ideas on a page:

Point Form
This is the most common form of note-taking. Summarize your ideas in a few words and use bullets to separate your ideas.

Diagrams and Word Webs
A Venn diagram allows you to compare ideas. In a Venn diagram, you put ideas that are different in the separate parts of the circles and ideas that are the same in the parts of the circles that overlap.

A word web is helpful when you have to answer many questions at once. It allows you to organize the information according to the question asked, quickly and easily.

Charts
You can use a simple chart to help you organize your ideas into lists and then compare ideas.

You can also use a KWL chart to reflect on what you already **K**now, what you **W**ant to know and what you have **L**earned about a topic.

Strategies

Communication Strategies

Tricks to Help You When You Are Speaking

1 Use gestures.

Use your body and your facial expression to express a message. They speak too.

2 Repeat what the person said to make sure you understand.

> **Sam:** *"It doesn't matter if you come after supper."*
>
> **Eve:** *"I am not sure I understand the expression: it doesn't matter. It means it's O.K., no problem?"*
>
> **Sam:** *"Yes, that's it!"*

3 Say it another way.

If people don't understand what you are saying, say it in a more simple way.

> **Eve:** *It's a quarter to nine.*
>
> **Sam:** *Excuse me. Can you repeat please?*
>
> **Eve:** *It's eight forty-five.*

4 Take your time.

Take your time to think before you give an answer.

> **Sam:** *What do you think about video games?*
>
> **Eve:** *One moment please, let me think …*

5 Substitute.

Replace the word you want to use by other words.

> **Eve:** *I have to go to see the boss of the school …*
>
> **Sam:** *Oh, you have to go and see the principal.*

6 Don't panic.

Try not to be stressed when you are speaking English. Learning a new language is difficult for everyone. Relax.

7 Ask the person to repeat.

Don't be shy. When you are learning English, you hear a lot of new sounds. Ask the person to say it again. Maybe you will understand the second time if the person speaks slowly.

Can you repeat, please?

Excuse me, what did you say?

8 Take a risk.

Even when you are not sure, try to say it in English. Do not say it in French. Make an effort!

Learning Strategies

Tricks to Help You Learn Better and Faster

1 Direct your attention.

Focus on your work. Don't let the distractions affect your concentration.

2 Plan what you have to do.

Ask yourself: What do I have to do? What resources do I need? Plan in steps:
- First, I will find ideas on the Internet.
- Second, I will write a draft.
- Third, I …

3 Self-evaluate.

Reflect on what you learned.

What are my strong points? What do I need to improve? How do I learn?

4 Set goals.

Give yourself some objectives for each semester or each week. What do you want to improve?

5 Pay attention.

Decide in advance what you will notice while reading or listening to a text.

6 Create opportunities to practise English outside of the classroom.

Watch TV shows and movies, read magazines, surf the Internet, speak in English with people you know.

7 Self-monitor.

Check and correct your mistakes. If you realize that you made a mistake when you are speaking, correct it right away.

She like pizza; no, excuse me, she likes pizza.

Tricks to Help You When You Are Working

1 Start with what you know.

Start with what you know when:
- you are reading a text
- you are listening to an audio recording or watching a video
- you are starting a project

2 Infer.

Make guesses based on the context, on words you know, on visual clues.

3 Recombine.

Use what you learned in a new way:

Sam: *I'll call you tonight.*

Eve: *O.K., I'll wait for your call!*

4 Take notes.

Write down the important information, highlight the difficult words, use a colour code, use abbreviations, connect ideas together, use cue cards when you are presenting.

5 Compare.

Note similarities and differences in a text. Use a Venn diagram.

6 Practise.

Use English all the time. Practice is the best way to learn!

7 Scan.

Look for specific information in a text (you don't always have to read the entire text). For example, find the date, the address, the name of the boy …

8 Transfer.

Use what you learned in a new context.

9 Delay speaking.

Take time to listen and speak when you are ready!

What do you think, Tony?

I am not sure. Give me some time to think about it.

10 Predict.

Make hypotheses with what you know: the title, the subtitles, and with pictures …

11 Skim.

Read through a text quickly to get a general overview.

12 Use graphic organizers.

Group ideas in a clear way.

Tricks to Help You Encourage Yourself and Ask for Help

1 Ask for help, repetition, clarification.

Never hesitate to ask for further explanations.

Can you explain this to me again?

2 Cooperate.

Work with others to achieve a common goal.

3 Encourage yourself and others.

Talk to yourself and others in a positive way.

Here are some things you can say to encourage yourself and others:
Don't give up!
You are doing really well!
Keep going!
I am getting better!
I did it!
I can do it!

4 Reward yourself.

Congratulate yourself when you are finished with a task.

5 Ask questions.

When you don't understand something, ask your teacher or partner to answer your questions.

What is my role?

When will we meet for the project?

What is your phone number?

6 Develop cultural understanding.

Talk to English speakers. Learn about English culture.

7 Lower anxiety.

Do not panic when you are speaking English. Remind yourself of your goals and the progress you made.

8 Take risks.

Experiment with English without the fear of making errors.

Processes

Response Process

There are different ways you can respond to a text:

> You can write your notes in a journal.
> You can answer reflection questions.
> You can discuss it with your class partners.
> You can write a sketch or do an improvisation about what you learned.
> You can put the new information in graphic organizers (word webs, Venn diagrams, timelines).
> You can do a collage of important illustrations.

Step 1 Explore the text individually.

Before You Read

> Think about what you know.
> Make predictions based on the title, the illustrations, the sounds.
> Make sure that you know which information you need to find. Read the comprehension questions.
> Decide which strategies you will use (skim, scan, direct attention, …).

While You Read

> Confirm or reject predictions.
> Answer questions.
> Identify elements that are important.
> Visualize the people, places or events in the text.
> Pause to reflect on what is difficult to understand.
> Look for words that are similar to French words.
> Use a graphic organizer.
> Look up difficult words in the dictionary.
> Make personal connections.
> Ask for help if you don't understand.

After You Read

> Answer questions.
> Write down notes, reactions, opinions, questions, information.
> Organize information.
> Make links with the text.
> Reread the text if necessary.

Examples of sentence starters:

I learned / noticed that …
I did not understand …
I found … very interesting …
I relate to the main character …
I agree / disagree …

Step 2 Explore the text with partners.

> Share what you think is important in the text.
> Ask questions.
> Give feedback to others.
> Take notes.
> Leave traces of what you understood.

Step 3 Establish a personal connection with the text.

> Make links to the text with your opinion, experiences, interests and feelings.
> Use learning strategies (compare, recombine).
> Use resources (a dictionary, other texts).
> Share your opinion with others.

Examples of sentence starters:

I experienced something similar …
I know someone who …
If I were in that situation, …
Now that I know this, I will …

Step 4 Generalize beyond the text.

> Learn about yourself.
> Think about how you can use what you learned in other situations.
> Develop a sense of community.

Examples of sentence starters:

This problem also exists …
This is caused by …
I think people should …
We could …

Writing Process

Step 1 **Prepare**

> Think about what you already know about the topic.

> Brainstorm topics and ideas.

> Define your purpose. Why are you writing this text? To express an opinion? To inform? To influence?

> Define your target audience. Who are you writing this text for? Teens? Adults? Children?

> Plan. Decide how you will present your project (an informative text, a letter, a poem …).

> Organize your ideas into an outline.

> Do research. Use resources (books, magazines, newspapers, the Internet).

Step 2 **Write**

> Write down ideas, opinions, thoughts and feelings.

> Write a rough draft based on your plan.

> Review your plan and adjust it.

> Ask partners for their opinions. Ask for help.

Step 3 **Revise**

> Reread your text and verify the organization of your ideas.

> Reflect on what you wrote.

> Clarify your ideas to express the purpose of your text.

> Ask someone to look at your text and give your feedback. Consult your teacher.

> Add, substitute or remove ideas and words. Rewrite your draft with the change.

Step 4 **Edit**

> Use resources to help you correct grammar and spelling (Smart Reference section, dictionaries, grammar references).

> Correct spelling mistakes, capital letters, punctuation and sentence structure.

> Check if you used the correct verb tenses.

> Write a final copy.

Step 5 **Publish**

> Present your text to your teacher and your classmates.

> Reflect on and evaluate your work.

Production Process

Step 1 Prepare

> Find a group to work with and distribute roles.

> Think about what you already know about the topic.

> Brainstorm topics and ideas.

> Define your purpose. Why are you producing this text? To express an opinion? To inform? To influence?

> Define your target audience. Who are you producing this text for? Teens? Adults? Children?

> Plan. Decide how you will present your project (poster, video, audio recording, web page, …).

> Organize your ideas into an outline.

> Do research. Use resources (books, magazines, newspapers, the Internet).

> Use strategies (take notes, use a graphic organizer).

> Validate your ideas and make adjustments to your plan.

Step 2 Produce

> Create the media text using strategies and resources.

> Use media conventions and techniques.

> Use information and communication technologies (ICT).

> Present your media text to a small group and ask for feedback.

> Make changes based on the feedback you receive.

> Edit and add final touches.

Step 3 Present

> Present your media text to the class.

> Reflect on the audience's reaction, cooperation in your group, the final product and your goals for future productions.

Ideas to Improve Your English

All the Time

Be confident when you speak even if you make mistakes.
Take your time when you speak.
Practise English every time you can.
Use gestures when you speak.
Practise useful expressions.
Spell new words in your head.
Set goals for yourself.
Encourage yourself.
Have fun!

In the Classroom

Be attentive.
Take notes when your teacher is speaking.
Read out loud with a partner.
Use an English dictionary.
Ask questions.
Help students that are weaker than you.
Be open to learning something new.
Do your homework regularly.
Use the resources in this book.

At Home

Read English magazines and newspapers.
Read English cartoons and stories.
Watch English TV and movies.
Find an English pen pal or e-pal.
Surf the Internet in English.
Play English video games.
Play a board game in English.
Talk to your pet in English.
Decorate your room with posters of English movies.

Out with Friends

Order a meal in a restaurant in English.
Learn an English joke and tell it to your friends.
Listen to and sing English songs.
Make a friend whose mother tongue is English.
Learn an English tongue twister.
Make a list of English words that you want to learn.

Travelling

Travel to a city where people speak English.
Read signs and advertising in English.

Photo Credits

ALAMY
p. 81: AA World Travel Library

ART RESOURCE, NY
p. 6 (left): Marc Chagall's Estate, SODRAC (2008), E. Lessing
p. 17: E. Lessing
p. 34: Marc Chagall's Estate, SODRAC (2008), Giraudon
p. 41: Emmanuel Bellini's Estate, SODRAC (2008), Image Bank ADAGP
p. 52: Salvador Dalí, Fundació Gala-Salvador Dalí, SODRAC (2008), E. Lessing
p. 56: HIP
p. 64 (top): Alberto Giacometti's Estate, SODRAC (2008), E. Lessing
p. 78 (left): E. Lessing
p. 80: H. Lewandowski
p. 91: E. Lessing
p. 94: E. Lessing
p. 98: Max Ernst's Estate, SODRAC (2008), The Metropolitan Museum of Art
p. 106 (right): Bildarchiv Preussischer Kulturbesitz
p. 109: Picasso's Estate, SODRAC (2008), Réunion des Musées Nationaux
p. 129: Réunion des Musées Nationaux
p. 141: Fine Art Photographic Library, London
p. 156: Réunion des Musées Nationaux
p. 180: E. Lessing

BILL HALL
p. 131

CNAC/MNAM
p. 48 (bottom): J.-C. Planchet

CORBIS
p. 1: W. Morgan
p. 2 (top): Comstock
p. 5 (bottom): G. Brown
p. 5 (top): R. Faris
p. 12 (bottom): Images.com
p. 12 (top): V. Berger, zefa
p. 14: B. Pepone, zefa
p. 18: Somos Images
p. 19 (bottom): R. Faris
p. 20: D. Mason
p. 23: A. Strack
p. 24: Somos Images
p. 26: Comstock Select
p. 27 (top): M. Stuckey, Comstock
p. 36: D. Stewart, Photex, zefa

p. 38: Moodboard
p. 39–40: R. Holz, zefa
p. 42: H. Winkler, zefa
p. 45 (bottom, right): B. Bird/zefa
p. 45 (centre, right): C. Boisvieux
p. 47 (bottom, right): O. Graf, zefa
p. 53: J. M. Foujols, zefa
p. 55: R. Friedman
p. 57: G. Steinmetz
p. 65 (bottom, right): P. Guis, Kipa
p. 65 (top, right): Image Source
p. 69: Bettmann
p. 70 (bottom, left): R. Hamilton Smith
p. 70 (top, right): M. Bolton
p. 71: H. Armstrong Roberts
p. 73 (top): Image 100
p. 75: T. Grill
p. 76: R. Estall
p. 77 (below): W. Lockwood
p. 77 (top): B. Krist
p. 83 (bottom): A. Schein Photography
p. 83 (top): R. Faris
p. 84: R. Faris
p. 96 (top): Creasource
p. 100 (right): K. Dodge
p. 100 (left): Bettmann
p. 104: Ausloeser, zefa
p. 108: P. Beck
p. 115: R. Faris
p. 116: J. Hollingsworth
p. 117 (right): B. Thomas
p. 117 (left): P. Saloutos, zefa
p. 118: N. Wheeler, Sygma
p. 122 (left): Duomo
p. 124: Asian Art & Archaeology, Inc.
p. 125: T. Lang
p. 126: D. Ramazani, zefa
p. 128 (right): A. Inden, zefa
p. 128 (left): T. Pannell
p. 130 (right): Duomo
p. 132: E. Hurd
p. 133: M. McGill
p. 134 (top): T. Pannell
p. 135: D. Madison
p. 136 (bottom)
p. 136 (top): K. Dodge
p. 139: J. Hollingsworth
p. 140: K. Singer, bilderlounge
p. 142 (right): L. Aigner
p. 143: J. Craigmyle
p. 144: S. Grewel, zefa
p. 145: A. Peisl, zefa
p. 146: H. Benser, zefa
p. 148: Move Art Management

p. 150: F. G. Mayer
p. 151 (top): A. Strack
p. 152: R. Botterell
p. 157 (bottom): J. L. Pelaez, Inc.
p. 157 (top): T. Pannell
p. 162(1): T. Hase, dpa
p. 162(3): F. Lanting
p. 162(4): Firefly Productions
p. 163: Free Agents Limited
p. 164: D. Tardif, LWA
p. 165: F. McMahon
p. 166 (bottom): P. Turnley
p. 166 (top): M. Reynolds, epa
p. 175 (bottom)
p. 176: Duomo
p. 177: A. Strack
p. 178: Car Culture
p. 179 (top): Car Culture
p. 181 (bottom): epa
p. 181 (top): Car Culture
p. 185 (bottom, right): R. Botterell
p. 185 (bottom, left): S. Westmorland
p. 185 (centre, right): B. Vogel, Solus-Veer
p. 185 (centre, left): B. Krist
p. 185 (top, right): J. & L. Merril
p. 185 (top, left): N. Wier
p. 186: B. Luxmoore, Arcaid
p. 187(5): A. Maher, Sygma
p. 187(6): K. Ward
p. 187(4): C. Morris
p. 187(2): Bettmann
p. 187(1): Bettmann
p. 189 (top): D. Boylan, Reuters
p. 196: C. Savage
p. 198: S. Marcus
p. 199 (bottom): RNT Productions
p. 202 (left): K. Dannemiller
p. 209: CKDJ, zefa
p. 210 (centre, right): W. Whitehurst
p. 211 (centre): B. Smith
p. 212 (top): S. Vidler, Eurasia Press
p. 213: J. Hollingsworth
p. 214: J. Henley
p. 215 (centre): Digital Art
p. 216 (right): M. Costantini, San Francisco Chronicle
p. 218: R. Ressmeyer
p. 219 (bottom): S. D. Warren, zefa
p. 219 (centre): Digital Art
p. 219 (top, right): T. McConville, zefa
p. 222: T. Pannell
p. 224: R. Gomez

p. 226: L. Hebberd
p. 227: Images.com
p. 228: T. McConville, zefa

COURTESY OF JON STEIN
p. 31

CP IMAGES
p. 105
p. 105 (bottom)
p. 187(3): F. Chartrand
p. 97 (bottom): Brand X
p. 119
p. 120 (right)
p. 123 (bottom): P. Karadjias, AP Photo
p. 123 (bottom, right): A. Sancetta, AP Photo
p. 123 (right, centre-top): H. Deryk, 1992
p. 123 (right, centre-below): A. Forget, COC
p. 123 (right, top): K. Frayer
p. 123 (left, centre-bottom): C. Stoody
p. 123 (left, bottom): A. Medichini, AP Photo
p. 123 (left, centre-top): E. Thompson, AP Photo
p. 123 (left, top): AP Photo
p. 134 (bottom)
p. 190

DORLING KINDERSLEY
p. 210 (centre, top): S. Gorton, Courtesy of Leica UK Ltd

FREMANTLE MEDIA
p. 197

GETTY IMAGES
p. 211 (bottom): Hulton Archive, Stringer

ISTOCKPHOTO
p. 2 (bottom, centre): W. Rennick
p. 2 (bottom, right): C. Carroll
p. 3 (top): V. Loiseleux
p. 3 (centre): L. Gough
p. 6 (right): T. Gentuso
p. 9: J. Tyler
p. 10: G. Hall
p. 13: C. Schmidt
p. 33: Z. Kolundzija
p. 47 (bottom, left)
p. 48 (top): N. Monu
p. 64 (bottom): T. Bryngelson
p. 65 (right, bottom-centre): L. K. Young
p. 65 (right, top-centre): T. Lorien
p. 70 (bottom, centre-left)
p. 70 (top, centre-left): N. Gleave
p. 73 (bottom): T. Stalman

p. 74 (centre): A. Manley
p. 78 (right): G. Barskaya
p. 86 (top)
p. 97 (top): C. Schmidt
p. 107: O. Williams
p. 151 (bottom): T. Bryngelson
p. 155
p. 162(2): R. Vernede
p. 162(7): R. Hackett
p. 162(8): G. Randles
p. 171 (top): R. Legg
p. 175 (top)
p. 176: S. Jastrzebski
p. 191 (bottom): J. Wackerhausen
p. 202 (bottom): C. Schmidt
p. 204
p. 205: R. Tahilramani p. 210
(bottom, left)
p. 210 (centre, bottom): T.
Segundo
p. 210 (centre, right): R. Cano
p. 212–214 (bottom): J.
Wackerhausen
p. 220: J. Wackerhausen

JASPER
p. 92 (top)

KEN DANBY STUDIOS
p. 122 (right): Ken Danby, 1984,
Used with permission

MAXX IMAGES
p. 45 (centre, left): Creatas
p. 45 (top, right): Image Source
p. 46 (bottom, right): N. Katano
p. 47 (centre, bottom): L.
Williams
p. 47 (centre, right): J. Arbogast
p. 96 (bottom): E. Ereza
p. 105 (top): J. Gual

p. 110: SuperStock
p. 121: D. MacDonald
p. 142 (left): ImageSource
p. 153 (top): Stockbyte
p. 161: Glowimages
p. 162(5): S. Grandadam
p. 162(6): Merten
p. 168: F. Whitney
p. 169: SuperStock
p. 171 (bottom): Inspirestock
p. 173 (top): Corbis
p. 179 (bottom): D. Hammond
p. 188: J. Feingersh

MICHEL BOULIANNE
p. 70 (bottom, right)

**MINISTRY OF PUBLIC WORKS
AND GOVERNMENT SERVICES
CANADA**
p. 173–174 (bottom)

**NATIONAL GALLERY OF
CANADA, OTTAWA**
p. 85: Photo National Gallery of
Canada, National Gallery of
Canada, Ottawa, Thomas Gardiner
Keir Bequest, 1990

PAUL KRONENBERG
p. 194
p. 195

PHOTOTHÈQUE ERPI
p. 45 (top, left)
p. 58
p. 73 (top, right)
p. 74 (left)
p. 89
p. 93 (bottom)
p. 149
p. 153 (bottom)

p. 154 (right)
p. 158
p. 181 (centre)
p. 187 (bottom, right)
p. 187 (bottom, left)
p. 187 (top, left)
p. 200 (bottom)
p. 200 (top)
p. 215 (top)
p. 216 (left)
p. 219 (top, left)

**PUBLIPHOTO PHOTO
RESEARCHERS**
p. 70 (bottom, centre-right): J. W.
Bova
p. 70 (top, centre-right): Y.
Momatiuk and J. Eastcott
p. 70 (top, left): Nature's Images

RADIO-CANADA
p. 120 (left)

**RÉUNION DES MUSÉES
NATIONAUX**
p. 48 (right, centre): Photo
CNAC/MNAM, Dist. RMN—Jean-
Claude Planchet

REUTERS
p. 51: N. Elias

SHUTTERSTOCK
p. 19 (top): T. Trojanowski
p. 32: H. Maes
p. 45 (bottom, left): N.
Mikhaylova
p. 46 (top, right): P. Aleksey
p. 74 (right): R. Jansa
p. 86 (bottom): A. Blazic
p. 90 (bottom): M. Vasily
p. 90 (top): Palto

p. 93 (top): P. Feteka
p. 101: I. Sergey
p. 106 (left): O. Lis
p. 187 (bottom, centre): R. G.
Santa Maria
p. 187 (centre, top-right): R. G.
Santa Maria
p. 204: N. Edmund

**THE BRIDGEMAN ART
LIBRARY**
p. 15–16: Private Collection
p. 27 (bottom): Private Collection
p. 28: Succession Picasso,
SODRAC (2008), Museo Picasso,
Barcelona, Spain, DACS, Giraudon
p. 47 (top, right): Private
Collection, Peter Willi
p. 130 (left): Wimbledon Lawn
Tennis Museum, London, UK
p. 191 (top): Private Collection
p. 199 (top): Bibliothèque des
Arts Décoratifs, Paris, France,
Archives Charmet
p. 203: Kunsthistorisches
Museum, Vienna, Austria
p. 217: Hamburger Kunsthalle,
Hamburg, Germany, DACS

**THE GRANGER COLLECTION,
NEW YORK**
p. 154 (left)

THE KOBAL COLLECTION
p. 210 (top, left): DANJAQ, EON,
UA

THOMAS VALLIÈRES
p. 201

WAR CHILD CANADA
p. 189 (bottom)